Who Stole My Religion?

REVITALIZING JUDAISM AND APPLYING JEWISH
VALUES TO HELP HEAL OUR IMPERILED PLANET

By Richard H. Schwartz
with Rabbi Yonassan Gershom
and Rabbi Dr. Shmuly Yanklowitz

KTAV

URIM PUBLICATIONS
Jerusalem • New York

Who Stole My Religion?
Revitalizing Judaism and Applying Jewish Values
to Help Heal Our Imperiled Planet
by Richard H. Schwartz, PhD
Foreword by Rabbi Dr. Shmuly Yanklowitz

Copyright © 2016 Richard Schwartz

All rights reserved

Typeset by Ariel Walden

Printed in United States of America

ISBN 978–965–524–234–8

Published by
KTAV Publishing House
527 Empire Boulevard
Brooklyn, NY 11225
www.ktav.com

Urim Publications
P.O. Box 52287,
Jerusalem 9152102, Israel
www.UrimPublications.com

Contents

Dedication

To Yosef Ben Shlomo Hakohen (Jeff Oboler *z"tl*), who passed away as this book was being completed. Yosef was the author *The Universal Jew*, a friend and valuable advisor to me and to many others, a true *tsaddik*, a bridge between Orthodox and non-Orthodox Jews and between Jews and others, a person dedicated to Torah learning and teaching, and widely spreading Judaism's universal messages through the work of his Hazon website. We will miss Yosef and his wisdom, joy, and *niggunim* (tunes), and we must try to apply his insights and nudging to the tasks of outreach and organizing to which he dedicated his too-brief but shining life.

To all Jews (and others) working to apply Jewish values toward seeking a more just, compassionate, healthy, peaceful, and environmentally sustainable world, may this book help inspire more people to engage in these vital pursuits and help make their work more effective and accomplished, so that we help shift our imperiled planet onto a sustainable path.

Foreword

By Rabbi Dr. Shmuly Yanklowitz

I N AN AGE OF extremism and self-absorption, Dr. Richard Schwartz's crucial book *Who Stole My Religion?* reminds us of our global responsibilities. In a tragic world overflowing with poverty, cruelty, destruction, and war, voices of faith and reason must remind us of our core values. In times of despair, Jewish leadership must unequivocally stand with courage in a fight against oppression and injustice. Dr. Schwartz helps us to remember that the Jewish tradition can be a guide to liberation and healing in our complex, interconnected world.

We must work to prevent Jewish thought from being hijacked to the monastic serenity of quiet mountaintops where peace is chosen over truth and the self over the collective. Authentic religion today is lived in the hustle and bustle of the streets, and it is here that Torah can be most transformative for 21st century Jews. We must also call a moratorium on the perpetuation of partisan markers as the primary images of Jewish political identity. In lieu of continuing to construct the monolithic traditional, liberal, and conservative identities that have become so pervasive throughout the Jewish community, we need more radicals! Liberals and Conservatives are too frequently content with bumper stickers, quoting stats at meals and in emails, cultivating animosity for the opposition, and then doing *bubkis*, doing nothing, from a distance. Radicals, on the other hand, ensure that they win in the streets. It isn't enough to care and to talk. We must transform.

Our theological calling to the public arena is not inherently a political summons. Rabbi Abraham Joshua Heschel argued in the first half of the twentieth century: "We affirm the principle of separation of church and state. We reject the separation of religion and the human situation." So too, for religion to matter, it must be deeply responsive to and molded by the

9

society in which we are embedded. As Rabbi Yisrael Salanter once argued, "The physical needs of another are my own spiritual needs." Spiritual life is embedded in the presence of the crude realities before our eyes, and to neglect them is to resemble a fish unaware of the very water it swims in. Dr. Schwartz reminds us that we must take ownership of our Judaism and stand up courageously to address the greatest moral challenges of our time. We should heed this call! Dr. Schwartz urges us all to step up!

Rabbi Dr. Shmuly Yanklowitz is the Executive Director of the Valley Beit Midrash, the Founder & President of Uri L'Tzedek, the Founder and CEO of The Shamayim V'Aretz Institute, and the author of eight books on Jewish ethics. Newsweek named Rav Shmuly one of the top 50 rabbis in America.

Author's Preface

*I*n this hour we, the living [post-Holocaust Jews], are "the people of Israel." The tasks begun by the patriarchs and prophets and continued by their descendants are now entrusted to us. We are either the last Jews or those who will hand over the entire past to generations to come. We will either forfeit or enrich the legacy of ages.

– RABBI ABRAHAM JOSHUA HESCHEL[1]

*O*n some positions, Cowardice asks the question "Is it safe?" Expediency asks the question "Is it politic?" And Vanity comes along and asks the question "Is it popular?" But Conscience asks the question "Is it right?" And there comes a time when one must take a position that is neither safe, nor politic, nor popular, but he must do it because Conscience tells him it is right."

– DR. MARTIN LUTHER KING, JR.[2]

*R*abbi Tarfon said: "The day is short, the work is urgent, the workers are lazy but the reward is great and the Owner is insistent . . . It is not for you to complete the task [of perfecting the world], but neither are you free to desist [from doing all you can.]"   – Pirkei Avot 2:17–18

---

1. Abraham Joshua Heschel, *The Earth is the Lord's* (New York: Harpers, 1966) 107.
2. Martin Luther King, Jr., "Remaining Awake Through a Great Revolution," an address at the Episcopal National Cathedral, Washington D.C., March 31, 1968.

HERE IS MY LONG-HELD VISION FOR JUDAISM
IN THIS TIME OF MULTIPLE CRISES:

To be a Jew is to see the world through the eyes of God, to be unreconciled to the world as it is, to be discontented with the status quo, and to be unafraid to challenge it.

To be a Jew is to be a co-worker with God in the task of perfecting the world, to know that the world remains unredeemed and that we must work with God to redeem it.

To be a Jew is to feel deeply the harms done to others, to speak out in the face of wrongdoing, and to prod the conscience of those who passively accept the status quo.

To be a Jew is to stand apart from the world, to be a non-conformist, to shout "NO" when others murmur "yes" to injustice, and to actively help uplift those in need and try to correct injustices, even if others stand idly by.

To be a Jew is to be intoxicated with a dream of social justice, to have an abiding concern for others, and to have compassion without condescension for people who are poor, weak, and suffering.

To be a Jew means to know that God's name can be sanctified by our actions, and to try to live a life compatible with being created in God's image by doing justly, acting kindly, and in all ways imitating God's attributes.

To be a Jew means to believe in the unlimited potential of people in spite of the evil and injustice around us, and recognizing that we have been chosen to serve as an example, to strive to be "a light unto the nations."

To be a Jew means of course many specific practices concerning Shabbat, kashrut, and much more. It means study and worship, and most of all action and observance. It means all these things and far more. It is not always easy to be a Jew, but it is always a very significant and worthwhile endeavor.

T HIS BOOK IS MEANT to be a wake-up call – the most urgent that I can make – to alert Jews and others that we must do all we can in applying Jewish values to help shift our imperiled planet onto a sustainable path. Its primary aim is to show that the world is heading toward a "perfect storm" of existential crises: sudden, catastrophic climate change; severe environmental degradation; devastating scarcities of food, water and energy; widening terrorism; and other critical threats to life as we know and value it. The application of Jewish values can make a major difference in shifting our imperiled world away from its present perilous path. It is meant to represent a cause and a crusade, in the best sense of that term.

Please consider the following brief discussions of some issues that are explored more thoroughly later in this book:

The climate crisis: There is a very strong scientific consensus, involving science academies worldwide and 97% of climate scientists, that the world is rapidly approaching a climate catastrophe, which is largely due to human activities. Glaciers and polar icecaps are rapidly melting, and there has been a significant recent increase in the number and severity of droughts, wildfires, storms, and floods. The world has already reached atmospheric CO_2 levels beyond what climate experts think are safe.

Threats from radical Islamists: As I review and update this material on December 17, 2015, ISIS has become increasingly aggressive, holding territory and attracting many alienated young people. They have recently taken credit for downing a Russian passenger plane and for murdering many people in terrorist attacks in Lebanon and Paris. An attack by a radical Muslim couple that was inspired by ISIS in San Bernardino, California on December 2, 2015, which killed 14 people and injured 21, sparked a major campaign to demonize American Muslims, including a widely criticized statement by Donald Trump that no Muslim should be permitted to enter the U.S. The U.S. and countries worldwide have increased efforts to guard against additional terrorist attacks.

World hunger: There is the potential for major food shortages due to (1) increasing population (projected to rise by about 50% by 2100), (2) increasing affluence, leading to an escalation in grain-intensive meat consumption, and (3) increased production of corn-based ethanol. There is also the potential for a decreased production of food due to (1) the conversion of farm land into land used for houses, roads, parking lots, factories, and other needs of the growing population, and (2) the negative effects of heat waves, droughts, floods, and other effects of climate change.

Running out of water: The world is also experiencing increasing water shortages. Climate change causes severe droughts in many parts of the world, even as it is causing flooding in other areas. Trying to grow adequate food for the world's increasing population (and the growing appetite for water-intensive meat production in the developing world) through irrigation of feed crops causes aquifers to shrink in many countries, and some may soon be completely depleted. In addition, because of global warming, glaciers that replenish water to rivers in the spring are receding rapidly.

Meeting energy needs: Because the burning of coal and oil contributes to climate change and other environmental problems, and there are dangers related to nuclear energy, it is essential that renewable sources of energy – solar, wind, and hydroelectric – be rapidly developed

Climate wars: Many military leaders and security experts are increasingly concerned about the national security implications of climate change. They are concerned that tens of millions of hungry, thirsty, desperate refugees fleeing from droughts, floods, heat waves, storms, wild fires, and other effects of climate change will increase the likelihood of instability, violence, terrorism, and war. Many military and strategic experts believe that major droughts caused by severe climate change resulted in failed farms with many farmers moving to cities, contributing to the start of civil wars in the Sudan and in Syria.

Other threats: Unfortunately, there are many other threats to humanity's future. These include: deforestation, desertification, rapid species extinction, pollution, increasing poverty, soaring financial deficits in some countries, and the inability of many countries to meet the needs of their people.

Everything possible must be done to avert the potential catastrophes indicated above, since they threaten humanity and all life on the planet.

This book argues that the application of Jewish values, such as pursuing justice and peace and working as partners with God in protecting the environment, can contribute greatly to solving these problems. Fortunately, other religions have similar values, and hopefully others will increase efforts to encourage their co-religionists to apply their religions' values to today's crises.

A main theme of this book is that, in the face of today's urgent problems, Jews must return to our universal Jewish values and to our missions: to be "a light unto the nations," a kingdom of priests and a holy people, descendants of prophets, champions of social justice, eternal protestants against a corrupt and unjust world, and dissenters against destructive and unjust systems. Jews must become actively involved in the missions of global survival and Jewish renewal, working for major changes that will lead to a society where there is far less oppression, injustice, violence, hunger, poverty, and alienation.

Unfortunately, as with other religions (with significant exceptions), there has been too little effort by Jews to apply Jewish values to the many critical problems that threaten the world today. In fact, as discussed in Chapters 1 and 2, along with the many positive developments in Jewish life today there has been a shift by many Jews away from these basic Jewish values just when the world needs them more than ever before.

I hope that this book will contribute to help expand widespread open dialogues about Jewish teachings concerning these critically important issues and will play a part in moving our precious planet away from its present perilous path onto one that is more just, humane, peaceful, and sustainable.

THE CHALLENGE OF WRITING THIS BOOK

This is my fourth book, not counting revised editions and shorter booklets, and it has been by far the hardest to complete. It took me about ten years to write the first edition, and I had many stops and starts along the way before I mustered enough courage and momentum to complete it.

Although I have become increasingly frustrated as many Jews are passive and/or have moved toward disturbingly conservative, often non-traditionally-Jewish, positions, I wondered if it would be *chutzpah* to challenge the prevailing views in much of the Jewish community, including sometimes those of members of my own family and of many of my friends and fellow congregants. At a time when the State of Israel is so threatened, anti-Semitism is increasing in many countries, terrorism is becoming an increasing concern, and Jews (among others) are facing economic and other challenges, would I be worsening the situations?

On the other hand, I thought about the importance of trying to make Jews (and others) more aware of Judaism's eternal teachings and how essential it is to apply Judaism's basic values to today's critical issues. And I wanted to try to counteract conservative forces that have been shifting Judaism away from its historic, progressive roots. Taking all this into account, and knowing that I am sure to stir up criticism of some of my views, I decided that it was important to go ahead, because it is essential that there be respectful dialogues on how the application of Jewish values can help shift our imperiled planet onto a sustainable path.

FOR WHOM IS THIS BOOK INTENDED?

For Jews who look to Judaism for moral and spiritual guidance, but who find that contemporary interpretations of our faith and traditions do not address the pressing issues of today. For Jews who are seeking a Judaism that will make a difference in responding to the crises of today and will help guide humanity in directions that can bring a more just, compassionate, peaceful, and environmentally sustainable future for generations to come. For Jews who recognize that the Jewish calling to be a light unto the nations gives them a special responsibility to live in ways that benefit all of God's creation. And, since other religions have similar problems and concerns, I believe that many non-Jews will also find this book interesting, challenging, informative, and valuable.

More information about the issues in this book can be found in the sources mentioned in the bibliography, including my books *Judaism and Global Survival* and *Judaism and Vegetarianism*. Both of my books are available to read freely online at www.Jewishveg.com/Schwartz, where you can also find over 200 related articles written by me as well as about 25 podcasts of my talks and interviews. These issues are also presented in a documentary called *A Sacred Duty: Applying Jewish Values to Help Heal the World* that I helped produce with multiple-award-winning producer, director, writer, and cinematographer Lionel Friedberg. It can be viewed for free at www.aSacredDuty.com.

This is a book about Jewish values and ethics, not a work of Jewish law, concerning which I do not claim to be an expert. Anyone who desires practical guidance in these matters should consult a qualified rabbi. If you have specific questions, points of disagreement (or of agreement that you would like to share), suggestions about promoting the ideas in this book or just points you would like to discuss, please contact me at veggierich@ gmail.com. I welcome your comments and suggestions, especially about how to get dialogues started about the application of Jewish values to current critical issues. Many thanks!

Acknowledgments

F
IRST, I WISH TO express my thanks to God by reciting the traditional Jewish blessing (*shechiyanu*) pronounced when a person reaches a milestone in life: "Blessed are you, Lord our God, King of the universe, Who has kept us alive and sustained us, and brought us to this season."

While I strongly believe it is essential that the issues discussed in this book be put on the Jewish agenda, I recognize my limitations in presenting this material. Fortunately, I have received input and suggestions from a wide variety of dedicated and extremely knowledgeable individuals.

I especially want to thank Rabbi Yonassan Gershom for his superb contributions. I started this book many years ago but found it difficult to complete, because much of the material is very controversial, and I was not sure how to best convey the ideas. After many unsuccessful attempts to complete the manuscript, I decided to ask Yonassan – a Breslov Hasid, peace activist, and storyteller – to work with me and write the book in dialogue form. We had previously been sharing ideas on these issues for almost a decade, and I had been working with Yonassan on several other projects. He was particularly helpful in providing valuable suggestions for my book *Judaism and Vegetarianism,* especially on the Kabbalistic concept of raising holy sparks by eating meat and other foods. I felt that his mystical, story-telling, Hasidic approach would complement my more factual, statistical approach.

We worked very well together for over a year, and Yonassan added much valuable material and superb editing to the original manuscript. As the project progressed, however, we realized two things: (1) feedback from our preliminary readers indicated that the dialogue mode was not working out as well as we had hoped and (2) we have some disagreements on our writing styles and on how to approach certain issues.

Yonassan eventually decided it was best that he pull back from the project and let me be the primary author for the good of the book and for our mutual efforts for *tikkun olam.* The original 2011 edition of this book contained several of our dialogues as Appendices, but when the current publisher requested us to shorten the book, Yonassan and I mutually agreed to remove the dialogues. Much of that material was later adapted for his 2015 book, *Kapporos Then and Now: Toward a More Compassionate Tradition.* Nevertheless, a great deal of his writing from the early dialogues was incorporated verbatim (with his permission) into the present text. He continued to help me behind the scenes with editing and research, as well as formatting the book for publication. His addition of appropriate photographs, as well as the cover design, added a much-appreciated dimension to the first edition of this book. I am extremely grateful for the hundreds of hours that Yonassan put into our collaboration and for his many valuable contributions.

Much of Yonassan's wisdom – especially his skill at applying Jewish stories to social action – is reflected in the chapters of this book. He played a very important role in balancing my more mainstream academic approach. There were many times when his down-to-earth, practical experience with nature, animals, and the outdoors made me stop and think, which led to the great improvement of the book.

I also want to express special thanks to Rabbi Dr. Shmuly Yanklowitz for his very thought-provoking foreword and his valuable suggestions. He is a very special person, and his activities give me hope for the future of Orthodox Judaism. By the age of thirty-five he has already written eight books on Jewish ethics and organized two important groups: Uri L'Tzedek, which focuses on Jewish teachings and activities related to social justice, and Shamayim v'Aretz, which focuses on Jewish teachings and activities related to veganism and related issues. His willingness to apply Jewish values to current situations is indicated by his donation on June 16, 2015 of a kidney to an Israeli whose life would be greatly shortened without the donation.

I am honored to be able to include Rabbi Gershom and Rabbi Yanklowitz as contributors on the cover of the book.

The following people (in alphabetical order) reviewed at least part of the manuscript for the first and/or second edition and made helpful suggestions: Syd Baumel, Patti Breitman, Dan Brook, Karima Vargas Bushnell, Aviva Cantor, Robert Cohen, Rina Deych, Lionel Friedberg, Bruce Friedrich, Sally Gladstein, Kris Haley, Susan Harris, Roberta Kalechofsky, Steve Kaufman, Ari Knoll, David Krantz, Jay Lavine, Mendy Mirocznik, Vasu Murti, Nina Natelson, Charles Patterson, Norm Phelps, Professor Joe Regenstein, Lewis Regenstein, Stewart Rose, Rabbi David Rosen, David Rosenfeld, Rabbi Simcha Roth, Steven Schuster, Rabbi David Seidenberg, Rabbi Gerry Serotta, Steve Sheffey, Rae Sikora, Rabbi Barry Silver, Professor Alon Tal, Aharon Varady, and Pauline Dubkin Yearwood.

The reviewers named above do not necessarily agree with everything in this book, nor did I always use their suggestions. Although every one of them was very helpful in the writing process, I take full responsibility for the final selection of material and interpretations, as well as any errors. I apologize in advance to any contributors that I might have inadvertently omitted.

I wish to express deep appreciation to my dear wife, Loretta, our children Susan (and David Kleid), David, and Devorah (and Ariel Gluch), and my grandchildren: Shalom Eliahu, Ayelet Breindel, Avital P'nina, and Michal Na'ama Kleid, and Eliyahu, Ilan Avraham, Yosef, Yael Shachar, Talya Nitzan, and Ayala Neta Gluch for their patience, understanding, and encouragement as I took time away from other responsibilities to gather and write this material.

Special thanks to Tzvi Mauer, Sarit Newman, Michal Alatin, and others at KTAV and Urim for their splendid cooperation in all phases of the production of this book, and for their valuable suggestions that greatly improved the book.

Finally, I wish to thank in advance everyone who will read this book and send me ideas and suggestions for improvements, so that this book can more effectively help revitalize Judaism and show how the application of Jewish values can help move our endangered planet onto a sustainable path.

Richard Schwartz

Chapter 1

Who Stole My Religion?

1 am a Jew because the faith of Israel [Judaism]
   demands no abdication of my mind.
I am a Jew because the faith of Israel asks every
   possible sacrifice of my soul.
I am a Jew because in all places where there are tears
   and suffering the Jew weeps.
I am a Jew because in every age when the cry of
   despair is heard the Jew hopes.
I am a Jew because the message of Israel is the most
   ancient and the most modern.
I am a Jew because Israel's promise is a universal
   promise.
I am a Jew because for Israel the world is not finished;
   men will complete it.
I am a Jew because for Israel man is not yet fully
   created; men are creating him.
I am a Jew because Israel places man and his unity
   above nations and above Israel itself.
I am a Jew because above man, image of the divine unity,
   Israel places the unity that is divine.

— EDMOND FLEG, "WHY I AM A JEW"[1]

---

1. Edmond Fleg (1874–1963) was a French essayist, playwright, and poet whose main writings deal with Judaism and the Jewish people.

I FERVENTLY BELIEVE IN THE above sentiments and many other positive aspects about Judaism, and I am proud to be a Jew. Judaism has wonderful, powerful, and universal messages, and applying them is essential to move our precious, yet increasingly threatened, planet onto a sustainable path.

I wrote this book to urge Jews to apply basic Jewish teachings at a time when they are needed more than ever before to the many tumultuous crises facing humanity and all of God's creatures. By encouraging Jews to apply Judaism's eternal values to current issues, I hope this book will help revitalize Judaism and will make Judaism more attractive to many disaffected Jews.

ABOUT MY MODERN ORTHODOX[2] SYNAGOGUE

I have been a member of Young Israel of Staten Island, a modern Orthodox synagogue, since 1968, and I have served as Vice President for Youth, Cultural Director, and co-editor of the synagogue's newsletter. Over the years I have seen the dedication of members of my congregation to Judaism and Jewish issues. The amount they donate to charity is truly outstanding. The acts of kindness and concern for the well-being of fellow congregants are also remarkable, and there is always great communal sharing at occasions of joy and sorrow. There are *gemachs* that provide free wedding and other gowns, furniture, centerpieces for celebrations, and clothing for people who need them, and there is a food pantry. There is a unique group called Nachas (joy) Unlimited that collects money to help cover medical expenses for ill children.

Especially commendable are the actions of the voluntary group Hatzolah, whose members will drop whatever they are doing at a moment's notice – whether they are at work, taking part in a Passover seder, or just relaxing with their families or friends – to respond to medical emergencies. Many synagogue members make weekly visits to patients in hospitals and nursing homes. Many of the synagogue's young attendants work with great compassion and dedication at special summer camps, taking care of children with cancer and other health problems.

---

2. Modern Orthodox Judaism attempts to combine traditional practices and values with involvement in the modern, secular world.

The commitment of my synagogue's community to learning and to prayer is also outstanding. There are well-attended classes and *minyanim* (prayer services) throughout the week, and often there are scholars in residence on Shabbat and guest speakers during the week who enlighten the members on a variety of issues. This is typical of other Orthodox synagogues throughout the United States and in other countries.

There are also many positive things happening in the wider Jewish community, including the Orthodox community. Appendix C provides information about many Jewish groups that are helping Jews with special needs.

IS ENOUGH BEING DONE TO APPLY JEWISH VALUES TO CURRENT THREATS?

Many Jews today are appropriately concerned about Jewish survival and the flourishing of Jewish culture and learning. And, as delineated in Appendix C, some Jewish groups are indeed attempting to apply Jewish values to today's critical issues. However, much more needs to be done in the face of the many threats to the world today.

Unfortunately, too many Jews today, especially among the Orthodox, seem to be paying insufficient attention to the words of Jewish prophets and sages, whose teachings resound with a passionate concern for justice, peace, and righteousness. There is too little active involvement or protest against injustice in the world at large. Instead, there is much complacency and conformity.

While there are many acts of kindness, charity, and learning within Jewish communities, many Jews have forgotten the Jewish mandate to strive to perfect the world. Today's synagogues and rabbinic pronouncements are often unrelated to the critical issues that face the world's people. God requires that we pursue justice and peace, and that we exhibit compassion and loving kindness. God demands that we protest against evil, but our synagogues have too often focused on ritual, self-interest, and parochial concerns.

A person who takes Jewish values seriously would be alienated by much of what goes on and is sanctioned in Jewish life today. As Rabbi Abraham Joshua Heschel stated, "One is embarrassed to be called religious in the face of religion's failure to keep alive the image of God in the face of man . . . We have imprisoned God in out temples and slogans, and now the word of God is dying on our lips."[3] Many idealistic Jews have turned away from Judaism, because Judaism's teachings about active involvement in the crucial challenges of today are not adequately disseminated or practiced.

For observant, caring Jews the acts of helping the needy and caring for the world are not voluntary options but responsibilities and divine commandments. These are not only individual responsibilities, but also obligations of every Jewish community and indeed of the entire Jewish people – obligations, in fact, upon the entire world. Our tradition understands this principle as a covenant – a mutual agreement that binds us to God. In this covenant we assume the task of caring for and improving the world and, in return, receive the Divine promise that the world will be redeemed. The Jewish message is not only one of responsibility, but also one of hope.

Unfortunately, some Jewish leaders and institutions have forgotten that the practical expression of justice has been and must continue to be a major emphasis of Jewish living. It is a tragedy that the Jewish community has generally failed to apply our rich theology to the preservation of the environment. Too often the Jewish establishment has been silent while our atmosphere warms, contributing to severe climate events. Our air is bombarded by poisons that threaten life, our rivers and streams are polluted by industrial wastes, our fertile soil is eroded and depleted, and the ecological balance is endangered by the destruction of rain forests and other indispensable habitats.

The Jewish community must become more actively involved. We must proclaim that it is a desecration of God's Name to pollute the air and water, to slash and burn forests, to mistreat animals, and to wantonly waste the abundant resources with which God entrusted us. We cannot allow any other needs or fears or concerns, however legitimate, to prevent us from applying fundamental Jewish values to the critical problems of today.

It is also unfortunate that many Jews are unaware of the rich legacy of the Jewish tradition and its focus on justice for both the individual and society. Indeed, Judaism provides a pragmatic path for implementing its progressive ideas. The Talmud and other rabbinical writings are filled with in-depth discussions, advice, and legal decisions on how to apply the principles of the Torah and the prophets to everyday situations. Judaism

---

3. Fritz A.Rothchild, Between God and Man: An Interpretation of Judaism, From the Writings of Abraham J. Heschel (New York: The Free Press, 1959), 240.

also offers the richness and warmth of an ancient historical community, a meaningful inheritance for each Jew.

Religious practitioners frequently mischaracterize God's demands. Instead of crying out against immorality, injustice, deceit, cruelty, and violence, they too often condone these evils through silence, while instead emphasizing formulaic ceremonies and ritual. For many Jews today, Judaism involves occasional visits to the synagogue or temple, prayers recited with little feeling, rituals performed with little meaning, and socializing. And all too many Jews who are commendably committed to learning and *davening* (praying) are not relating their Jewish knowledge to addressing current societal threats. To the prophets, worship accompanied by indifference to evil is an absurdity, an abomination to God (Isaiah 1:13). Judaism is mocked when Jews practice empty rituals side-by-side with apathy to immoral deeds.

Rabbi Heschel blames religion's losses to its failure to speak out and be involved in critical current issues:

> Religion declined not because it was refuted but because it became irrelevant, dull, oppressive, insipid. When faith is completely replaced by habit, when the crisis of today is ignored because of the splendor of the past, when faith becomes an heirloom rather than a living fountain, when religion speaks only in the name of authority rather than with the voice of compassion, its message becomes meaningless.[4]

WHY I BELIEVE MY RELIGION HAS BEEN STOLEN

Despite all the positive activities by members of my Orthodox synagogue and other Jews mentioned above, I think that my religion has been stolen. Why? It is largely because many in the Orthodox community – the group of Jews most involved in Jewish religious life, the group most steeped in Jewish learning and observance, the Jewish group that is growing most rapidly and having a major impact in the Jewish world and on the outside society, the group of Jews with whom I am most involved – has, I believe, gone astray by not adequately applying our traditional Jewish values to the critical issues facing the world today. Instead, there has been a major shift,

---

4. Abraham Joshua Heschel, *The Insecurity of Freedom* (New York: Ferrar, Strauss, and Giroux, 1967), 3–4.

primarily among Orthodox Jews, towards support of very conservative policies and a Republican Party in the U.S. that puts a priority on helping corporations and wealthy people rather than the majority of people.

A few clarifications: I am mainly focusing on Orthodox Jews for the reasons indicated above, but of course they are not the only ones who are not adequately addressing current threats. Other Jews and people of other religions, as well as secularists, should also do far more to address current challenges.

Recognizing my own limitations, I am reluctant to be critical of others, but I feel some respectful criticism is called for in an effort to try to start meaningful dialogues that will help galvanize Jews and others to actively confront the major crises mentioned in the preface. I strongly believe the fate of humanity is at stake now and everything possible must be done to improve the situation. We need to reawaken the spirit of the prophets of old in the Judaism of today.

As indicated above, Appendix C discusses Jewish groups that are doing many positive things to improve the world, but far more is necessary at this critical time. I wish to clarify that while I might not agree 100% with everything each of these groups stands for (in many cases they don't even agree with each other), I do believe it is imperative that we examine the issues from many different perspectives and not get locked into one "party line" or another. More information about why I think my religion has been stolen is in later chapters, especially Chapter 2.

Chapter 2

The Political Shift of Orthodox Jews to the Right and its Effects

*T*here is no precedent, whether in the European experience or Israel, for the nasty political and ideological
writing that has become standard fare in U.S. fervently
Orthodox publications, particularly the stream of vitu-
peration directed against the Obama administration and
the collateral adoption of far right positions. . . . I believe
that the embrace of right-wing attitudes is a factor in the
high rate of attrition among younger Orthodox, a rate
that dwarfs any gains achieved through outreach. . . . In
view of the still too recent history of persecution and
genocide, how can any who are Orthodox have a comfort
level with the far right? The answer appears to be that
Rush Limbaugh, Sarah Palin and other right-wingers
have become their ideological guides. This needs to be
challenged.

—MARVIN SCHICK[1]

I N THE 2008 U.S. election, while about 78% of Jews voted for
Barack Obama, roughly that same percentage of Orthodox Jews
voted for the Republican can4didate John McCain. This vote by
Orthodox Jews was despite the horrendous economic condition the Bush
administration left the country in, with the United States on the brink of a
financial depression, and the fact that strong opposition from conservative
Republicans forced McCain to drop his plans to choose Jewish Senator
Joseph Lieberman as his running mate. This led to McCain picking the

---

1. "Right is Not Right" *The Jewish Week.* January 21, 2010.

unqualified, untested, and very conservative Sarah Palin to be potentially one heartbeat away from the U.S. presidency, under an aging president with a history of heart problems.

As further proof of the political shift, consider these results from exit polls during the 2010 U. S. midterm elections:[2] Jewish voters voted for Democrats for Congress over Republicans on November 2, 2010 by a margin of 66% to 31%, or more than two-to-one, according to an election-night exit poll conducted by the progressive group J Street. Reform, Reconstructionist, Conservative, and secular Jews supported Democrats far more than Orthodox Jews. Nationwide, J Street's polling numbers show that Democrats won among Reform Jews by 72% to 24% and among Conservative Jews by 58% to 39%, but lost the Orthodox Jewish vote by 53% to 44%.

In some races, there was an even greater gap. In New York's fourth congressional district on Long Island, Democratic incumbent Carolyn McCarthy bested Republican Fran Becker among Jewish voters by about two to one, according to a Republican Jewish Committee survey.[3] McCarthy won Reform Jewish voters by 80% to 11% and Conservative Jewish voters by 61% to 21%. Among Orthodox Jewish voters, however, she lost by a lopsided 64% to 15%. Similar results occurred in other races.

A Pew Research survey released in October, 2013 reinforced the view that Orthodox Jews are more conservative than other Jews.[4] They reported that while 70% of Jews are Democrats or lean Democratic and only 22% are or lean Republican, 57% of Orthodox Jews are either Republican or lean toward the Republican Party.

A personal experience reinforced my perception that Orthodox Jews increasingly support conservative candidates and positions. During the primary election in my district for the Republican nomination for Congress in 2010, a Republican candidate spoke at my synagogue after a Shabbat afternoon service. During the question period following the talk, I asked the candidate what policies he supported that differed from those of the Bush administration that had proved so disastrous and left the country

---

2. The poll results are from an article by J. J. Goldberg in the November 19, 2010 issue of the *Jewish Forward*, "Jewish Voters, Obama and the Great Elephant Hunt."

3. *Ibid.*

4. Alan Cooperman and Greg Smith, "Eight facts about Orthodox Jews from the Pew Research survey," October 17, 2013.

in great economic peril. One member of the congregation applauded my question. When the candidate said to the applauder, "Oh, you liked that question," another congregation member called out, "They are the only two liberals in the synagogue." This was, of course, an exaggeration, but not by much, based on my many conversations with synagogue members.

For some time I thought that perhaps my modern Orthodox synagogue might be an outlier, out of the mainstream of the views of most Orthodox Jews. Then I read the article by Jerome A. Chanes, "Orthodox and Liberal, And Lonely On The West Side," in the New York Jewish Week (October 26, 2012). The article starts as follows:

> Looking around at my fellow worshippers at the late Maariv services at the Carlebach Synagogue the other night, I pondered political affiliation. Who, mused I, are the Obama supporters, and who are in the Romney camp? When I nudged my pew-mate, a prominent West-Side MD, and asked him "65 percent Romney?" he sputtered, "Get real! We're talking 90 percent, maybe 99 percent. The 1 percent Obama is you!"

Another indication that Orthodox Jews have moved to the right is the large readership in that community of the conservative *Jewish Press*, which claims to be "the largest independent weekly Jewish newspaper in the United States." Its editorials and articles generally support conservative political positions. Other Jewish periodicals read by many Orthodox Jews are also generally very politically conservative. An example of the extreme conservative views in such publications was the title of the December 7, 2015 online *Jewish Press* article: "Liberals: Disease of the Mind, Sickness of the Soul." Yet, as I argue in the next chapter, Judaism is not just a liberal religion, but is a radical religion, in the best sense of "radical."

One factor that impelled me to continue working on this book was an article by a *Jewish Press* columnist calling environmental activists "*tikkun olam* pagans."[5] He openly ridiculed Jews who apply the term *tikkun olam* (repairing the world) to ecology and social action. When I challenged him in a letter to the editor, several readers defended his reactionary stance.

The article's position is inconsistent with that of contributors to the Orthodox Forum Series volume *Tikkun Olam: Social Responsibility in*

---

5. Steve Plaut, "The Rise of Tikkun Olam Paganism," *Jewish Press*. January 23, 2003.

Jewish Thought and Law, who clearly apply *tikkun olam* to social issues. The book cites many distinguished Orthodox rabbis, including Samson Raphael Hirsch, Abraham Isaac Kook, Joseph B. Soloveitchik, and Lord Immanuel Jakobovits, all of who stress that Jews have a religious and ethical responsibility to work with others to promote the welfare of society. In his anthology, *Compassion for Humanity in the Jewish Tradition,* Rabbi Dovid Sears, a Breslov Hasid, discusses numerous source texts that indicate our responsibility for working to benefit all people. The phrase *tikkun olam* is not an invention of the modern liberal mind, but occurs many times in the *Mishnah* and later rabbinic literature.[6] Nevertheless, reactionaries continue to be hostile in connecting Jewish progressive teachings, such as *tikkun olam* with social action. A recent example was at a rally against the Iran nuclear deal in Manhattan on July 22, 2015 when the largely Orthodox crowd booed every time the names of liberals Chuck Shumer, Hilary Clinton, and Barack Obama were mentioned.[7]

Another example was the wave of ugly, very harsh criticism of Jewish Congressman Jerrold Nadler from members of his largely Orthodox Jewish district and other Orthodox Jews when, after much review and soul searching, he supported the Iran nuclear deal[8]. Although Nadler has been a consistent, very strong supporter of Israel for over 50 years, he was called a "traitor to your people and to Israel," a kappo, a Jew who worked on behalf of the Nazis in a concentration camp, and one who "endangered the existence of the state of Israel." Zev Brenner's radio program, which has a large Orthodox audience, received so many calls and emails that he could not respond to all of them, and they all opposed Nadler's decision. This reaction is despite the fact that the vast majority of U.S. and Israeli strategic, military experts and diplomats, most Democratic senators, and many former Jewish leaders, including a former head of AIPAC, supported the nuclear deal.

While Nadler expected criticism, he was stunned by the viciousness of the attacks on him. He told a *Jewish Week* reporter:

---

6. Rabbi Jill Jacobs, "The History of 'Tikkun Olam,'" *Zeek,* June, 2007.

7. Gary Rosenblatt, "How Not To Influence Friends In Congress," *The Jewish Week,* July 31, 2015, p. 7.

8. Stewart Ain, "Nadler's Iran Vote Unleashes Vitriol," *The Jewish Week,* August 26, 2015

It's one thing to be told you are wrong, it's another to say you know you are wrong and that you are doing it for terrible motives. . . . People are entitled to their views, but what bothers me is that people are saying, 'You betrayed us.' I have been a supporter of Israel all my life. This is my decision and I think it is best for the U.S. and Israel. I could be right or wrong, but to conclude that anybody who supports the deal is opposed to the Jewish people and Israel's welfare is absurd.

My analysis in this section is reinforced by an article in the online *Forward* on August 26, 2015, "Pew Study Finds Orthodox Similar To Evangelical Christians – Not Other Jews," by Nathan Guttman. According to the article, the Pew Research Center reported that Orthodox Jews "vote, believe, worship, act and raise their children more like white evangelical Protestants than like their fellow Jews." The voting and acting (politically) are relevant to the present discussion.

WHY THE SHIFT TO THE PRESENT VERY CONSERVATIVE REPUBLICAN PARTY IS A PROBLEM

The recent shift of many Orthodox Jews to the Republican Party stands in sharp contrast to a long history of Jewish support for the Democratic Party. Of course, Orthodox Jews, like everyone else, are entitled to support any politician of their choice. And certainly there are problems with the Democratic Party, some of whose members also receive large contributions from highly profitable corporations that have spent billions of dollars in pursuit of obtaining "the best government that money can buy." Democratic platforms are no substitute for basic Jewish values, and I certainly don't agree with everything that Democrats advocate. But I wonder how the Republican philosophy, which has generally opposed Social Security, Medicare, Medicaid, workers' compensation, and other benefits that society now takes for granted, can be reconciled with Jewish teachings about concern for the poor, the stranger, the widow, and the orphan, and about working for a more compassionate, just, and peaceful world. In my opinion they *cannot* be reconciled.

Some might respond, "Yes, these goals are important to me, but the government should not be involved in implementing them – they should be left to individual initiatives and charity groups." Certainly these private efforts are important and must be supported and encouraged, but considering the magnitude of the problems, including poverty, unemployment, and homelessness, and the resulting physical and emotional problems, private efforts cannot be enough. The U.S. Constitution states that one of the functions of government is to promote the general welfare of the citizens.

Judaism sees taking care of the poor and powerless as important communal and societal responsibilities. The Talmud and Codes of Jewish Law give broad authority to communal bodies to tax, regulate, and redistribute income.[9] I know that many Orthodox Jewish (and other Republican) supporters are intelligent, sensitive, and caring people, but I respectfully wonder how they can support the Republican Party in view of the following examples, more of which can often be found in news reports:

- Today's Republican Party has very few moderates like Nelson Rockefeller, Jacob Javits, John Heinz, Mark Hatfield, and Clifford Case, and the Tea Party's increasing involvement is shifting the Party even further to the Right.
- As of May 2016, there were no Republican Jewish senators (the Democrats have nine and there is one liberal independent) and only one Republican Jewish congressman (compared to 18 for the Democrats).
- The positions of today's Republican Party are generally consistent with the extreme, intolerant views of commentators like Glenn Beck, Rush Limbaugh, and Sean Hannity, people who often deny realities (like human-caused climate change) to favor conservative interests. The latest example of this is that at this writing on May 8, 2016, the presumptive Republican nominee for president is the racist, sexist, xenophobic Donald Trump and his main rival was the very conservative Senator Ted Cruz.
- Current Republican leaders propose policies similar to or worse than these of the Republican George W. Bush administration, which converted a three-year budget surplus on track to completely eliminate the federal debt into a major deficit, created very few net jobs (none in the private sector), and left the economy in a major downward-spiraling economic freefall, with an average of 750,000 jobs per month being lost in the administration's final three months.

---

9. There is much in the writings of Rabbi Aaron Levine and Dr. Meir Tamari on Jewish teachings on economic issues. Please see bibliography.

- Republicans have been doing everything possible to keep the Obama administration from pulling the country out of these terrible economic conditions, often voting against and filibustering legislation they had previously supported and sometime cosponsored, in attempting to undermine the president and regain power.
- Republicans generally support the wealthiest Americans and high profitable corporations, rather than the middle class and poor people.
- Republican senators were so committed to helping the wealthy that on December 1, 2010, all 42 Republican senators signed a letter indicating that they would block all pending legislation, unless the Senate approved continuing all Bush-era tax cuts, including those for the wealthiest two percent of Americans.[10]
- Republicans support gutting regulations that constrain Wall Street, crippling rules that promote worker safety and health, keeping the "starvation level" national minimum wage, and repealing the Affordable Care Act (Obamacare), even though it has sharply reduced the number of people without insurance and has significantly cut the rate of increase of medical costs. Yet they are doing so while they have no comprehensive plan to replace it, cutting back Medicare and Social Security, reducing corporate taxes, and, in general, moving the nation back to pre-New Deal days.
- Republicans oppose efforts to improve the nation's infrastructure despite the fact that the American Society of Civil Engineers gives the U. S. infrastructure a grade of D+, and they also oppose efforts to improve our educational system and research capacities and develop renewable energy sources. These activities would create many new jobs, bring in additional tax revenues, and help improve the economy, as well as save lives, improve the environment, and prepare the country for a far brighter future.
- In the summer of 2011, Republicans used the threat of a government default to hold the Congress hostage in order to force major cuts in essential programs, while making sure that there would be absolutely no tax increases for the wealthiest Americans or repeal of tax breaks for highly profitable corporations.

---

10. "Senate Republicans Vow to Block Dem Legislation Until Tax Cuts, Budget Pass," Fox News.com, December 1, 2010.

- In their 2015 budget proposals, Congressional Republicans continued their efforts to improve things for the wealthiest Americans, failing to consider benefits to average Americans. While proposing an additional $38 billion for the Pentagon and a continuation of major tax breaks for the wealthy, their plan would cut federal student loan programs and pre-school assistance for thousands of students, weaken the Consumer Financial Protection Bureau, and repeal Obamacare, even though millions of people received insurance from it, and the rate of healthcare costs has been significantly decreased.[11]

In view of the above and more, I would like to respectfully address the following questions to Jews who support the Republican Party:

- Are Jewish values of compassion, justice, environmental sustainability, and concern for the poor consistent with a Republican Party that seems mainly concerned with helping the wealthy become even wealthier beyond any need or reason, at the expense of the poor and the middle class, and with fighting to relieve corporations of legal accountability and social responsibility through deregulation?
- Is support for politicians who want to cut social services while keeping tax cuts for the wealthiest Americans consistent with Jewish teachings on caring for the most vulnerable members of society?

Some may feel that I am too harsh on Republicans, but please consider the following words of the prophet Isaiah:

Woe to those who make unjust laws, to those who issue oppressive decrees, to deprive the poor of their rights and withhold justice from the oppressed of my people, making widows their prey and robbing the fatherless. What will you do on the day of reckoning, when disaster comes from afar? To whom will you run for help? Where will you leave your riches? (Isaiah 10:1–3)

---

11. Associated Press, "Proposed GOP budget seeks Obamacare repeal and additional $38 billion to Pentagon," *The Guardian*, April 30 2015.

DENIAL ON CLIMATE CHANGE AND
OTHER ENVIRONMENTAL THREATS

Another important reason I believe my religion has been stolen is the widespread denial by so many Jews, especially Orthodox Jews, about climate change, at a time when Jews should be leading efforts to work toward stabilizing the world's climate. This issue is discussed in much greater detail in the chapter addressing the environment, so I will just mention here that (1) there is an overwhelming scientific consensus that climate change is happening, that it is driven by human activities, is a major threat to humanity, and could be close to a tipping point where it will spin out of control with disastrous consequences unless major positive changes soon occur; (2) reinforcing these views are the fact that polar ice caps and glaciers worldwide are rapidly melting, and there has been a recent increase in the number and severity of heat waves, droughts, wildfires, storms and floods; (3) atmospheric CO_2 levels reached 400 parts per million (ppm) in 2014, well above the 350 ppm that climate experts believe should be a threshold value to assure that the severest climate events will not occur; and (4) the Israeli Union for Environmental Defense has projected that due to climate change Israel will face many more heat waves, an average decrease of precipitation of up to 30%, increasing desertification, and a possible inundation of the coastal plain where most Israelis live from a rising Mediterranean Sea.

The many positive side effects of working to reduce climate change include a less polluted world with massive public health benefits, lessened dependence for oil on foreign countries (some of whom are leading supporters of terrorism), healthier people, new business opportunities, and the timely creation of a twenty-first century "green collar" workforce at a time of high unemployment. These are all good things to do even outside of the issue of climate change, as Pulitzer Prize-winning cartoonist Joel Pett illustrated in his now-famous cartoon of a climate-change skeptic saying, "What if it's a big hoax and we create a better world for nothing?"[12]

One has a choice of believing mostly ideology and industry-driven "skeptics," with little or no relevant scientific background, or the true experts: climate scientists and the world's official scientific bodies, informed by the overwhelming cumulative weight of research and em-

---

12. http://www.gocomics.com/joelpett/2009/12/13/

pirical evidence dating back to the nineteenth century. In other words, the simplistic rhetoric of misinformed conservative pundits or the sober consensus of the world's leading scientists. Later chapters offer additional information about climate change and why Jews should be actively involved in responding.

SHOULD JEWS SUPPORT REPUBLICANS WHO ARE IN DENIAL ABOUT THE ENVIRONMENT AND CLIMATE CHANGE?

In view of the fact that, as discussed in Chapter 11, Judaism has very powerful teachings about environmental sustainability, and considering the climate threats mentioned above, I find it very difficult to understand how so many Orthodox Jews can ignore the reality that the Republican Party is so out of touch with current environmental issues. The following are a sampling of the many facts that illustrate the negative approach of most conservatives about climate change and other environmental threats:

- When the Republicans took over the US Senate in 2015, the strongest climate denier in national politics, Senator James Inhofe, became head of the Senate's Environment and Public Works Committee, the committee that deals with climate and environmental matters. His eccentric, strong views about climate change are detailed in his 2012 book *The Greatest Hoax: How the Global Warming Conspiracy Threatens Your Future*. On February 26, 2015 he brought a snowball onto the Senate floor to demonstrate his belief that climate change is a hoax.
- In a Senate vote in January 2015, 49 of the 54 Republican senators voted against a Sense of the Senate amendment that human activities are a major contributor to climate change.
- In addition to ignoring the strong scientific and military consensus on climate threats, Republican lawmakers shrugged off Pope Francis' powerful June 18, 2015 encyclical on climate change.[13]
- In June 2015, Congressional Republican legislators promoted appropriation bills that promoted corporate interests at the expense of public health and safety, sharply cutting environmental spending and repealing major parts of regulatory authority, including the ability of the

---

13. Edward Werner and Matthew Daly, "Republican Lawmakers Shrug off Pope Francis Climate Message," Associated Press, June 18, 2015.

Environmental Protection Agency to use the Clean Air Act to regulate greenhouse gas emissions.[14]

- On November 17, 2015, 51 of the 54 Republican senators voted to scuttle President Obama's tough climate change efforts, hoping to weaken the ability of the U.S. to be effective at the Paris climate change conference in December. Fortunately their efforts failed and Obama's efforts were a major factor in leaders of 195 nations agreeing to what many climate experts consider a historic, game changing, climate change agreement, an essential step toward reducing climate change. The Republican presidential candidates have vowed to end U.S. cooperation with the agreement if they are elected, a step that would make avoiding a climate catastrophe even more unlikely.

In summary, it seems incredible that so many Orthodox Jews and others are in denial about climate change at a time when leaders at the Paris climate change conference, major science academies, and almost all the world's climate experts agree that urgent steps are needed to reduce greenhouse gas emissions. Especially at a time like this when glaciers and polar ice caps are rapidly melting, when there has been an increase in the number and severity of storms, floods, droughts, wildfires, and other effects of climate change, and when atmospheric CO_2 levels are far higher than the value climate experts deem to be safe.

Unfortunately, "denial is not just a river in Egypt," and most people, including Orthodox Jews, are "rearranging the deck chairs on the Titanic as we head toward a giant iceberg." When I talk to members of my modern Orthodox synagogue about climate change and other environmental threats, almost all deny there is a problem that requires a major response or tell me that God or a future Messiah will take care of the threat. Perhaps they should consider the following story:

A man's house was caught in a big flood, but when the order to evacuate came he refused. "Don't worry about me," he said, "I'll be safe. I am very pious, so God will protect me."

The floodwaters rose higher and higher, eventually forcing him to climb up to the roof. But still he kept turning down the rescuers who

---

14. Ben Adler, "Congressional Republicans: Damn the environment, full cuts ahead!," *Grist*, June 22, 2015.

came – first in a rowboat, then a motorboat, and finally a helicopter. Each time the man told them, "No thank you, I'm fine here; God will save me." But the waters rushed over the roof and he drowned.

When he got to the Next World he asked God, "How could you abandon me like that? How could you let this happen to such a pious person as me?" God replied, "What more did you want? I sent two boats and a helicopter."

Jews are not supposed to rely on miracles. A good approach I once read in a collection of statements given out in a synagogue for Rosh Hashanah and Yom Kippur inspirational readings suggested that we should pray as if everything depends on God, and act as if everything depends on us. The key point here is that because of increasing evidence that the world is rapidly approaching a human-created climate catastrophe and faces many other environmental crises, it is extremely urgent that the Jewish community play a leading role in responding to these threats.

Since I have been especially critical of the lack of involvement of Orthodox Jews in responding to environmental threats, I would like to stress that there are Orthodox Jews who are actively working for a better environment. Especially noteworthy is the Orthodox group Canfei Nesharim (Wings of Eagles), which organizes events, produces considerable literature, and manages an excellent website to increase awareness of Torah teachings on environmental sustainability. More information about them and other activist Jewish groups is in Appendix C.

HOW SUPPORT FOR ISRAEL IS RELATED TO THE ABOVE ISSUES

As I will discuss in Chapter 6, I am a strong supporter of Israel. My wife and I visit family members there at least twice a year. Having a grandson in the Israeli Defense Forces, another in the reserves after serving for three years, and other grandsons who will soon be old enough to join the IDF, I pray especially hard for peace in Israel. I feel that the best way to support Israel is to promote a peaceful resolution of conflicts between Israel and its neighbors, while recognizing the many difficulties in bringing this about.

Members of my modern Orthodox congregation and other Orthodox Jews are properly strong supporters of Israel. A major reason they support Republican politicians is that they consider them to be fervent backers of Israel, which they often define as supporting extremely hawkish Israeli positions. They frequently disregard politicians' positions on economic, environmental, and social issues. Fellow congregants have often told me that the only issue they care about is Israel. Many of my Orthodox co-congregants and other Orthodox Jews support conservative Republicans because these politicians will support hawkish Israeli policies, even though they might be counterproductive to the peace process and to other Israeli and American interests.

These Jews ignore the statements by the Bush administration in its final year about the need for a two-state solution, the very same policy for which they now oppose Obama. If you are a Republican leader, it seems you are given a free pass on positions for which Democrats are severely criticized. Conservatives also fail to consider that Israel urgently needs peace to avoid another intifada or war, halt her increasing diplomatic isolation, help address her many economic, environmental, and other domestic problems, and remain both a Jewish and a democratic state. Israel's need to be constantly on the alert for possible terrorist acts and war makes it very difficult to meet her domestic needs and threatens her future economic well-being. Bottom line: a politician can be a denier of climate change and can support reactionary social and economic positions, but can still gain support from many U.S. Jews if his or her position on Israel is in support of Israeli hard-liners.

Larry Derfner's July 7, 2010 *Jerusalem Post* article, "Israel is waiting for Palin," indicates that many Israelis felt that Israel would benefit from the Republican Party's being in power and were arguing — absurdly — that "you're for Israel or you're for the Democrats, you can't be both." Since when does a person's political party define whether or not one supports Israel? Years ago, such a claim would have been unheard of. In any case, are the Republicans *really* that good for Israel if they blindly support Israeli policies that can have negative consequences?

Evidently, many Jews are ignoring (or simply do not care about) reactionary and/or outdated Republican positions on the environment, health care, education, helping the poor, and other domestic issues. Their position is largely based on a belief that a president who does not push Israel to make any concessions for peace is the best president for Israel. They fail to recognize that Hamas, Hezbollah, and Iran all became significantly stronger during the eight years of the George W. Bush administration's mainly hands-off policies concerning Israel.

It is also important to consider that the major budget cuts that Republicans, especially Tea Party politicians, are promoting may have a major negative impact on foreign aid for allies, including Israel. According to many economists, such cuts will harm the U.S. economy, possibly making it more difficult for the U.S. to support Israel during difficult economic times.

I want to stress that there are Orthodox individual Jews and groups that have been actively involved in promoting a two-state solution of the Israeli/Palestinian conflict. One such group, Oz v'Shalom/Netivot Shalom, is discussed in Chapter 7.

ANTI-OBAMA ATTITUDES OF MANY RELIGIOUS JEWS

Many Israelis and conservative American Jews, especially among the Orthodox, have very negative views about President Obama. Of course, like previous presidents, he has been far from perfect in trying to deal with some very complex problems. So, of course, some criticism is understandable, but not the outrageous charges that have no basis in fact or reason that I often read in Jewish publications for primarily Orthodox Jewish audiences or hear from members of my Orthodox synagogue. Some of these claims are listed below. (While Obama will no longer be president shortly after this book is published, I still think it is important to refute the false claims about him. Trying to demonize Democrats – not only Obama – by repeating false claims is a Republican policy, and it is important to not let them become common wisdom.)

Outrageous claim 1: President Obama has negative feelings about Jews and favors Muslims.

Facts in response: Obama's initial chief of staff Rahm Emanuel is Jewish and the son of Israelis. One of his former key advisors, David Axlerod, is Jewish, and he was also a key strategist for Obama's 2012 re-election campaign. Obama appointed a Jew, Elana Kagan, as a Supreme Court Justice (even though that left the nine-member Court with three Jews and no Protestant members). Most recently, Obama nominated Jewish Merrick Garland to fill a Supreme Court vacancy, which, if he was confirmed, would mean that four of the nine justices would be Jewish. (It is noteworthy that all the Jewish members of the Supreme Court in the past 80 years were appointed by Democratic presidents.) Obama also appointed another Jew, Janet Yellen, to be Director of the Federal Reserve, perhaps the most important economic post in the world. Orthodox Jew Jack Lew is currently Obama's Secretary of Treasury, and he formerly served as his Chief of Staff. Obama is the first president to have Passover seders in the White House, and he has done so for the eight consecutive Passovers that he has been president.

Outrageous claim 2: President Obama has consistently acted against Israel's interests.

Facts in response:
- Israeli strategic experts agree that strategic cooperation between the U.S. and Israel has never been better.
- The US has supplied funding for the "Iron Dome" missile defense system that has saved many Israeli lives.
- The Obama administration has consistently backed Israel at the UN and helped prevent a declaration of a Palestinian State by the UN, an effort that led Israeli Prime Minister Netanyahu to declare that Obama deserved a "badge of honor." Most recently, on July 3, 2015, the U.S. was the only country on the UN Human Rights Council to stand with Israel and oppose a resolution to investigate Israel for human rights crimes during the Gaza war during the summer of 2014. By contrast, 41 members of the Council supported the resolution, including England, France, Germany, and the Netherlands.
- Obama has supported Israel with regard to the Goldstone report that was critical of Israel's actions in the 2009 war and the Gaza flotilla events.
- Obama helped save six Israelis who were trapped in the Israeli embassy in Cairo in response to a frantic, middle-of-the night call from Netanyahu. Afterward, Netanyahu stated that Israel owes Obama, "a special measure of gratitude."
- In his talk to the U.S. Congress in March 2015, Netanyahu praised Obama warmly, indicating that Obama had done many additional things for Israel that only he and a few others know about.
- Some Jews have been critical of Obama because in 2009, his first year in office, he went to Cairo but did not visit Israel. However, his talk in Cairo was aimed at, among other things, improving relations with

Muslims in order to increase the chances for a settlement of Israel's conflicts with the Palestinians and neighboring Arab countries. It is noteworthy that Obama said the following in Cairo, a major Arab capital:

America's strong bonds with Israel are well known. This bond is unbreakable. It is based upon cultural and historical ties, and the recognition that the aspiration for a Jewish homeland is rooted in a tragic history that cannot be denied. . . . Threatening Israel with destruction – or repeating vile stereotypes about Jews – is deeply wrong and only serves to evoke in the minds of Israelis this most painful of memories while preventing the peace that the people of this region deserve.[15]

Many who are critical of Obama's behavior toward Israel generally forget or overlook the many times that Republican presidents treated Israel badly. For example,[16] In 1956 Eisenhower forced Israel to withdraw from the Sinai, Nixon postponed the sale of and delivery of 25 Phantom jets and 80 Skyhawks to Israel in 1970, and Gerald Ford stopped all major arms transactions with Israel for six months in 1975, while calling for a "total reassessment" of the U.S.-Israel relationship. Reagan condemned Israel at the UN, suspended military aid to Israel, and sold arms to Saudi Arabia over AIPAC's strong objections. George H. W. Bush denounced Israeli settlements, opposed loan guarantees to Israel, and publically declared that he was just "one lonely little guy" up against "a thousand lobbyists on the Hill." George W. Bush abstained on UN resolutions condemning Israel, suspended cooperation on a fighter jet, and rescinded loan guarantees to Israel.

Outrageous claim 3: President Obama is a socialist.

Facts in response: Obama has appointed several members from Wall Street to his cabinet and other important positions, including his first Secretary of the Treasury Tim Geitner. The president has had great eco-

---

15. "Text: Obama's Speech in Cairo," International New York Times, June 4, 2009.
16. The examples that follow are from (1) Peter Beinart, "Michael Oren's wildly unconvincing, deeply trivial attack on Obama," Haaretz, June 17, 2015, and (2) Steve Sheffey's June 16, 2015 "Michael Oren 's Misleading Op-Ed" National Jewish Democratic Council.

nomic success turning a country on the brink of a depression when he entered office – with an average of 750,000 jobs being lost per month, and stock and housing values sharply decreasing – into one that has seen 73 consecutive months of private sector job growth (as of May 2016), record breaking stock values, a restored housing market, a revitalized auto industry, and greatly increased consumer confidence. Perhaps we need more such "socialists"!

Outrageous claim 4: President Obama is an ineffective leader with few accomplishments.

Facts in response: Like all previous U.S. presidents, Obama is far from perfect, but this claim ignores that Obama got the U.S. economy back on track from the very severe recession that he inherited from the George W. Bush administration. Despite consistent Republican efforts to obstruct Democratic proposals, Obama saved the U.S. auto industry, oversaw efforts that killed Osama bin Laden, put together a coalition of nations that applied the largest ever boycott of Iran, resulting in their reducing their nuclear weapon capacity, and played a major leadership role in getting 195 nations to support the historic climate change agreement in Paris in December 2015.

Long-time Orthodox commentator Marvin Schick reinforced many of the responses above in his article "Right Is Not Right" in the January 21, 2010 issue of the New York *Jewish Week*. He sharply criticized the viciousness directed against President Obama by many Orthodox Jews who are "in bed with the far right" in an "unholy alliance," which "means that, unbeknownst to them, they are in bed with tens of thousands of crazies, anti-Semites, and outright Nazi lovers." Our moral and ethical guides should be Moses and the Prophets, not extreme conservatives like Limbaugh and Palin. In the next chapter, we will explore how Jewish leaders of old responded to social injustices.

Chapter 3

Is Judaism a Radical Religion?

*T*here are no words in the world more knowing, more disclosing, and more indispensable. Words both stern and graceful, heart-rending and healing. A truth so universal – Elohim [God] is One. A thought so consoling – He is with us in distress. A responsibility so overwhelming – His Name can be desecrated. A map of time – from creation to redemption. Guideposts along the way: The Seventh Day; An offering – contrition of the heart. A utopia – would that all people were prophets. The insight – man lives by his faithfulness, his home is in time, and his substance in deeds. A standard so bold – ye shall be holy. A commandment so daring – love thy neighbor as thyself. A fact so sublime – human and divine pathos can be in accord. And a gift so undeserved – the ability to repent.

—RABBI ABRAHAM JOSHUA HESCHEL[1]

B
ASED ON THE VERY powerful quote above by Rabbi Heschel, and so much more in the Jewish tradition, I believe that Judaism *is* a radical religion in the best sense of 'radical.' However, most Jews nowadays would probably disagree with this assertion. Even the word "liberal" has become a negative word for some Jews. So I think it is important to explore why Judaism is a radical religion, and why applying basic Jewish values and teachings could greatly improve the world.

---

1. Abraham Joshua Heschel, *God in Search of Man* (New York: Harper and Row, 1955), 239.

JUDAISM'S RADICAL HISTORY

From its beginning, Judaism has often protested against greed, injustice, and the misuse of power. Abraham, the first Hebrew, smashed the idols of his father even though his action challenged the common belief of the time. He established the precedent that a Jew should not conform to society's values when they are evil. Later he even challenged God, exclaiming "Shall the Judge of all the earth not do justly?" when God informed him of His plans to destroy Sodom and Gomorrah (Genesis 18:25). By contrast, Noah, though personally righteous, was later rebuked by some Talmudic sages because he failed to criticize the immorality of the society around him.

At the beginning of the book of Exodus, the Torah relates three incidents in Moses' life before God chose him to deliver the Israelites from Egypt. They teach that Jews must be involved in fighting injustice and helping to resolve disputes, whether they are between Jews, Jews and non-Jews, or only non-Jews.

On the first day that Moses goes out to his people from the palace of Pharaoh in which he was raised, he rushes to defend a Hebrew against an Egyptian aggressor (Exodus 2:11–12). When Moses next goes out, he defends a Jew being beaten by another Jew (Exodus 2:13). Later, after being forced to flee from Egypt and arriving at a well in Midian, Moses comes to the aid of the shepherd daughters of Jethro who were being harassed by other shepherds (Exodus 2:17). In all three cases, Moses pursues justice, no matter whom the victims are or what group they belong to. One could argue it was these three actions that demonstrated to God that Moses was the right person to confront Pharaoh and later lead the Israelites out of Egypt.

The story of Moses has become an archetypal model for liberation movements today. This is a great gift from the Jewish people to the world. When Dr. Martin Luther King said to a gathering of civil rights activists in Memphis, Tennessee on April 3, 1968, the night before he was assassinated, "I've seen the Promised Land. I may not get there with you. But I want you to know that we, as a people, will get to the Promised Land," he was evoking the eternal story of Moses as a model for the United States civil rights movement. Like Moses, Dr. King was confronting the Pharaoh of his own day with "Let my people go!"

Balaam, the biblical pagan prophet, intended to curse Israel, but ended up blessing them. He described the role of the Jewish people as: "Lo, it is a people dwelling alone, and not reckoning itself among the nations" (Numbers 23:9). For Jews both then and now, the keynote of their existence is: "I am the Lord thy God, who has separated you from the nations that you should be Mine" (Leviticus 20:26). Throughout their history, Jews have often been nonconformists who refused to acquiesce to the false gods and values of the surrounding communities.

When the Jews were in Persia, Mordechai refused to defer to an evil ruler. As the book of Esther tells us: "And all the king's servants . . . bowed down and prostrated themselves before Haman. . . . But Mordechai would not bow down nor prostrate himself before him" (Esther 3:2). Mordechai believed that bowing down to a human being was inconsistent with his obligation to worship only God. Later Mordechai condemned inaction by urging Esther to take personal risks to save the Jewish people (Esther 4:13–14).

The greatest champions of protest against unjust conditions were the Hebrew prophets. Rabbi Abraham Heschel summarizes the attributes of these spokespeople for God. They had the ability to hold God and people in one thought at the same time; they could not be tranquil in an unjust world; they were supremely impatient with evil, due to their intense sensitivity to God's concern for right and wrong; they were advocates for those too weak to plead their own cause (the widow, the orphan, and the oppressed); and their major activity was involvement, remonstrating against wrongs inflicted on other people.[2]

So prophets, in Judaism, are not fortunetellers. They are social activists, protesters, and yes, radicals. They care about the common people in the here and now and call the community to decisive action. They do not claim that human suffering is some sort of karma to be accepted with resignation. They challenge us to change ourselves, change the fabric of society, and make the world a better place in which to live. The prophets rage against injustices and demand that we fix them in the here and now. In the words of Rabbi Heschel:

What manner of man is the prophet? A student of philosophy who turns from the discourses of the great metaphysicians to the orations of the

---

2. Abraham Joshua Heschel, *The Prophets* (Philadelphia: Jewish Publication Society, 1962), and *The Insecurity of Freedom* (Noonday Press, New York, 1959), 9–13 and 92–93.

prophets may feel as if he were going from the realm of the sublime to an area of trivialities. Instead of dealing with the timeless issues of being and becoming, of matter and form, of definitions and demonstrations, he is thrown into orations about widows and orphans, about the corruption of judges and affairs of the marketplace. . . . Prophecy is the voice that God has lent to the silent agony, a voice to the plundered poor, to the profaned riches of the world. It is a form of living, a crossing point of God and man. God is raging in the prophet's words.[3]

In sharp contrast to this prophetic heritage, today's Jewish communities (and most others) often ignore or respond placidly to immoral acts and conditions. We try to maintain a balanced tone while victims of oppression are in extreme agony. But it is not so with the prophets. Isaiah cries out:

> Cry aloud, spare not, Lift up your voice like a trumpet, and declare unto My people their transgression. . . . Is this not the fast that I have chosen? To release the chains of wickedness, to undo the bonds of oppression, to let the crushed go free, and to break every yoke of tyranny.
>
> (Isaiah 58:1,6)

The prophet Amos berates those who are content amidst destruction and injustice:

> Woe to those who are at ease in Zion,
> And to those who feel secure
> on the mountains of Samaria . . .
> Woe to those who lie upon beds of ivory,
> And stretch themselves upon their couches,
> And eat lambs from the flock,
> And calves from the midst of the stall;
> Who sing idle songs to the sound of the harp . . .
> Who drink wine in bowls,
> And anoint themselves in the finest oils,
> But are not grieved on the ruin of Joseph!
>
> (Amos 6:1,4–6)

---

3. Abraham Joshua Heschel, *The Prophets* (Philadelphia, Jewish Publication Society, 1955), 3,5.

In order to carry out their mission to be a kingdom of priests and a light unto the nations, Jews throughout history were compelled to live in the world, but apart from it – in effect, living on "the other side," that is, opposing wickedness. This, the sages comment, is implied in the very name "Hebrew" (*ivri*), from *ever*, "the other side." "The whole world is on one side [idolaters] and he [Abraham, the Hebrew] is on the other side" (Midrash Genesis *Rabbah*). Jacques Maritain, a French Catholic philosopher, wrote in 1939 that the Jewish people were

> found at the very heart of the world's structure, stimulating it, exasper-ating it, moving it. . . . It [the Jewish people] gives the world no peace, it bars slumber, it teaches the world to be discontented and restless as long as the world has not accepted God.[4]

Several distinguished Orthodox rabbis of the past two centuries, including Rabbis Samson Raphael Hirsch, a leading 19th century German Orthodox theologian; Jonathan Sacks, former Chief Rabbi of the United Kingdom; Joseph B. Soloveitchik, known as the Rav; and Lord Immanuel Jakobovits, former Chief Rabbi of the United Kingdom have stressed that Judaism has a message for their surrounding cultures and that Jews should convey it to their host societies.[5] Rabbi Soloveitchik, one of the foremost Torah leaders of the twentieth century, believed that Jews have a responsibility to work with others to promote the welfare of civilization. He felt that Jews must aid the needy and protect human rights because such obligations are "implicit in human existence."[6] He states: "We stand shoulder to shoulder with the rest of civilized society over against an order that defies us all." Rabbi Sacks believes that working for *tikkun olam* (healing and repairing the planet) can be an antidote to religious isolationism:

> One of the most powerful assumptions of the twentieth century is that faith . . . belongs to private life. Religion and society, many believe, are

---

4. Quoted in Norman Lamm, *The Royal Reach* (New York: Feldheim, Inc., 1970), 131.
5. David Shatz, Chaim I. Waxman, and Nathan J. Diament (eds.), *Tikkun Olam: Social Responsibility in Jewish Thought and Law* (Northvale, NJ: Jason Aronson, 1997), 3
6. Ibid, 4; also see Joseph B. Soloveitchik, "Confrontation," *Tradition* 6:2 (1964), 5–29.

two independent entities, so we can edit God out of the language and leave our social world unchanged.[7]

In contrast to society's conforming attitude, and based on Jewish tradition and values, Jews have been active in many protest movements. Some of these movements have been on behalf of Jewish causes, such as the effort to rescue European Jews from the Holocaust, the battle to support Jewish independence and survival in Israel, and the struggles for Soviet Jewry and later for Syrian and Ethiopian Jewry. But Jews also have been actively involved in struggles for a more peaceful world, human rights, and a cleaner environment. A group of rabbis, acting in accordance with the Jewish ethic of protest, explained why they came to St. Augustine, Florida in 1964 to demonstrate against segregation in that community:

> We came because we could not stand silently by our brother's blood.
> We had done that too many times before. We have been vocal in our
> exhortation of others but the idleness of our hands too often revealed
> an inner silence. . . . We came as Jews who remember the millions of
> faceless people who stood quietly, watching the smoke rise from Hitler's
> crematoria. We came because we know that second only to silence, the
> greatest danger to man is loss of faith in man's capacity to act.[8]

SOME OF JUDAISM'S RADICAL TEACHINGS

The Uniqueness and Sanctity of Each Person

Judaism teaches that every person is created in God's image (Genesis 1:27), and therefore is of supreme value. This is a truly radical statement, considering that many ancient civilizations (and even some people today) considered their race or nation superior to all others. The English word "barbarian" comes from the ancient Greek *barbarous*, meaning "not a Greek." Judaism expresses the concept that Jews are a chosen people.

---

7. Jonathan Sacks, *The Persistence of Faith*, (London, Jews College, 1990), 27.
8. "Why We Went," (paper of the Social Action Commission, Union of American Hebrew Congregations, New York); quoted in Rabbi Henry Cohen, *Justice, Justice: A Jewish View of the Black Revolution* (New York: Union of American Hebrew Congregations,1969), 18.

This does not imply any special favoritism, but rather obligations and responsibilities, a call to greater involvement, in being a "light unto the nations" in working to improve the world. As Rabbi Ahron Soloveichik expressed it, "The distinction between Jew and non-Jew does not imply any concept of inferiority, but is based primarily upon the unique and special burdens that are incumbent upon Jews."[9]

Imagine if people really took the claim of Genesis 1:27 seriously and viewed each person as created "in the image of God." We would likely not have so much hatred, bigotry, animosity, and violence toward each other. We would not have so much oppression of the poor and underprivileged – "the widow, the orphan, and the stranger" – so often invoked in Scripture.

Do Not Oppress the Stranger

There is a commandment in Exodus that is repeated in various formulations 36 times in the Hebrew Bible, more often than any other mitzvah: "You shall not oppress a stranger, since you yourselves know the feelings of a stranger, for you were strangers in the land of Egypt" (Exodus 23:9). Having historically been aliens in a foreign land ourselves, we should know what it is like to be oppressed and looked down upon simply for being foreigners.

Based on this frequent scriptural repetition, Rabbi Emanuel Rackman, former Chancellor of Bar Ilan University in Israel, points out that Judaism teaches a special kind of justice, an "empathic justice," that seeks to make people identify themselves with each other's needs, each other's hopes and aspirations, and each other's defeats and frustrations. Because Jews have known the distress of being slaves and the loneliness of having been strangers, we are to project ourselves into the souls of others and make their plight our own. We are to empathize – literally "to feel with" – the lonely stranger among us. Rabbi Levi Yitzchak Horowitz, the Bostoner Rebbe, reinforces this concept:

> The fact that the Jewish people had to experience 400 years of Egyptian exile, including 210 years of actual slavery, was critical in molding our

---

9. Rabbi Ahron Soloveitchik, *Logic of the Heart, Logic of the Mind: Wisdom and Reflections on Topics of Our Times* (Jerusalem: Genesis Jerusalem Press, 1991), chapter 5, Civil Rights and the Dignity of Man, 61.

national personality into one of compassion and concern for our fellow man, informed by the realization that we have a vital role to play in the world. . . . For this reason, God begins the Ten Commandments with a reminder that "I am the Lord, your God, who took you out of Egypt" (Exodus 20:2). We must constantly remember that we were slaves in order to always appreciate the ideal of freedom, not only for ourselves but also for others. We must do what we can to help others to live free of the bondage of the evil spirit, free of the bondage of cruelty, of abuse and lack of caring.[10]

Helping the Poor and Hungry

To help the poor and hungry and to support communal purposes and institutions, Judaism places great stress on the giving of charity as an act of righteousness. The Hebrew word for charity, *tzedakah*, literally means "righteousness" and is derived from the same root as *tzedek* – justice. In the Jewish tradition, giving *tzedakah* is not an act of condescension by one person to another who is in need. Rather, it is the fulfillment of a mitzvah, a holy commandment, to a fellow human being, who has equal status before God. The beggar has the *right* to ask for help, and the person asked is often *obligated* to give it. All wealth ultimately belongs to God, so if you prosper, that good fortune is meant to enable you to be a steward of God's wealth and to take care of the less fortunate. In so doing, you yourself are also blessed. And everyone, even a beggar, is obligated in turn to give to others, because there is always someone worse off than he is.

For this reason, many Torah laws are designed to aid the poor: the produce of corners of the fields are to be left uncut for the poor to take (Leviticus 19:9); the gleanings of the wheat harvest and fallen fruit are to be left for the needy (Leviticus 19:10); and during the sabbatical year, the land is to be left fallow so the poor (as well as animals) may eat of whatever grows freely (Leviticus 25:2–7). In the same chapter of Leviticus in the Torah portion *Kedoshim* ("You shall be holy"), in which "Love your neighbor as yourself" (19:18) appears, the Torah outlines some specific ways that this mandate can be put into practice:

---

10. Rabbi Levi Yitzchak Horowitz, the Bostoner Rebbe, "And You Shall tell Your Son," *Young Israel Viewpoint*, Spring, 1997. Quoted in David Sears, *Compassion for Humanity in the Jewish Tradition* (Northvale, New Jersey/Jerusalem: Jason Aronson, 1998), 22.

You shall not steal; nor shall you deal falsely nor lie to one another
. . . You shall not oppress your neighbor, nor rob him . . . You shall
not curse the deaf, and you shall not put a stumbling block before the
blind . . . You shall do no injustice in judgment; be not partial to the
poor, and favor not the mighty; in righteousness shall you judge your
neighbor. You shall not go up and down as a talebearer among your
people; neither shall you stand idly by the blood of your neighbor: I
am the Lord.   (19:11, 14–16)

Proper Treatment of Non-Jews

Judaism is concerned with the proper treatment of non-Jews as well as
Jews. The Talmud contains many statutes that require Jews to assist and
provide for non-Jews as well as Jews:

We support the poor of the non-Jew along with the poor of Israel and
visit the sick of the non-Jew along with the sick of Israel and bury the
dead of the non-Jew along with the dead of Israel, for the sake of peace.
                                                        (Talmud *Gittin* 61a)

In a city where there are both Jews and Gentiles, the collectors of alms
collect from both; they feed the poor of both, visit the sick of both,
bury both, comfort the mourners whether they be Jews or Gentiles,
and restore the lost goods of both, *mipnei darchei shalom*: to promote
peace and cooperation.   (*Yerushalmi Dmai* 4:6 24a)

Jewish Teachings on Involvement and Protest

Judaism teaches that people must struggle to create a better society. The
Torah frequently admonishes: "And you shall eradicate the evil from
your midst" (Deuteronomy 13:6, 17:7, 21:21, 24:7). Injustice cannot be
passively accepted; it must be actively resisted and, ultimately, eliminated.
The Talmudic sages teach that one reason Jerusalem was destroyed was
because its citizens failed in their responsibility to constructively criticize
each other's improper behavior (Talmud *Shabbat* 99b). They indicate that
"love which does not contain the element of [constructive] criticism is
not really love" (Midrash Genesis *Rabbah* 54:3).

Among the many powerful rabbinical teachings about the importance of active involvement are the following:

> Whoever is able to protest against the transgressions of his own family and does not do so is punished [held liable, held responsible] for the transgressions of his family. Whoever is able to protest against the transgressions of the people of his community and does not do so is punished for the transgressions of his community. Whoever is able to protest against the transgressions of the entire world and does not do so is punished for the transgressions of the entire world. (*Shabbat* 54b)

> If a person of learning participates in public affairs and serves as judge or arbiter, he gives stability to the land. But if he sits in his home and says to himself, "What have the affairs of society to do with me? . . . Why should I trouble myself with the people's voices of protest? Let my soul dwell in peace!" If he does this, he overthrows the world.
> (Midrash *Tanchuma* on *Mishpatim* 2)

While the essential elements of Jewish practice include devotion to Torah, study, prayer, performing good deeds and other *mitzvot* (commandments), and cultivating a life of piety, Judaism teaches that to be considered truly pious, a person must also protest against injustice in society (*Shabbat* 55a). Moses did not simply sit and study after encountering the burning bush. He returned to Egypt to confront Pharaoh and to help free the Hebrew slaves.

Judaism teaches that it is not sufficient merely to perform *mitzvot* while passively acquiescing to unjust conditions. The Maharal of Prague, a sixteenth-century sage, said that individual piety pales in the face of the sin of not protesting against an emerging communal evil, and a person will be held accountable for not preventing wickedness when capable of doing so.[11] Holocaust survivor and author Elie Wiesel said: "Take sides. Neutrality helps the oppressor, never the victim. Silence encourages the tormentor, never the tormented."[12]

---

11. R. Judah Loew, Netivot Olam, Shaar Hatochahah, end of chapter 2.
12. Nobel Prize speech by Elie Wiesel, December 10, 1986, http://www.eliewieselfou ndation.org/nobelprizespeech.aspx

One of the most important dangers of silence in the face of evil is that it implies acceptance, or possibly even support. According to Rabbenu Yonah, a medieval sage, sinners may think to themselves, "Since others are neither reproving nor contending against us, our deeds are permissible" (*Orchot Tzaddikim* 24).

"JUSTICE, JUSTICE SHALL YOU PURSUE" (DEUTERONOMY 16: 20)

The pursuit of a just society is one of the most fundamental concepts of Judaism. The prevalence of injustice in today's world makes Judaism's emphasis on the importance of actively seeking justice all the more urgent. To practice justice is considered among the highest demands of prophetic religion.

> It has been told to you, O human being, what is good
> And what the Lord requires of you:
> Only to do justly, love *chesed* (mercy, kindness),
> And walk humbly with your God. (Micah 6:8)

The prophets constantly stress the importance of applying justice.

> Learn to do well – seek justice, relieve the oppressed, judge the fatherless, plead for the widow. . . . Zion shall be redeemed with justice, and they who return to her with righteousness. (Isaiah 1:17, 27)

> The Lord of Hosts shall be exalted in justice, the Holy God is shown holy in righteousness. (Isaiah 5:16)

The prophet Amos warned the people that without the practice of justice, God is repelled by their worship:

> Take away from Me the noise of your songs
> and let Me not hear the melody
> of your stringed instruments,
> but let justice well up as waters,
> and righteousness as a mighty stream. (Amos 5:23, 24)

The practice of justice is even part of the symbolic betrothal between the Jewish people and God:

> And I will betroth you unto Me forever; And, I will betroth you unto Me in righteousness, justice, loving kindness, and compassion. And I will betroth you unto Me in faithfulness. And you shall know the Lord.
>
> (Hosea 2:21–22)

Many other statements in the Jewish tradition emphasize the great importance placed on working for justice. For example, the book of Proverbs asserts: "To do righteousness and justice is preferred by God above sacrifice" (Proverbs 21:3). The Psalmist exhorts: "Give justice to the weak and the fatherless; maintain the right of the afflicted and the destitute" (Psalms 82:3).

The prophets of Israel were the greatest champions of social justice in world history. Jeremiah rebukes the Jewish people when they fail to plead the cause of the orphan or help the needy (5:28). He castigates an entire generation, for "in your skirts is found the blood of the souls of the innocent poor" (2:34). Ezekiel rebukes the whole nation for "using oppression, robbing, defrauding the poor and the needy, and extorting from the stranger" (22:29). Isaiah (5:8) and Micah (2:2) criticize wealthy Jews who built up large holdings of property at the expense of their neighbors. The prophetic books are filled with such moral admonitions.

Based on these teachings, Jews have regarded the practice of justice and the seeking of a just society as divine imperatives. This has inspired many Jews throughout history to be leaders in struggles for better social conditions. The teachings of the Torah, prophets, and sages have been the most powerful inspiration for justice in the history of the world.

Seek Peace and Pursue it (Psalms 34:15)

Judaism describes a special obligation to strive for peace. Our tradition commands that Jews actively pursue peace. The Midrash states that there are many commandments that require a certain time and place for their performance, but with regard to the mandate to "seek peace and pursue it," (Psalms 34:15) we are to seek it in our own place and pursue it everywhere else (Midrash *Leviticus Rabbah* 9:9). The famous Talmudic sage Hillel states that we should "be of the disciples of Aaron, loving peace and pursuing peace" (*Pirkei Avot* 1:12). There is a rabbinic story of how Aaron the Priest would go back and forth between adversaries, gradually bringing them together in peace. He was the model peacemaker. The only other value that Judaism teaches us to *pursue* is justice. The Jewish sages stressed the importance of peace:

> Great is peace, for God's name is peace ... Great is peace, for it encompasses all blessings ... Great is peace, for even in times of war, peace must be sought ... Great is peace for when the Messiah comes, he will commence with peace, as it is said [in Isaiah 52:7]: "How beautiful upon the mountains are the feet (footsteps) of the messenger of good tidings, who announces peace." (Leviticus *Rabbah* 9:9)

> Great is peace, for with peace the Holy One, Who is to be blessed, will announce the Redemption of Israel, and with peace He will console Jerusalem ... See how beloved is peace! When the Holy One, Blessed be He, wished to bless Israel, He could not find a vessel great enough to contain their blessings, except for peace. (Deuteronomy *Rabbah* 5:15)

It is significant that many of the most important Jewish prayers conclude with a supplication for peace. These include the *Amidah* (silent prayer – also known as the *Shmoneh Esrei* – which is recited three times daily), the *Kaddish*, the Grace After Meals, and the Priestly Blessing.

The Jewish tradition does not mandate pacifism or peace at any price, although some Jews do become pacifists based on Jewish values.[13] The Israelites frequently went forth to battle and not always in defensive wars. But they always held to the ideal of universal peace and yearned for the day when there would be no more bloodshed or violence and when the instruments of war would be converted into tools of production:

---

13. Rabbi Yonassan Gershom is a pacifist. He considers pacifism to be his personal *chumra* – an extra strictness – voluntarily taken on in the service of God. In the course of helping me write this chapter, he explained, "Some people are extra strict with such *mitzvot* as observing the Sabbath, keeping glatt kosher, dressing very modestly, etc. In the same spirit, I choose to be extra strict in pursuing peace. The role of a pacifist is to remind people that war is not a normal condition of human existence, and that we should all be striving for peace."

And they shall beat their swords into plowshares,
And their spears into pruning hooks;
Nation shall not lift up sword against nation,
Neither shall they learn war any more.
But they shall sit every man under his vine and under his fig tree;
And none shall make them afraid;
For the mouth of the Lord of hosts has spoken.

(Isaiah 2:4; Micah 4:3–4)

Rabbi Albert Axelrad, former Hillel director at Brandeis University, argued that Jews should be "pacifoids." This means doing everything possible to avoid war, but also recognizing that in extreme cases war may be tragically necessary. Such an approach would likely have avoided recent United States wars in Vietnam, Iraq, and Afghanistan, and recent Israeli wars in Gaza and Lebanon, with all the resulting damage and tragedy from which we are still suffering.

*

IN SUMMARY, Judaism stresses that we are to love other people as ourselves, to be kind to strangers "for you were strangers in the land of Egypt," and to act with compassion toward the homeless, the poor, the orphan, the widow, even toward enemies, and to all of God's creatures. The Torah also teaches us how to be activists and not "stand by our neighbor's blood," which means not allowing evil to happen to others while doing nothing to stop it. We are, as the account of Cain's question in Genesis implies, "our brother's [and sister's] keepers." The Prophets understood this, and so did our Sages throughout the centuries.

These are only a few of the many authentic concepts and references in the Jewish tradition that can be cited to prove the radical nature of Judaism as an activist religion. More information about these and other radical Jewish teachings can be found in my book, *Judaism and Global Survival.*

In later chapters these concepts, as well as additional radical teachings from the Torah, the prophets, the Talmudic sages and some recent rabbis, will be discussed in more depth. For now, it is enough to say that these ethical principles helped to shape my own activism. Now it is for us – all of us, Jews and Gentiles alike – to pick up this thread of "justice, justice shall you pursue" and carry it into the future.

Chapter 4

Should the Holocaust
Be a Spur to Activism?

For me the Holocaust was not only a Jewish tragedy, but also a human tragedy. After the war, when I saw that the Jews were talking only about the tragedy of six million Jews, I sent letters to Jewish organizations asking them to also talk about the millions of others who were persecuted together with us – many of them only because they helped Jews.

— SIMON WIESENTHAL[1]

Every year around *Yom Hashoa*, Holocaust Remembrance Day, my Orthodox synagogue has a memorial commemoration. It is a well-planned event, featuring a talk by a Holocaust scholar or survivor, appropriate songs by local yeshiva choirs, and the lighting of candles by descendants of Holocaust victims or survivors. Similar events are held at many other synagogues, Jewish community centers, and other communal venues on or around that day. This is very appropriate, since it is essential that the horrors of the Holocaust never be forgotten and that younger generations be educated about why and how this cataclysm happened.

But there is seldom an attempt to use the Holocaust as a spur to action against other injustices. Of course, there should not be any attempt to equate events, but there should be recognition that some of the mindsets behind the Holocaust are still causing much harm to people, and it is important not to repeat the apathy that was so prevalent during the Holocaust.

In his book *The Dignity of Difference*, Jonathan Sacks, former Chief

---

1. http://thinkexist.com/quotation/for-me-was-the-holocaust-not-only-a-jewish/348597.html

Rabbi of the United Kingdom, argues that there can only be reconciliation and an end of war and violence through forgiveness. But his awareness of Jewish history involving centuries of exiles and expulsions, pogroms, and persecutions – starting with the first crusade and culminating with the murder of two-thirds of European Jews during the Holocaust – makes him wonder how he can let go of the pain that is written into his very soul.

> And yet I must. For the sake of my children and theirs, not yet born. I cannot build the future on the hatreds of the past, nor can I teach them to love God more by loving people less.... The duty I owe my ancestors who died because of their faith is to build a world in which people no longer die because of their faith. I honour the past not by repeating it but by learning from it – by refusing to add pain to pain, grief to grief. That is why we must answer hatred with love, violence with peace, resentment with generosity of spirit and conflict with reconciliation.[2]

What a sharp contrast with the attitude of so many people who generally think in terms of revenge, and often revert to hateful attitudes and violent reactions in response to actual or perceived harms.

Instead of learning universal lessons from the Holocaust and making sure that all injustices are actively responded to, many Jews have adopted the view that the whole world is against us, or, at best, does not care about us. Therefore, they believe they need only be concerned about their own welfare and that of other Jews, while ignoring problems that do not specifically affect Jews.

The Holocaust was an unprecedented catastrophe in which six million Jews were slaughtered simply because of their ethnic identity, and at least five million others were also killed because of who they were. It is important that there be annual commemorations of the Holocaust and that people continue visiting Holocaust museums, so that the unspeakable horrors are not forgotten. It is also important to avoid simplistic comparisons with the Holocaust, lest its meaning be diluted and the suffering of those who perished or were tortured in the Holocaust be minimized.

However, we should not try to build a wall around the Holocaust, and turn it into a sacred shrine that is isolated from the rest of history and the

---

2. Jonathan Sacks, *The Dignity of Difference: How to Avoid the Clash of Civilizations* (London/New York: Continuum, revised edition 2003), 190.

rest of the world. We should not use the Holocaust to silence thought about how the mentalities and methods analogous to those that produced the Holocaust continue to promote other injustices and atrocities. We should not let the Holocaust and our respect for the memory of its victims and survivors inhibit us from confronting the issue of how the Holocaust came about, especially since the attitudes that led to it are still prevalent in the world today. We should not keep the lessons of the Holocaust in a narrow straitjacket in the name of remembering the victims.

I believe that the best way to honor the memories of Holocaust victims is to work against the ideologies and techniques that helped produce it and still continue, although to a lesser degree, to inflict tremendous damage on people, animals, and the entire planet. We honor the lives and deaths of Holocaust victims by working to combat all injustice and oppression. We owe it to them to make the world a better place.

The greatest tribute we can give to the victims and survivors of the Holocaust is to confront the fascist, might-makes-right mentality that produced the Holocaust, wherever such attitudes and behavior appear, so that nothing remotely like the Holocaust ever happens again to Jews or to anybody else. Doing this will be a *kiddush HaShem* (a sanctification of God's name) that will greatly benefit the world. We should learn from the Holocaust and be impelled by it to work for a more just, non-violent world. Apathy to current oppressions of people and animals does not honor the memory of Holocaust victims. Letting the Holocaust be a spur to action to try to make positive changes is a much better way to honor the martyrs of the Holocaust.

And, of course, the Holocaust should not be used to justify acts of oppression against others, or to keep Jews from responding swiftly and effectively to the oppression of others. If we look at modern studies about the cycles of bullying and abuse, the sad fact is that the abused often grow up to become abusers unless there is conscious intervention to break the cycle.

While it is true that the Holocaust was an unprecedented catastrophe, it is also true that there have been other genocides in recent years, such as the calculated mass murder of two million Cambodians in the 1970s, the "ethnic cleansing" in Bosnia and the Balkans in the 1990s, the murder of over 800,000 Tutsi tribes-people by the Hutus in Rwanda in 1994, and the killings recently taking place in Darfur. The world sees these events as reminiscent to the Holocaust because they are genocides, even though the numbers of dead are not as great and the victims are not Jews. As Jews, we are obligated not to stand idly by and let these murders unfold. We should be among the first to protest and get involved in efforts to stop them.

We should not feel that the suffering during the Holocaust was so great that any current suffering is minor by comparison, and therefore we do not need to be concerned about it. We should not feel that because the world was silent when Jews were being massacred, we have a legitimate excuse for inaction today. We should instead make sure that the stirring motto "Never again!" is applied not only to Jews, but to all people everywhere.

Looking at the Holocaust as an impetus to activism can help revitalize Judaism by showing how Jewish eternal values can be addressed to current threats to humanity, such as hunger, environmental degradation, racial profiling and other prejudices, terrorism, war, and genocide.

Elie Wiesel has pointed out that there can be no analogies to the Holocaust, but that it can be used as a reference point. In that context, we can consider the millions of people, many of whom are infants, who die each year due to malnutrition. Of course, victims of hunger are not singled out because of their religion, race, or nationality, but, like Holocaust victims, they die while the world goes about its business, grumbling about personal inconveniences, indifferent to the plight of the starving people.

Rabbi Abraham Joshua Heschel, himself a refugee from Europe just before the Holocaust, applied this reasoning to the Civil Rights Movement. He marched with Dr. Martin Luther King to help end segregation in the United States. He saw the parallels between making Jews wear a "badge of shame" (Star of David identifying them as Jews) and singling out African Americans because of their skin color.

The Mishna teaches that if one saves a single human life, it is as if one has saved the entire world (Sanhedrin 4:5).[3] What then if one fails to save a single life? Or fails to help save millions of lives? Although Elie Wiesel argues that the Holocaust cannot be compared to any other event, he does believe in caring about and being involved in working to end other genocides, oppressions, and other tragedies.

---

3. This quote appears in multiple places in Jewish texts with variant versions. Some versions read "whoever saves a single *Jewish* soul," leading anti-Jewish critics to claim that Jews do not value the lives of Gentiles. However, when Jews cite this sentence as a maxim, it is always the universalist version. The Qu'ran also cites the universalist version of this Mishnah (*Sura* 5:32)

In deciding if we should help others who are being oppressed or slaughtered, we should consider the famous statement by Pastor Martin Niemöller (1892–1984) about the inactivity of Germans after the Nazis rose to power and purged one group after another.

> They came first for the Communists, and I didn't speak up because I wasn't a Communist. Then they came for the Social Democrats, and I didn't speak up because I wasn't a Social Democrat. Then they came for the trade unionists, and I didn't speak up because I wasn't a trade unionist. Then they came for the Jews, and I didn't speak up because I wasn't a Jew. Then they came for me, and by that time no one was left to speak up.[4]

An excellent example of using the Holocaust as a spur to action is the life of Alex Hershaft, PhD. He visited Israel from May 2 to May 13 in 2015 to explain how his experience in the Warsaw Ghetto was a major factor in his becoming a leading animal rights activist. With the theme, "From surviving the Warsaw Ghetto to co-founding the U.S. animal rights movement," he gave several talks and met with Israeli Jewish and Arab animal rights activists.

In his lectures, Hershaft discussed how dealing with the trauma and grief over the loss of his family during the Holocaust shaped his values and outlook on life, and increased his sense of compassion. When his life was no longer in danger, he felt guilty that he survived when so many others had perished. He felt that in response to his miraculous survival, he should devote himself to repaying a debt to society by devoting his life to helping the helpless, and to working to reduce the oppression in the world. After visiting a slaughterhouse where he saw piles of hooves, skins, hearts, livers, and skulls that he felt bore silent witness to evil, he became a vegetarian (and later a vegan). He felt that the challenging mandate, 'never again,' should apply to us not oppressing others as well as us not being oppressed.

With a PhD in chemistry, Hershaft could have had a career that would have provided him with a comfortable life. But he gave that up to devote his life to ending the mistreatment of farmed animals. He founded the Farm Animal Reform Movement (FARM), which later became the Farm

---

4. http://www.history.ucsb.edu/faculty/marcuse/niem.htm

Animal Rights Movement. The group has many activities, including an annual animal rights national conference that now attracts almost 1,500 attendees to hear leading animal rights activists, and to visit booths that provide much information about other animal rights and vegan groups as well as information about the latest vegan products, books, and videos. Since their beginning in 1976, and official formation in 1981, FARM has launched a variety of grassroots campaigns in pursuit of their mission: World Day for Farmed Animals, Great American Meatout, Gentle Thanksgiving, 10 Billion Lives Tour, Letters from FARM, Sabina Fund, Meatout Mondays, and Live Vegan. I am proud to be on the Board of this wonderful organization.

In an interview with the Israeli publication Ynet magazine during his visit,[5] 81 year-old Hershaft stated:

> As a Holocaust survivor, I have found a way to repay my debt to the world. There's a reason why I survived. The way (to pay my debt) is to fight for the animals.
>
> The Jewish Holocaust was a unique event in history – a unique event for the Jewish people and for me personally. Apart from the Holocaust, there's never been another act of systematic and industrial inhumanity on the part of one nation towards another. The holocaust of the animals is also unique and systematic – yet it continues unabated. Hundreds of millions of animals are brutally slaughtered around the world every day.
>
> The best way to honor the Holocaust is to learn from it and to fight all forms of oppression. We may have been victorious in World War II, but the struggle against oppression and injustice is far from over. For me, the Holocaust isn't a tool in the struggle, but an experience that shaped my personality and my values, made me who I am today, and drove me to fight all forms of oppression, including the oppression of the weakest creatures, the animals.
>
> It's important for us to think about the oppression that exists everywhere, to emphasize the silent cooperation of the masses. The Holocaust, too, would not have taken place without the silent consent, the lack of opposition, the disregard of the nations of the world that simply stood by and allowed it to happen.

---

5. Moshe Ronen, "Holocaust survivor in defense of the animals," *Ynet magazine,* May 10, 2015.

And the same goes for eating meat and other animal products. We support it without seeing the abuse with our own eyes. The masses that stand on the sidelines and remain silent facilitate this abuse and oppression. The emphasis shouldn't be on the victims, but on us. We have to ensure that we never repeat the horrors that the Nazis perpetrated against us.

The following statement by Rabbi Philip Bentley, former Chair and now Honorary President of the Jewish Peace Fellowship, in his essay "Fixing the World" from the book *Roots of Jewish Nonviolence*, is a good summary of the arguments in this chapter:

> There are two ways to respond to the lessons taught [to] us by the Holocaust. We can say, "No one is our true ally, therefore we must concern ourselves only with ourselves." Or we can say "The Nazis were able to demonize the Jews and then murder millions of us because we were unable to bring others to our cause. We must therefore fight every kind of bigotry and tyranny from the outset, lest we also become victims." A national trauma like the Holocaust brings out the best and the worst in people. The hard lesson of the Holocaust is that we must be quick to respond to every threat to ourselves, but also to every kind of racism and bigotry, no matter who its victims are.

The world is threatened today as perhaps never before. The potential catastrophes threaten not only Jews, but all of humanity as well. Therefore, it is essential that the Holocaust not be used as a reason to avoid involvement, but just the opposite – as a spur to consistent activism, to create a more just, humane, peaceful, and environmentally sustainable world.

Chapter 5

How To Reduce Anti-Semitism

*A*nti-Semitism is not to be overcome by getting people to forget us, but to know us.   – Meyer Levin

*T*he worst mistake I ever made was that stupid, suburban prejudice of Anti-Semitism.   – Ezra Pound

*T*hou shalt not be a victim, thou shalt not be a perpetrator, but above all, thou shalt not be a bystander.

– YEHUDA BAUER

ANTI-SEMITISM, A EUPHEMISM FOR Jew hatred that was coined in the 19th century, has existed in nearly every age and nearly every country, generally irrespective of circumstances, even where there have been few or no Jews. Anti-Semitism, like racism, is not based on reason. It sets up Jews as scapegoats for current problems, and lets those who are really responsible for society's ills off the hook. Whatever the current social order does not like (or feels threatened by) is projected onto the Jews.

In the 19th century, with the rise of nationalism, Jews were portrayed as "universalists" with no loyalty to any country. In the mid-20th century when global consciousness increased, Jews began to be negatively portrayed as "separatists" who only care about themselves and not the rest of the world. Neither of these stereotypes about Jews is true – in fact, they are incompatible opposites – but they serve to give simplistic explanations for complex problems to the more gullible sectors of society. Similarly, Jews have been portrayed simultaneously as greedy, wealthy bankers and capitalists and as revolutionary, subversive Marxists. This scapegoating has often caused great pain, oppression, and hardship for the Jewish people.

Jews have probably suffered more from prejudice throughout Western history than any other group. The Crusades, the Inquisition, and the Holocaust are just three of the most horrible examples. Many times Jews have been killed, expelled from countries where they had lived and contributed to society for many generations, subjected to pogroms, or converted at sword point (or died resisting) solely because they were Jewish. Whenever conditions were bad, the economy suffered, or there was a plague blaming "the Jews" provided a convenient scapegoat. In parts of medieval Europe, long before the discovery of bacteria, it was commonly believed that the very presence of a Jew would sour the milk and spoil the crops. Jews often paid with their lives for these superstitions.

RECENT INCREASES IN ANTI-SEMITISM

Unfortunately, in the 21st century anti-Semitism has gone global and is increasing in many areas of the world. Neo-Nazis, Skinheads, Muslim extremists, and other hate groups use the Internet and other modern means to spread their hateful messages. Old lies and forgeries, such as *The Protocols of the Elders of Zion,* have been "rediscovered" and posted on the web, complete with pseudo-intellectual analyses. People don't always use critical thinking about what they read, and some take these canards at face value. There are also many groups and even some government leaders, like former President Ahmadinejad of Iran, who claim that the Holocaust never occurred or has been wildly exaggerated.

This prejudice is not limited to right-wing fanatics. Some segments of the anti-war movement have conspiracy theories that blame the Jews for pushing the United States into invading Iraq and controlling other aspects of U.S. foreign policy. Other examples of anti-Semitism are protest signs and speeches that equate Zionism with Nazism, Jewish leaders with Hitler, and the Star of David with a swastika. There have been many examples of increased anti-Israel statements and actions that are rooted in anti-Semitism in the Arab world and among some Muslim communities in many countries.

Recently there has been an increase in anti-Semitism in several European countries, to such an extent that many European Jews have left for Israel or are seriously considering doing so. An especially serious example that was a wake-up call to many in France was the killing of four Jews in a kosher supermarket shortly before Shabbat on January 9, 2015, confirming the worst fears of an already tense Jewry, due to previous acts of terrorism.

MISUSE OF CLAIMS OF ANTI-SEMITISM

It is very important to distinguish between genuine anti-Semitism – which is discussed above – and *perceived* anti-Semitism, which may or may not be the same thing. Of course, we must do everything possible to reduce genuine anti-Semitism and respond to it whenever it occurs. However, there are some segments of the Jewish community that regard any criticism of Israel or Judaism as "anti-Semitism." This approach is actually counterproductive, because if you define any criticism of anything that Jews do as anti-Semitism, you close off the possibility of dialogue. Some non-Jews then write off real anti-Semitism as "there go those Jews again, always playing the anti-Semitism card," and the term loses meaning.

Unfortunately, people challenging policies of the Israeli government, no matter how justified or reasonable these challenges may be, are often labeled as anti-Semitic, or, if they are Jewish, as self-hating Jews. Certainly some criticism of Israel is based on anti-Semitism, and some anti-Semites have used the Palestinian cause to mask their hatred of Jews, but this is not always the case. To be critical of Israel continuing to build settlements, or of some Israelis destroying Palestinian olive groves – an act arguably forbidden by the Torah (Deuteronomy 20:19–20), or of disrespectful behavior of some Israeli soldiers at checkpoints, is not necessarily anti-Semitic. As long as these criticisms are not generalized to demonize Israel or "the Jews," they should be seen as a legitimate exercise of the democratic right to criticize one's society or government.

Being critical of one's government does not mean that one is unpatriotic or hateful. I believe that the highest form of patriotism is to challenge one's country to live up to its highest ideals. Criticism of some Israeli actions is not necessarily anti-Semitic, just as criticism of some U.S. policies is not necessarily anti-American. Painting every criticism of Israel as anti-Semitic can have the same effect as crying "wolf" when there is no wolf around. It may turn off people to real cases of anti-Semitism. I believe that one's country or group should be applauded when right and constructively criticized when wrong.

When people see a spectrum of respectful dissent, when they see a variety of opinions being expressed by different groups of Jews, then it's much harder for anti-Semites to paint "the Jews" with a broad brush. But when dissent is stifled, and the public hears only the most extreme opinions, people may assume that all Jews think alike.

For many years, as discussed in Chapter 6, certain strong supporters of Israel have used aggressive tactics to try and shut out contrary opinions about Israel. However, there are also Jews, both in America and in Israel, who love Israel *but* want Israel to end the occupation and take greater steps toward peace. The two are not mutually exclusive, and it is not proper to label such Jews as "self-hating."

REDUCING ANTI-SEMITISM

While there will always be some anti-Semitism (and other prejudices) in the world, there are things that can and should be done to reduce it. While some people will hate Jews regardless of the actions of Jews, this should not deter us from taking actions that can help reduce anti-Semitism. This requires both vigilance against bigots and the willingness to work cooperatively with people of good will to create a world where all forms of discrimination are reduced or eliminated.

Below are some suggestions of ways to reduce anti-Semitism. I hope others will build on these suggestions and suggest additional approaches. All of the suggestions below have additional benefits, so it would be important to act on them even if there was no anti-Semitism.

1.   *Apply Jewish values to help reduce poverty, hunger, illiteracy, and other social ills.*

One prime example of a group that is doing this is the American Jewish World Service (AJWS), which, as described on their website, "funds hundreds of grassroots organizations working to promote health, education, economic development, disaster relief, and social and political change in the developing world." Besides fighting to reduce hunger, poverty, and disease in poorer countries, AJWS advocates for global change and educates the American Jewish community on global issues.

A Jewish group that does similar work is Ve'ahavta (the first Hebrew word in the verse "You shall love your neighbor as yourself"), a Canadian Jewish Humanitarian and Relief Committee. As they state on their website, they are "motivated by the Jewish value of *tzedakah* – the obligation to do justice – by assisting the needy in Canada and other countries through volunteerism, education, and acts of kindness, while building bridges between Jews and other peoples worldwide." Their motto is: "Repairing the world through volunteerism, kindness, and building global bridges."

Another Jewish group that helps needy people worldwide is Mazon. Founded in 1985 as "A Jewish Response to Hunger," Mazon "is a national nonprofit organization that allocates donations from the Jewish community to prevent and alleviate hunger among people of all faiths and backgrounds." Information about these and other Jewish activist groups is in Appendix C.

While it is essential to educate all people – Jews and non-Jews alike – about anti-Semitism and how to combat it, and to openly confront and oppose anti-Semitism, racism, and other forms of discrimination, it is also necessary to work to reduce and eliminate poverty, unlivable housing, hunger, illiteracy, unemployment, homelessness, and other social ills and injustices that lead to discontent and scapegoating. Since half the world's population does not even have the basic human needs of food, clothing, and shelter, it's all too easy for demagogues to deflect the blame onto Jews and other minorities.

Just, democratic societies will be far safer for everyone, including Jews. Jewish organizations, such as the Anti-Defamation League, are working to reduce anti-Semitism, but much more needs to be done to eliminate this ancient, persistent bigotry. Imagine if thousands of synagogues, Jewish schools, and other Jewish institutions, while continuing the many positive things they are already doing, made *tikkun olam* their central focus. Not only would this have very positive benefits for the world, but it would likely help greatly reduce anti-Semitism, because people could see Jews in a positive light, working constructively to help others.

2.   *Spotlight the many positive things that Israel does.*

Israel is always among the first countries to respond when there are natural disasters, such as the earthquake in Haiti, the Asian tsunami, and Hurricane Katrina that devastated New Orleans and the Gulf Coast. Israeli hospitals provide Israeli and Palestinian Arabs as well as Jews with the best medical care possible.

In addition to improving Israel's image, such efforts can also benefit

Israel in times of crisis. When Israel had the worst forest fire in her history near Haifa in December 2010, she received much help from many countries, including the Muslim countries of Turkey, Egypt, and Jordan, as well as the Palestinian Authority.

Another major example of Israeli help occurred in response to the major volcanoes and aftershocks in Nepal in April 2015.[1] As soon as Israel recognized the seriousness of the situation, they sent Nepal 260 Israel Defense Force (IDF) members, 40 doctors, and 95 tons of supplies. When they arrived, the Israeli team set up a field hospital with operating rooms, X-ray equipment, and pediatric care, so that wounded Nepalese could be provided with emergency medical care. Some of the Israelis helped with search and rescue efforts. In addition, the Chabad Center in Israel provided 2,000 meals daily to Nepalese. It is important that information about such generous activities be widely shared to improve the image of Israelis and Jews, and hopefully to reduce anti-Semitism.

3.   *Increase efforts to resolve conflicts between Israel and the Palestinians and other Arab nations.*

I recognize this is a very difficult, controversial issue, but I believe that it should be addressed, with the hope that it will help to reduce anti-Semitism and have other positive benefits.

In addition to spotlighting the many positive things that Israel does, we should honestly examine certain aspects of Israeli policies that are painful to face. If we do not resolve the problems between Israel and the Palestinians, this conflict will continue to overshadow much of the good that Israel does.

Some of Israel's actions may fuel anti-Semitism, especially when Arabs and other third world populations, as well as western social activists, see TV footage of the infrequent poor Israeli behavior in the West Bank. While it is true that certain networks play the same unrepresentative, violent footage over and over to inflame their viewers, it is also true that if this conflict were to be resolved, such footage would not exist. In this day of satellite communications, it's often impossible for events to be hidden from the public. In the electronic age, secrecy seldom works, and the

1. Ben Sales, "After Nepal quake, some 100 Israelis are reported missing," JTA, April 26, 2015.

negative things emphasized in the Palestinian media overshadow many of the positive things that Israel does.

So we must ask ourselves with regard to the recent increase in anti-Semitism, how much do Israeli policies with regard to the Palestinians and Israeli Arabs contribute to it? This is a very difficult question, one that the Jewish community has insufficiently considered.

Former Israeli Prime Minister Ehud Olmert stated in 2009 that the occupation was a factor behind worldwide anti-Semitism. He said, "As long as this reality [occupation] continues, it makes it possible to attack Israel and gives anti-Jewish sources the opportunity to be heard. The complicated situation we're in encourages anti-Semitism. . . . As long as we continue to be presented as occupiers, we'll continue to suffer from anti-Semitism."[2] He was reacting to reports of an increase in anti-Semitism worldwide after Israel's Operation Cast Lead in Gaza. Former prime minister Ariel Sharon stated, "You cannot like the word, but what is happening is an occupation – to hold 3.5 million Palestinians under occupation. I believe that is a terrible thing for Israel and for the Palestinians." Former Israeli general, defense minister, and prime minister Ehud Barak once said that, "If I were a Palestinian of the right age, I would join, at some point, one of the terrorist groups." He recognized that being ruled by another people, no matter how benign the treatment, can produce humiliation, rage, and a desire for revenge. There is absolutely no excuse for terrorism or anti-Semitism, but it is important to recognize that certain actions and conditions can make them more likely.

Because of modern communications, people are much more aware of injustices in other parts of the world than they were in the past. Anybody can now post raw footage on YouTube for all to see. So when people hear that there are separate villages for Arabs and Jews, even separate roads and buses in the West Bank (Judea and Samaria), they interpret this as segregation and develop a less favorable attitude toward Israel and Jews.

Israel should not use the fact that Palestinians are teaching hatred and carrying out terrorist acts, or that some other nations are oppressing their people, as an excuse to justify unnecessarily harsh measures against Palestinians. As the old saying goes, two wrongs do not make a right. Of course, Israel must always continue to guard against possible terrorist

---

2. Maayama Miskin, "Olmert: Occupation in Gaza Causes anti-Semitism," *Arutz Sheva*, February 22, 2009.

acts, but in ways that minimize the negative images and avoidable harms. The importance of resolving the Israeli/Palestinian conflict in reducing anti-Semitism is discussed further in Chapter 7.

4. *Israel should announce that once the Middle East conflict is settled, she will, hopefully along with the United States and other nations, devote a percentage of the money now being used for her military to the improvement of the lives of all of the people in the region by working to reduce poverty, hunger, pollution, illiteracy, and other social problems.*

This has the potential of greatly improving Israel's image. Instead of Palestinians and others focusing on negative things about Israel and Israelis, they would see positives, and their feelings of despair, anger, and hopelessness would be replaced with visions of hope, reconciliation, cooperation, and peace. A model for this idea is the proposal by the Network of Spiritual Progressives and *Tikkun* magazine, led by Rabbi Michael Lerner, for a "Global Marshall Plan," in which the U.S. (and possibly other wealthy nations) would "use one to two percent of [their] Gross Domestic Product each year to reduce global poverty, disease, illiteracy, and environmental destruction."[3] This idea is discussed in more detail in Chapter 8, where I explore ideas about a foreign policy consistent with Jewish values.

5. *Israel and Jews worldwide should work actively with others to reduce climate change and other environmental threats.*

An excellent start at this was discussed in an October 27, 2010 Environmental News Network report, "Israel and Palestine Declare War . . . Against Climate Change." This report discussed an agreement between Israel, thirteen other Mediterranean-bordering nations, and the Palestinian Authority to reduce greenhouse gas emissions. Many people were encouraged by this example of Israel and the Palestinians working together to try to avert a common threat. There have also been other examples of recent cooperation between Israel, Jordan, and Palestinians on other

---

3. More information about the Global Marshall Plan proposal is at http://www.spiri tualprogressives.org/article.php/gmp_one.

environmental issues of joint concern, such as ways to conserve and share water and other resources.

In November 2010, in the midst of Israel's worst drought ever, Jewish, Muslim, and Christian religious leaders in Israel put aside their differences and united for a first-time-ever joint prayer service for much-needed rain.

Working together on common problems provides an ideal way to build bridges of understanding among different cultures. People fear what they do not know, so getting to know each other on a personal level is a positive step toward understanding each other on a cultural level and ultimately living together cooperatively and harmoniously. Working to stabilize climate would have additional benefits for Israel. The Middle East is a semi-arid area and climate experts are predicting that the region will become even hotter and drier. Military and strategic experts fear that there will be many desperate, hungry, thirsty refugees fleeing from heat waves, droughts, wildfires, floods, and other effects of climate change, making instability and violence more likely. With tensions and animosities already widespread in the Middle-East, Israel could be very badly affected if temperatures continue to rise. Experts think that the civil war in Syria was largely caused by a four year drought that prompted farms to fail, causing farmers and others to flee into already overcrowded cities, fueling animosity and violence. This is discussed in more detail in Chapter 11.

6.   *There should be increased efforts to create and support groups working for Israeli/Palestinian and Jewish/Muslim harmony and peaceful cooperation.*

In his book *Eight Candles of Consciousness: Essays on Jewish Nonviolence,* Rabbi Yonassan Gershom tells the following true story, which helps show the value of constructive dialogues:

> In Israel, there are a number of peace programs trying to bring Arab and Jewish youth together in cooperative projects. This is important work, because these two groups rarely mingle socially otherwise.
>
> On the first day of such programs, leaders can barely get the teens to call each other by their names instead of racial slurs. But by the end of the week, most of the hostility is gone, and some real sharing has taken place. At the last session, each side is allowed to ask the other any question – no holds barred – about being an Arab or Jew.

There are, of course, the usual teenage questions about dating habits, favorite music, etc. But on one occasion someone said, "Now that we have become friends, what will we do if we meet on the battlefield?"

Another teenager answered, "Then I would have to kill you."

There was a long silence. Then softly, almost in a whisper, another voice said, "I would lay down my gun and cry."

The enemy, once humanized, could no longer be the enemy.[4]

An example of Jews and Muslims working together is the Arava Institute for Environmental Studies located at Kibbutz Ketura in the Negev Desert. The institute has Israeli Jews and Palestinians, Jordanians, and international students. I had the pleasure of visiting there on March 10 and 11, 2015 where I spoke and interviewed the director David Lehrer and some faculty, students, and staff members. The interviews were posted on YouTube. The people I spoke to were unanimous in extolling the cooperative efforts of the wide variety of students studying and working together, and also indicated that their experiences at the institute made them feel more tolerant of other groups and more confident that a resolution of the Israeli/Palestinian conflict was possible.

Another example of Jews and Muslims working together is the experience of David Krantz, president of Aytzim: Ecological Judaism. After representing Aytzim's Green Zionist Alliance project at the Muslim Jewish Conference in Sarajevo, he wrote:

And I have found that after talking – when we get to know each other as people – a transformation takes place: We stop seeing each other as the "other" and start seeing each other as people, and sometimes even as friends.

I asked a participant from Saudi Arabia how she felt speaking with a self-identifying Zionist. She didn't understand why it should be a big deal, she said, because in her mind, she wasn't speaking with a Zionist or a Jew but a new friend who happened to be Jewish and Zionist.

Over and over, I have seen this through not just the Muslim Jewish Conference, but also Hartford Seminary's Building Abrahamic Partnerships program, as well as the inter-religious environmental

4. Yonassan Gershom, "After September 11," in *Eight Candles of Consciousness: Essays on Jewish Nonviolence* (New York: Lulu Press, Inc., 2009), 91–92.

networks with which I work, Interfaith Moral Action on Climate, and the National Religious Coalition for Creation Care. Through interfaith dialogue, we transcend our titles of Jew and Muslim and Christian, and become known to each other as David and Ahmed and Alison. We develop empathy for each other. And empathy is at the heart of peacemaking.[5]

One more example is the recent cooperation of American-born Orthodox rabbi and settler Hanan Schlesinger and leading Palestinian activist Ali Abu Awwad, who formed the group Roots, an initiative for "understanding non-violence and transformation."[6] They believe that "reconciliation begins with seeing the humanity of your enemy." Awwad said, "we need each other – there is no other way." An especially heartwarming example of Jewish/Muslim cooperation was the July 24, 2015 march of 1,000 Jews and Arabs in Haifa in support of veganism. The slogan "We Are All Their Voice: Coming Together for the Animals," showed the result of two years of close collaboration between Jewish and Arab animal rights activists.[7]

7.   *Jewish schools, synagogues, community centers and other groups should increase efforts to visibly perform services for people of other religions and for the general community.*

Of course, we should not do these things "visibly" just for the publicity – that would be crass and self-serving. We should do them *lishmah*, for their own sake, as a mitzvah. But it doesn't hurt to let people know that Judaism is where we get these positive values, especially in these times when people are focused on inclusiveness and expect to see identifying logos for various helping organizations. Rabbi Gershom, cited above, shared the following story with me:

A few years ago, a big tornado touched down and devastated a whole town not far from where I live. All kinds of groups showed up in their official T-shirts, hard hats and such, ready to help with cleanup, manage

---

5. Aytzim website http://www.aytzim.org/resources/articles/335
6. Gary Rosenblatt, "Unlikely Partners for Peace," *New York Jewish Week*, July 5, 2015, 7.
7. "Jews and Arabs March Together For Veganism and Animal Rights," The Vegan Woman, July 28, 2015.

the soup lines, and comfort those who had lost their homes. Well, a group of Jews from Minneapolis got the idea that they should go, too – *and that they should be visible as Jews.* So they made signs for their van, wore their yarmulkes, and pitched in.

For most of the people in that small Midwestern town, it was the first time they had ever met a Jew. And it was probably the first time that members of those other humanitarian organizations realized that Jews are willing to dig in and get their hands dirty, just like everybody else. Today, there is a permanent response team called *Nechama* (Comfort), officially sponsored by the Minneapolis Jewish community, which goes to help after such disasters.

Here is another example of a positive Jewish local effort that is making a difference. In Atlanta, there is a group organized by the local B'nai B'rith and known as "Pinch Hitters," composed mainly of Jews, who volunteer to work in hospitals on Christmas day (unless it occurs on Shabbat, in which case they volunteer on December 24 before sundown), so that Christians can take the day off and enjoy their holiday with their families. This engenders much good will with universal praise by the hospital staff for the volunteers' presence, attitude, and work ethic. Many recipients of the kindness from the Pinch Hitters consider them to be more like "Hall-of-Fame Sluggers." It would be wonderful if such things happened more often all over the United States and in other countries.

Rabbi Gershom also related to me that in Minneapolis one of the local synagogues hosts a dinner for the homeless on Thanksgiving. Only it's more than just a soup line. It's a very nice dinner with white tablecloths, flower centerpieces, and a live band. It's all done voluntarily, including rides to and from the homeless shelters. For families in crisis, such an event can be a big ray of hope that is not soon forgotten.

Yet another illustration of how such actions can convey a favorable image of Jews and Judaism and produce positive results was described in a front page article, "Presbyterians Tone Down Report on Israel After Jewish Lobbying," in the July 14, 2010 issue of the *Forward.* It reported that some delegates to a Presbyterian conference changed their position on a proposed boycott of Israel partly because of the help that Jews provided after Hurricane Katrina devastated New Orleans. One person recalled the Jews who worked with his church after the 2005 disaster: "The richness and diversity of points of view in the Jewish community really became clear to us when Jewish college groups started arriving." He said that his experience working side-by-side with Jews motivated him to want to provide some balance to the Israel report. Many synagogues across the U.S. already host homeless shelters and soup kitchens.

8.   *Jewish groups should increasingly arrange community events that involve leaders and lay people of other religions in shared activities, such as Thanksgiving services, community Seders, forums, Earth Day events, World Peace Day gatherings, etc.*

We should take advantage of such opportunities to show that we are part of the community, sharing common values and willing to cooperate.
In summary, instead of looking at anti-Semitism as something that has always occurred and will always occur no matter what we do, we should realize that there are many ways to reduce it that also have many other benefits, such as building bridges of understanding between Jews and the other peoples of the world.

Chapter 6

Israeli Policies and Diaspora Jews

*F*or *Zion's Sake I will not keep silent, and for Jerusalem's sake I will not rest, until her vindication goes forth as brightness, and her salvation as a burning torch.* — Isaiah 62: 1–2

*I*f *I forget you, o Jerusalem let my right hand wither. Let my tongue cleave to the roof of my mouth if I do not remember you, if I do not set Jerusalem above my highest joys.*

— PSALMS 137:5–6

*P*ray *for the peace of Jerusalem; may those who love her prosper. May there be peace within her walls, prosperity within her palaces. For the sake of my brethren and friends, I shall speak of peace within her midst. For the sake of the House of the Compassionate One, our God, I will seek her good.* — Psalms 122: 6–9

JEWS HAVE ALWAYS CHERISHED Israel. Even when stateless and dispersed throughout the world, Jews constantly yearned to return to *Eretz Yisrael* (the land of Israel). The prayer "Next Year in Jerusalem," recited at the close of Yom Kippur services and Passover seders, became an axiomatic byword among the Jewish people. Now that the state of Israel exists, Jews consider her as the fulfillment of a once-elusive dream: a homeland where Jewish tradition and values can be applied, and a beacon for the world.

I love Israel and am happy to call myself a Zionist. I am proud of Israel's amazing accomplishments in its short existence in many areas, including agriculture, education, law, social integration, technology,

Torah study, and human services, and I pray they will continue and grow.

I have two daughters living in Israel along with their husbands and my grandchildren, including one who is now (May 2016) serving in the Israeli Defense Forces, another who completed his three years of service and is now in the reserves, and three granddaughters who performed voluntary service after high school graduation. My wife and I visit often, generally twice a year for Passover and Sukkot, as well as for special occasions, such as *brit milot* (circumcisions of baby boys), *simchot banot* (welcoming ceremonies for girls), and bar and bat mitzvahs. With our growing family in Israel, my wife and I have decided to make *aliyah* in the summer of 2016.

Whenever I go to Israel to visit family, I frequently give talks about Jewish teachings on vegetarianism, environmentalism, animal rights, and related issues, and I try to meet with environmentalists, vegetarian leaders, rabbis, and other influential people. The documentary that I helped produce, *A Sacred Duty: Applying Jewish Values to Help Heal the World*, contains significant material about environmental issues in Israel. I was a Green Zionist Alliance delegate to the World Zionist Congress in Jerusalem in June 2010, and I was the GZA liaison to the media, environmentalists, rabbis and other contacts in Israel prior to the Congress. I was on the GZA (now called Aytzim: Ecological Judaism) Green Israel slate as a potential delegate for the next World Zionist Congress in October 2015. Unfortunately the slate only got enough votes to have one delegate slot, which went to the director of Aytzim, but I was very active in writing up resolutions about improving Israel's environment, to be voted on at the Congress. I did attend the Congress as an observer for Aytzim, and I was very gratified that the resolution that I drafted on climate change passed with 96% approval.

I believe that for Israel's sake, Judaism's sake, and the world's sake, a frank, respectful, loving assessment of Israel's policies and its best future strategy is essential. As indicated in great detail in the next chapter, Israel's future well-being and that of Jews worldwide, and, indeed, that much if not all of the world's people depend on a just, comprehensive, sustainable resolution of the Israeli/Palestinian conflict.

While of course Israelis must make final decisions on Israel's future, I believe that Jews in the Diaspora should also have a say because we are concerned about what happens in Israel and are also affected by it. We should respectfully raise the question: "How will Israel avert renewed violence and continued – and possibly increased – diplomatic isolation, effectively respond to her environmental, economic, and other domestic problems, and remain both a Jewish and a democratic state without a proper resolution of her conflict with the Palestinians and the surrounding Arab nations?" The implications of this question are discussed further in the next chapter.

This chapter and the next one have been especially hard for me to write because they contain ideas that are not part of the common wisdom shared by some members of my family, many friends, most members of my modern Orthodox congregation, and many other Jews, especially Orthodox Jews. But I have become convinced that it is essential that these issues be addressed, because I believe, as discussed in the next chapter, that peace is essential to Israel's survival and well-being and the well-being of the entire world. Of course, it must be recognized that Israel's very existence since 1948 has been one of constant struggle; there are forces in the world that wish to totally destroy her, there have been many acts of terror carried out by Palestinians, and there is great hatred and negative teaching of Israel among Palestinians. Many arguments can be won by stressing these points, but, difficult as it will be, it is essential to go beyond them and find common ground and solutions.

Because I love Israel, I am very concerned about the direction in which she is heading. "An open rebuke is better than hidden love" (Proverbs 27:5). The Biblical prophets rebuked Israel, not out of hatred or abuse, but out deep love and of sincere concern. Although I am far from being on the level of a prophet, I try to take the prophets as my role models, as did Rabbi Abraham Joshua Heschel. I speak out against injustices precisely because I love Israel and care deeply about the future of the Jewish people.

Rather than supporting everything Israel does, I think it is more important to try to get her back on the right track, in a loving and respectful way, when we think she has gotten off it. And there is much in the Jewish tradition that supports this approach. Chapter 3 discusses many Jewish teachings on involvement and protest.

DEMONIZATION OR DIALOGUE?

I have found that there are, roughly speaking, two kinds of people when it comes to politics. The vast majority of people see things in terms of good and evil, black and white, "us versus them." Many of them delight in demonizing people who are not in their camp and in scoring debating points. The more negative things they can find about their opponents – whether they be Arabs or Jews, Republicans or Democrats, blacks or whites, religious or secular, Orthodox or Reform, hawks or doves – the stronger they feel in their beliefs. They generally speak only to others from their own group, listen to commentators who reinforce their own views, and read material consistent with their outlooks. The second type of people, by far the minority, while aware of realities and difficulties, seek to find common ground and solutions. Of course, nobody is completely one type or the other, but I think most people have strong tendencies in one direction, and the fact that the vast majority of people are closer to the former than the latter makes it difficult to have the kinds of dialogues that are necessary to find solutions to today's critical problems.

Rabbi Yonassan Gershom told me that years ago, when he was studying with Rabbi Zalman Schachter-Shalomi in Philadelphia, they performed an exercise where people would stand in a circle and chant the words "us and them." First the rabbi would have everyone place the emphasis on the "us" and the "them," which focused the energy on separation and opposites – "*us* and *them*." Then he would change the rhythm to put the emphasis on the "and" – "us *and* them." Without changing the words at all, the chant suddenly became one of inclusiveness and cooperation because the focus changed. This powerful experience that Rabbi Gershom outlined epitomizes what I think we need to do regarding the Middle East and life in general. Instead of living in adversarial mode, we need to somehow find a way to move into a mode of conciliation and cooperation, seeking common ground and solutions.

Judaism has traditionally been based on reconciling opposites. There is a basic principle of Torah interpretation that says when two verses seem to contradict each other, a third verse will come to reconcile them. Judaism teaches us to listen to all sides of an argument and then try to find a way to reconcile them. But in recent decades, we seem to have lost this principle.

Of course, this doesn't mean that there is nothing about the Palestinians to be critical of, or that one should be unnecessarily critical of one's own people or nation. What it does imply is that we should recognize our own faults as well as those of others, and seek common ground and solutions rather than to just win debates. Unless we can open our minds enough to listen to each other, we will never have peace.

Rabbi Gershom's anecdote about people in a circle chanting "*us* and *them*" and then "us *and* them" reminded me of one of my favorite poems by Edwin Markham called "Outwitted":

> He drew a circle that shut me out;
> Heretic, rebel, a thing to flout;
> But love and I had the wit to win;
> We drew a circle that took him in!

Imagine if this response to a difficulty were what most people practiced. What a far more tolerant, harmonious, and peaceful world it would be! But most people seem to be living in the adversarial mode, the "*us* versus *them*" mode, a mode that shuts people out rather than drawing them in.

To most of my fellow congregants and many other Orthodox Jews, Israel is almost beyond criticism, the world is generally against Israel, and the Palestinians and other Arabs represent evil forces that must be completely and unequivocally opposed. They believe that Palestinians and other Arabs are so devious and so evil that it is impossible to even consider negotiating with them. All news reports that reinforce this view are widely shared with others, and any reports of cooperation and progress are downplayed or ignored. They circulate material via email that puts Israel in the best possible light, immune from criticism, and puts the Palestinians, other Arabs, and Muslims in general in the worst possible light.

Often the information in these emails about Muslims is completely false. For example, several times I have received email messages claiming that the United Kingdom has banned Holocaust studies in its schools, to avoid offending Muslims. A quick check on Snopes.com, a website that investigates rumors on the Internet, reveals the falsity of this assertion. I have also several times received the same type of false message about the University of Kentucky dropping Holocaust studies, probably because it also has the initials UK, as does the United Kingdom. Again, this is not true; the university still offers a course called "History 323: The Holocaust," and they never considered removing it.

The widespread transmission of such false rumors makes a meaningful dialogue on solutions to real problems far more difficult. And as a people mandated to be "a light unto the nations" (Isaiah 49:6), we Jews must accept a real responsibility to take special care to not bear false witness. I think a quick minute or two invested on Google or Snopes to confirm or refute a story's validity is a reasonable expectation.

For many, the possibility of dialogue and other forms of cooperation are seldom if ever considered. I have been a member of my Modern Orthodox synagogue since 1968, and in all those years I have heard only one speaker stress the importance of reconciliation and peace in the Middle East. That person was permitted to speak only because his father-in-law was a prominent synagogue member, a former president of the synagogue. He was not permitted to speak in the main sanctuary to the whole congregation, but was relegated to a smaller room, to which people had to move after a Shabbat service. That meant a smaller audience. Although he spoke with the moral authority and credentials of having served in the Israeli Defense Forces (IDF) and having had a brother-in-law die in one of Israel's wars, he received very strong criticisms of his positions.

By contrast, many speakers at my synagogue have spoken about how Israel is threatened by terrorism and other Arab actions, about Jewish suffering, about how we must be strong, stand by Israel, protest to U.S. governmental officials, and support everything Israel does – especially the West Bank settlers. Of course these issues should be discussed, and Israel should be defended, but there should also be discussions of the possibilities of resolving disputes by peaceful means. I have not attended every talk at my synagogue, but I do know that the overwhelming preponderance of talks on Israel and literature available for pickup take hard-line positions, and there is little, if any, desire to have other points of view presented.

It is ironic that Israelis themselves criticize their government far more openly than American Jews can do in their own communities without getting criticized. Newspapers in Israel regularly carry critical articles that would seldom get into Jewish-American publications. There are sometimes major demonstrations for peace and justice in Tel Aviv and other Israeli cities. The late Israeli Major General Matti Peled once noted, "The United States is making Israel less and less secure by encouraging the reckless agenda of the Israeli right."[1]

Not only do Israeli columnists and editors openly criticize their own government, but they also are sometimes frustrated that Americans

---

1. "The Swing to the Right in U.S. Policy Toward Israel and Palestine," THE FREE LIBRARY.

idealize it. There are daily articles in the Israeli press that are critical of various Israeli policies. I think there is something seriously wrong when we are asked to support Israel but cannot take into consideration the critical opinions which Israelis express.

Despite the supportive views of most Israelis and most American Jews for a two-state solution, as repeatedly expressed in polls, most members of my synagogue are strongly opposed to any territorial compromises for the sake of a possible peace agreement. During the Oslo talks, one guest speaker at my synagogue stated that we should not be concerned about a proposed peace settlement involving withdrawing from much of the West Bank, because Israelis were taking over many hilltops in that area, which would make a territorial compromise very difficult. As far as I know, there was no objection to that statement or similar statements over many years that have downplayed the possibility of peace and/or encouraged steps that would make resolving the conflict more difficult.

The difficulties American Jews face in being lovingly critical of Israeli policies was discussed in an op-ed article "The 'Real Jews' Debate" by *New York Times* columnist Roger Cohen on December 9, 2010:

> The view that American Jews supportive of Israel but critical of its policies are not "real Jews" is, however, widespread. Israel-right-or-wrong continues to be the core approach of major U.S. Jewish organizations, from the American Israel Public Affairs Committee (AIPAC) to the Conference of Presidents of Major American Jewish Organizations.
>
> To oppose the continued expansion of settlements in the West Bank . . . or question growing anti-Arab bigotry as personified by Israel's rightist foreign minister and illustrated by the "loyalty oath" debate, or ask whether the "de-legitimization" of Israel might not have something to do with its own actions is to incur these organizations' steady ire.

In his op-ed, Roger Cohen quotes Jeremy Ben-Ami, president of J Street, the organization whose slogan is "The political home for pro-Israel, pro-peace Americans."

> These organizations' view remains essentially that any time you engage in an activity critical of Israel you are trying to destroy the state of Israel. Here are all these Jewish kids being raised on great liberal values

at Hebrew schools – walks for the homeless, Darfur, AIDS – but God forbid we talk about what's happening in Israel! It's a dynamic that cuts off discourse.

A film was shown at my synagogue entitled *Crossing the Line: The Intifada Comes to Campus*. It dramatically showed the great increase in anti-Israel activities at several American and Canadian campuses, and the difficulties several Israeli representatives have had getting their messages out without strong heckling from Muslim students. It is wrong and disgraceful that such bias and disruptions are happening, and certainly Jews and others should be aware of what is occurring on our college campuses and in other places. It is also important to counter anti-Semitism and unfair criticisms of Israel. But along with their benefits, such films also project an all-or-nothing, black-or-white picture that allows for no nuance or complexity. There is no attempt at balance, or to point out the many issues on which Jews and Muslims are cooperating (discussed in Chapter 10), or to consider steps that might reduce such hostilities and confrontation.

As I will discuss in more detail in the next chapter, a positive resolution of the Israeli-Palestinian conflict is vital for Israel, Jews worldwide, Palestinians and other Arabs, the United States, and the entire world. There are many obstacles to a just peace, including Arab intransigence and promotion of hatred toward Jews and Israel, but I believe these problems can be solved. Any ultimate agreement must firmly assure Israel's security. Israelis will of course make the final decisions about Israeli policies, but they should consider the potential effects of their actions on Jews throughout the world.

INTOLERANCE AT THE WORLD ZIONIST CONGRESS

I personally witnessed an example of the failure of Jews to engage in respectful dialogue when I was a Green Zionist Alliance (GZA) delegate to the World Zionist Congress in Jerusalem in June 2010. Because a GZA resolution was considered in the session that dealt with settlement issues in Israel, I was assigned to that committee. When the first two resolutions, supporting a settlement freeze, endorsing a two-state solution, and calling for the Israeli government to repair relations with the American government, were approved, hard-liners noisily left the committee meeting.

Some shouted insults on the way out, such as calling Jews who voted for the resolutions Hamas and Obama supporters.[2]

To their credit, most of the Zionist Congress members of the committee avoided such name-calling. People on both sides of these issues urged those walking out to stay, but to no avail. Even the committee chairperson, a member of the hawkish Israeli party Yisrael Beiteinu (Israel, Our Home) left, ironically leaving the chairing of the remainder of the meeting to his co-chair Hadar Susskind, then Vice President of Policy and Strategy of the dovish J Street.

To the credit of Susskind and the other remaining progressive committee members, who now had an even greater majority after the hard-liner walkout, they conducted a respectful, well-reasoned dialogue on the remaining resolutions. They sought to reach common ground, making changes and dropping some statements, as urged by opponents of the more liberal resolutions. As Susskind put it in his J Street blog:

> With progressive delegates outnumbering those representing pro-occupation parties, the committee could have easily descended further into the political abyss by ramming through resolutions and not taking into account the deeply held views of all in the room. We took a different tack, recognizing that chairing this committee was an opportunity to demonstrate to the Congress and the Committee that it was possible to have a serious, fact-based, and frank discussion on these incredibly contentious issues.

The situation became worse at the final plenary, when all the delegates voted on the resolutions. When the voting on the first resolution of the settlements committee again went against the wishes of the more belligerent delegates by a very decisive margin, many of them angrily got up on the stage and sang *Hatikvah* (the Israeli national anthem) at the top of their lungs as a form of protest. They ignored calls to step down and to permit the democratic voting to continue. One member of the conservative Shas

---

2. Hamas is the right-wing Palestinian party currently in power in Gaza. It is important to note here that President Obama has never supported or endorsed Hamas or its policies. Obama, like other presidents before him, has repeatedly called upon Hamas to renounce terrorism, recognize Israel's right to exist, and engage in the peace process – which Hamas has repeatedly rejected.

Party shouted out, "North Tel Aviv and North America have betrayed the State of Israel!" This almost precipitated a serious confrontation, but, luckily, cooler heads prevailed. However, the unruly protest effectively shut down the voting process, and the Resolutions Committee decided to halt the proceedings and refer all remaining resolutions to a later meeting of the Zionist General Council.

After the protesters left the stage, two young delegates from opposing political perspectives spoke to the plenum and sharply criticized the protesters for not living up to Theodore Herzl's dreams for respectful discussion and decision-making by Congress delegates. This and an additional statement, very critical of the protesters by the leader of the Meretz delegation, received loud applause by the majority of the delegates.

The strong disagreements at the conference were summed up in an op-ed article "We Have Met the Enemy . . ." in the July 2 issue of the New York *Jewish Week* by Rabbi Gerald Skolnik, a Conservative rabbi from Forest Hills, Queens. He wrote:

> As we approach Tisha B'Av, it is worth remembering what the rabbis taught long ago. The Romans destroyed the Second Temple in the year 70 CE because of *sin'at chinam* – senseless hatred among the Jews of that time that undermined their ability to effectively combat the Roman threat.
>
> Based on some of the behaviors that I witnessed during the Congress, I have to wonder if the senseless hatred among the Jews of our time will undermine our own ability to deal with the very real threats to Israel and the Zionist cause in the 21st century . . .
>
> It is with the greatest of sadness that I, more than once or twice, actually felt hated by some of my fellow Jews precisely because of the beliefs that I hold. And that, I think, is what has left me so unsettled in the aftermath of the recent Zionist Congress . . .
>
> When you have developed the capacity to countenance this kind of behavior without being horrified, something is terribly wrong. These are critical times for the Zionist enterprise. The Zionist ship is listing badly, taking on water, and mighty cannons are firing at it from all directions. We need to be talking about the issues that are facing Israel, not hurling insults at those who raise them.

SMEARING PROGRESSIVE JEWISH GROUPS

Recently, even groups that were created specifically to support Israel have been demonized, if they don't blindly adhere to the right-wing agenda. The New Israel Fund (NIF), whose motto is "Promoting Equality for All Israelis," strives for democratic change in Israel and for a state where all its citizens have equal rights, regardless of their religion, race, gender, or sexual orientation. Seeking to build a progressive Israeli society since their inception in 1979, they have provided hundreds of millions of dollars to over 800 grassroots Israeli organizations that are dedicated to social justice, equality, human rights, and tolerance.

I think NIF's values and approaches are commendable. Like the NIF itself, I do not necessarily agree with every position and action of all of the many groups they support, but I think their net effect is very positive for Israel. However, there are right-wing Israelis and Diaspora Jews who oppose NIF's support for groups that advocate territorial compromises for a two-state solution, improved Israeli/Palestinian relations, an end to settler harassment of Palestinians, greater recognition of non-Orthodox groups, and other causes. Because of this, the NIF has become a target of efforts to stifle dissent and muzzle the Israeli human rights community.

These efforts included a smear campaign by an Israeli right-wing group Im Tirtzu ("If You Will It") and a failed effort in the Israeli Knesset to establish a "commission of inquiry" to investigate NIF. Both are based on claims that some of the groups supported by NIF provided damaging information to the Goldstone Commission, which issued a report critical of Israeli (and Palestinian) actions during the January 2010 war in Gaza.

The weekly column of former NIF Chair Naomi Chazan in the *Jerusalem Post* was discontinued, even though she received no money from the newspaper for writing it. Gershon Baskin, a long-time Israeli peace activist, stated in an article in the *Jerusalem Post:* "The witch-hunt against Chazan and the New Israel Fund is reminiscent of the darkest days of McCarthyism in the United States and similar to the atmosphere of states with secret police forces and dark dungeons."[3]

Fortunately, there has been worldwide support for the NIF, and this was a factor behind the Knesset inquiry not going forward. Many Israeli leaders from many political perspectives indicated opposition to what

3. Gershom Baskin, "A Dark Day for Democracy," *Jerusalem Post*, February 10, 2010.

they viewed as a witch-hunt against progressive Israeli organizations. Many in the progressive U.S. Jewish community came to NIF's defense. For example, Rabbi David Saperstein, then-Director of the Religious Action Center of Reform Judaism, issued a statement saying, "In their twisted attribution of blame for the Goldstone Report to the NIF, these attackers are trying to delegitimize the New Israel Fund in much the same way that the Goldstone Report is being used to delegitimize Israel in the eyes of the world."[4]

Former NIF Chair Naomi Chazan argued that there is no direct correlation between the positions of the Fund and those of the grantees. "We really don't support every single thing these organizations say, but we support their right to say it. Some organizations' only sin was signing a call to set up an independent committee of inquiry [related to the Goldstone report]."[5]

Because of continued smearing of the New Israel Fund by right wingers, Deborah Lipstadt, Professor of Modern Jewish and Holocaust Studies at Emory University, and David Ellenson, Chancellor Emeritus of Hebrew Union College Jewish Institute of Religion, wrote an article in the March 13, 2015 issue of the *Forward*, "Echoes of McCarthyism in Smear Campaign Against New Israel Fund Backers." In defending Jewish leaders who were attacked because of their support of NIF, they stated, "Their decades of service to our community speak far better than any testimonial. Nevertheless, decency demands that the libels against them not remain unchallenged. We feel compelled to raise our voices, protest these attacks, and call for their cessation."

In an ad in the *Jewish Week* on November 20, 2015, the New Israel Fund defended its positions. Their statement included the following:

NIF opposes the BDS movement and invests tens of millions of dollars in Israel every year. We do not fund any group that supports the BDS movement.

NIF stands for democracy and equality. We support Israelis working for a shared society, against racism, and for greater solidarity among

---

4. "Reform Movement Condemns Attack on New Israel Fund," Religious Action Center report, February 3, 2010.
5. Jonathan Lis, "Amid row over contentious ad, Jerusalem Post fires Naomi Chazan of New Israel Fund," *Haaretz*, February 5, 2010.

Israel's Jewish and Arab citizens. We do not support any group that promotes racism, incitement, or violence against Jews or against Arabs.

POSITIVE EFFORTS TO FURTHER
UNDERSTAND THE OTHER'S NARRATIVE

Fortunately, some college professors and others are trying to make peace more likely by exploring each side's narrative and by searching for common ground. Professor Mark Rosenblum, founder of Americans for Peace Now, teaches a course on the Israeli-Palestinian conflict at Queens College that both Jews and Muslims attend. As part of the class, each student must research and present a report from the perspective of the other side. This has resulted in a much greater appreciation of the other side's outlook by many of the participating students.

Another example is a course team taught at Brandeis University by three scholars: an Israeli, an Egyptian, and a Palestinian. At a time when many Middle Eastern Studies courses have been accused of bias, this course challenges students to discuss controversial issues in a respectful way. The professors are trying to prove that it is possible to consider the complex issues without promoting a cause or consistently blaming one side or the other.

Dr. Irwin J. (Yitzchak) Mansdorf has taught and directed a program in Israel-Arab studies at Midreshet Lindenbaum in Jerusalem. In a letter in the December 24, 2010 New York Jewish Week, he states that the focus is on presenting "both sides" and says that the approach works. He indicates that, unlike pure advocacy approaches, "we emphasize activism through empathy, which translates into having a thorough and complete understanding of the Palestinian Arab viewpoint." His post-high school students meet and learn from Palestinian Arabs and achieve some insight into the Palestinian Arabs experience. These students later take on major leadership positions on campuses in the U.S., England, and Canada.

When we are willing to listen to the narratives – the life stories – of the other side, we often find that we can identify with them more than we expected. Unfortunately, the only kind of contact that some Palestinians have with Israelis is at checkpoints, where they are not always treated respectfully. An exhaustive collection of testimonies of 700 Israeli soldiers about such behavior is in the publication with the understated title, *Occupation of the Territories*, produced by the group Breaking the Silence.

Even though such improper behavior is an infrequent and unauthorized aberration, it still breeds anger and resentment among Palestinians, as it would among Jews if we were subjected to such treatment. Of course, there are also many examples of improper Palestinian actions against Jews, including terrorist acts, but mistreating mostly innocent Palestinians is not the solution to the problem.

The vast majority of Israelis certainly do not behave improperly to Palestinians, and most Israelis denounce and actively oppose such behavior. As a matter of fact, many Palestinians receive excellent care in Israeli hospitals. This includes not only Israeli Arabs but also Palestinians from the West Bank and Gaza. But the harsh treatment that does occur often overshadows such positive actions, creates frustration and anger, and poisons all relationships. As I stated before, and want to re-emphasize now, there is absolutely no justification for terrorist acts that target innocent people, including women and children. But we must recognize the rage and desire for revenge that sometimes trigger such acts and do what we can to minimize unnecessary antagonism.

RIGHT-WING OPPOSITION TO AMERICAN GROUPS PROMOTING MIDDLE EASTERN PEACE

For many years I have supported efforts to find common ground and solutions that would help end the Israeli/Palestinian conflict. I was involved in many U.S. groups seeking peace over the years, including Breira (Alternative, a name chosen in contrast to the Hebrew phrase *ein breirah* – there is no alternative), New Jewish Agenda, and, most recently, J Street. All of them met strong opposition from the Jewish establishment. For example, although Breira had the participation of over a hundred rabbis, as well as noted American Jewish writers and intellectuals, the Jewish establishment subjected the group to a vicious McCarthy-like smear campaign. Rabbi Alexander Schindler, then president of the Union of American Hebrew Congregations, called the attacks on Breira and the firings by major Jewish organizations of some of its rabbinic supporters, a "witch hunt,"[6] which led to Breira's dissolution by 1977. Similar attacks were made against New Jewish Agenda and are currently targeting J Street.

---

6. Gregory D. Slabodkin, "The Secret Section in Israel's U.S. Lobby that Stifles American Debate" Washington Report on Middle Eastern Affairs, July, 1992.

J Street, the largest active group currently supporting a two-state solution to the Israeli/Palestinian conflict, considers itself the political home for pro-Israel, pro-peace Americans. According to J Street's website:

> This moment presents immense opportunities and daunting challenges for Israel's future: Can Israel continue to live by the principles upon which it was founded as the homeland of the Jewish people and a democracy for all its citizens? Can Israel overcome the continued threat of violence, the moral decline of deepening occupation and unchecked settlement growth? Will the American Jewish community show the leadership that is so greatly needed to influence American and Israeli leaders? Will Israelis and Palestinians find the political will to compromise and secure peace, or will the region – once again – sink into a period of terrible violence?
>
> We have a stake, and we have choices: Will we engage or will we walk away? Will we fight for our beliefs or simply despair? Will we accept our own agency to act or will we slip into passivity? When and how will we speak up?
>
> Those invested in building an Israel that embodies the "freedom, justice, and peace as envisioned by the prophets," simply do not have the luxury of throwing up our hands. We must find hope by creating opportunities for change.

Unfortunately, the Jewish establishment has generally been successful in portraying J Street and other peace groups that promote Israeli/Palestinian reconciliation as outside the mainstream and/or anti-Israel. To many Jews, being pro-Israel today means supporting the most conservative, hawkish elements in Israel. J Street's slogan is "Pro-Israel and Pro-Peace," but to many Jews, anyone who supports territorial compromise in pursuit of peace and does not support conservative Israeli positions can't be considered pro-Israel, simply because they don't fit into a narrow right-wing agenda.

As will be discussed in more detail in the next chapter, Oz v'Shalom/ Netivot Shalom, an Israeli Orthodox peace group, warned years ago that trying to control another people would be counterproductive and lead to great problems in the future, but their voice went unheeded. Yet we see today that they were right. The more we try to control the Palestinians, the more they resist the occupation.

I believe that the highest form of loyalty is challenging your nation or your group to live up to its highest standards. To repeat the insight from Proverbs, "An open rebuke is better than hidden love." Blindly supporting Israel in all of her actions is not really helping her; it is enabling destructive behavior that, in the long run, is detrimental to Israel's well-being and possibly her survival. Yet it seems that while it is acceptable for Americans to be critical of U.S. actions, such as our involvements in Vietnam (including atrocities and massive napalming), Central America (including "death squads" and Iran-Contra), and Iraq (with the discredited rationale, mistreatment of prisoners, and unforeseen consequences, including strengthening Iran and leading to the formation of ISIS), the same is not true when it comes to Israel. When one disagrees with the conventional "wisdom" formulated by the most conservative elements in Jewish life today, and advocates other possible directions for Israel, one is immediately declared "out of bounds." Many will then label you an anti-Semite or a self-hating Jew.

EFFORTS TO SMEAR J STREET

There are other examples in the United States of attempts by conservative individuals and groups to silence dissent about Israeli policies. J Street director Jeremy Ben-Ami was scheduled to speak in November 2010 at Temple Beth Avodah in Newton, a Boston suburb, but a small group of Jewish right-wing activists intimidated the board into cancelling the event. When the cancellation was initially announced, a "We Will Not Be Silenced" petition was created in response and obtained over 10,000 signatures in ten hours.[7]

Ben-Ami ended up speaking at a nearby school to a large, enthusiastic audience. When he told them that thousands had signed a petition expressing opposition to the intimidation of communal leaders that is intended to silence their voices, the crowd applauded loudly. The event received widespread local publicity; Public Radio in Boston (WBUR) led with the story, the Boston Jewish Community Relations Council defended J Street's right to speak, the *Boston Globe* carried favorable commentary, and there was a positive editorial in the local *Jewish Advocate*. The Temple's

---

7. "Huge Turnout for Boston Event," J Street Blog, November 19, 2010.

rabbi expressed support for open dialogue and regretted that a small group of Temple members had been able to prevent the talk at the Temple.

Unfortunately, the cancellation of Jeremy Ben-Ami's talk is not an isolated example. All across the U.S, small numbers of hawkish activists and donors regularly intimidate synagogues, Hillels, and other communal institutions into stifling the presentation of views on Israel they don't approve of.[8]

The "We Will Not Be Silenced" petition was kept open to support other peace activists who are fighting similar battles to get their messages out. Promoters of the petition want others who run into the stonewall of resistance "to be able to say that they are not alone – that thousands upon thousands of pro-Israel, pro-peace Americans want our voices heard in the communal and national conversation on Israel," so that incidents like the one near Boston will never happen again.

After the news about the cancellation broke, there were heartening examples of community support for freedom of speech. Alan S. Ronkin, deputy director of the Jewish Community Relations Council (JCRC) in Boston, wrote, "It's deeply troubling that there are people in the community who would prefer to stifle debate, rather than engage."[9] Jesse Singal at the *Boston Globe* wrote, "[i]f a mere conversation featuring the head of a group that has become, for better or worse, part of the mainstream conversation on Israel would 'threaten the fabric of the congregation,' it says more about the congregation than it does about J Street."[10]

In another example of increasing disapproval of dissenting opinions, Abby Backer, a Columbia University student and the daughter of a Wisconsin rabbi, recounted what occurred at a debate about Israel at Temple Beth El in Stamford, Connecticut between the activist lawyer Alan Dershowitz and J Street President Jeremy Ben-Ami. In her 'Opinion' essay, "Exclude Me At Your Own Peril," in the October 29, 2010 New York *Jewish Week*, she wrote that her experience at the debate made her feel

---

8. There have also been terrible cases of Muslim students disrupting talks by Israeli officials and pro-Israel speakers. Hopefully there will soon be a just resolution of the Middle East conflict so that such disruptions by activists will end.

9. Lisa Wangsness "Newton synagogue cancels talk by critic of Israeli policies," *Hokusai*, November 17, 2010.

10. "Listen Vanessa," blog, November 21, 2010, http://robbie.listenvanessa.com /2010_11_01_archive.html

like a "stranger within my own community." Backer, who was present as a student leader of Just Peace, the J Street U affiliate at Columbia University, described how Ben-Ami was hissed, the J Street staff was booed, and, after the contentious debate was over, an elderly woman confronted Backer in the synagogue lobby. "I should spit on you!" the heckler yelled. "Are you a Palestinian? You must be a Palestinian!" In her op-ed essay, Backer wrote:

> I have given much thought over the last week about whether I can continue to be part of this conversation. If I am not welcome, why [should I] bother to fight for entry? . . . What was it that proved so horrifying to that woman and those that hissed at Ben-Ami? Was it his statement that all Jews should be troubled by the conditions of Palestinians living under occupation? Was it his insistence that placing of blame on one side or the other is counterproductive? Was it his defense of students, like me, who are concerned about the occupation, but fear that honesty will put them on the periphery of our community?

Coincidentally (or maybe not), there was a reference in the same issue of *The Jewish Week* by editor Gary Rosenblatt in a column entitled "Exploring The Generation Gap Among Jewish Leaders" that served to reinforce Becker's message. It described a study by the Avi Chai Foundation that found that Jews in their twenties and thirties who are leaders of "non-establishment" Jewish groups in America are critical of establishment institutions for not welcoming diversity and for not permitting younger Jews to have input.

Those who are lamenting the loss of Jewish youth to assimilation, or who wonder why fewer and fewer younger Jews are joining the mainstream institutions, would do well to listen to the voices of those youth. Excluding them from the conversation only reinforces Backer's impression that they are not welcome in the Jewish community. In rejecting these student activists, we may well be driving away the next generation.

BRIEF CONSIDERATION OF THE NEW ISRAELI GOVERNMENT: A REASON TO SPEAK OUT FOR PEACE, JUSTICE, AND CIVIL LIBERTIES

Partly because the emphasis on security and countering potential terrorist acts has caused a shift of many Israelis to more conservative positions, on

March 17, 2015 Benjamin Netanyahu's Likud Party received thirty Knesset seats and was able to form a very conservative government along with hawkish and religious parties, with a bare majority of 61 of the total 120 Knesset seats. Prospects for peace and expansion of democratic rights are reduced with the new government for the following reasons:

- In order to help attract voters to his Likud party, Netanyahu stated right before election day that there would be no Palestinian state formed if he were reelected and that right wing Israelis should vote for his party because Arabs were "voting in droves." Netanyahu tried to walk back from his statement about a two-state solution, but many feel that his initial statement represents his actual position.

- Netanyahu appointed Deputy Prime Minister and Interior Minister Silvan Shalom, someone who opposes a two-state solution and favors continued settlement in the West Bank, to be responsible for talks with the Palestinians, if negotiations are resumed. He shortly resigned after several sexual harassment charges against him.

- Netanyahu's coalition consists almost completely of conservative, hawkish, and religious Knesset members who are willing to curb civil liberties and democratic values if they think this will help minimize criticism. For example, the new Justice Minister Ayelet Shaked plans to reduce the Israeli Supreme Court's oversight power to curb the government's efforts to reduce civil liberties. Also, Israel's new Minister of Religious Affairs David Azulai has stated that Reform Jews are not really Jewish.[11]

The hawkish, conservative, intolerant nature of the new government has resulted in much criticism from many, including Israeli conservatives who formerly supported Likud. For example, Dan Meridor, who served the Likud and Centre parties in six Knessets and held a variety of ministerial posts, including Deputy Prime Minister, Minister of Justice, and Ministry of Finance, has become a leading critic of Likud for carrying out policies that he believes are increasing Israel's diplomatic isolation.[12] He feels that Israel's new government is on a collision course with the international

---

11. Isabel Kirshner, "Israeli Minister Says Reform Jews Are Not really Jewish," *International Jewish Times*, July 7, 2015.
12. Judy Maltz, "Ex-Likud official warns Israel, world on a collision course," *Haaretz*, May 5, 2015.

community, because of an "irreconcilable contradiction between what the world community wants and what a majority in this government think."

While formerly known as a major Likud leader, Meridor is now critical of Likud for moving away from its former commitment to human rights and democracy. He stated in an interview with Haaretz, "Today, in the party, when you use words like democracy, human rights and rule of law, they immediately depict you as a leftist."[13]

Conditions have become so bad that a December 30, 2015 article in *Haaretz* was titled, "Israel 2015: This Is What a Trump Presidency Looks Like." The author, Asher Schecter, argues that:

> Israel's current leadership rose to prominence on the wings of the same sort of bigoted spiel that has elevated Trump in the polls. Trump calls Mexican immigrants criminals and rapists? Israel's Culture Minister, Miri Regev, called African asylum seekers "cancer." Trump wants a database for tracking Muslims? Three months ago, the Knesset passed the first reading (out of three) of a draconian government-sponsored anti-terror bill that expands the definition of "terrorism" to such a farcical degree that it includes such actions as wearing certain t-shirts, flag-waving, and leaving [anti-government] comments online.

An important example of the current Israeli government's efforts to stifle dissent is a proposed law approved by Israel's cabinet that would require Israeli non-governmental organizations (NGOs) to prominently state if foreign governments provide most of their funding. This would primarily harm progressive NGOs, since they get most of their funds from governments, and not conservative NGOs, since they get most of their funds from foreign individuals, such as conservative American Sheldon Adelson. The purpose behind the law is to imply that progressive NGOs have agendas supported by foreign governments and not by Israel. The proposed law is opposed by centrist Jewish groups – the Anti-Defamation League, the American Jewish Committee, and the Union for Reform Judaism – and by progressive Jewish groups – J Street, Americans for Peace Now, and Ameinu. In its statement of opposition, URJ stated:

---

13. *Ibid.*

In an open society, NGOs from across the political spectrum are constantly engaged in *machloket l'shem hashamayim*, an argument for the sake of heaven, and for the sake of improving Israel's security and institutions. Attempts to silence one side of the debate weaken Israel's democracy, civil society and its support abroad, making it even more difficult for Israel to defend herself against a swelling cohort of detractors.

The negative effects of American Jews failure to speak out respectfully and lovingly about Israeli policies was indicated in the January 4, 2015 *Haaretz* article, "The Great Betrayal: American Jews Stay Silent as Israeli Democracy Withers." The author, Chemi Shalev, criticizes "the deafening silence of most American Jews in response to the waves of chauvinistic antidemocratic legislation and incitement in which Israel is increasingly drowning." Shalev, U.S. editor for Ha'aretz, stresses the urgency of responses by American Jews: "By staying silent, by refraining from the kind of forceful, game-changing protest that the current situation warrants, American Jews . . . are betraying Israel itself. They don't owe it to Israeli liberals to come to their aid: They owe it first and foremost to themselves."

I am reluctant to criticize the Israeli government in this book and seriously considered removing the material in this section. However, because the present government, possibly the most rightwing in Israeli history, has the potential of harming Israel and Jews worldwide, I think it is important to stress that Diaspora Jews speak out respectfully and lovingly for positive changes. In doing so, one should keep in mind Israel's many positive acts, including helping other countries in times of trouble and helping Palestinians in Israeli hospitals, the effects of Palestinian terrorism; and that many other countries have worse human rights records than Israel.

For many years conservative American Jews have tried to influence Israeli policies. One significant example that might have been decisive in the last election is the providing of free copies of the very conservative daily publication *Israel Hayom* (Israel Today), paid for by Sheldon Adelson, who is also investing huge sums of money supporting Republican politicians in the U.S. It is essential that progressive Jews be actively involved in providing a counterbalance to the activist conservatives. One way we can do that is to support progressive groups that are concerned about Israel's future, such as the New Israel Fund, J Street, Americans for Peace Now, and Partners for Progressive Israel. Information about these and other progressive groups is in Appendix C.

The message in this chapter can be summarized by the title of an article by Seymour D. Reich, former chairman of the Conference of Presidents of Major Jewish Organizations in the April 29, 2016 Jewish Week, "Israel's Assault On Democracy: Time To Speak Out." Reich concludes, as I and many Israeli military and strategy experts have, "Ultimately [Israel's] policies and Israel's anti-Democratic practices will undermine Israel's security. That is why American Jewish leaders must speak out."

Chapter 7

Seeking Peace in Israel

It shall come to pass in the latter day ... that out of Zion shall go forth Torah, and the word of the Lord from Jerusa-lem....   – Isaiah 2:2–3

And I will bring back the captivity of My people Israel, and they shall build the wasted cities, and dwell therein; and they shall plant vineyards, and drink their wine; and they shall lay out gardens and eat their fruit.   – Amos 9:14

Until Israelis and Palestinians are able to listen to each other, hear each other's anguish and anger and make cognitive space for one another's hopes, there is no way forward.   – Rabbi Lord Jonathan Sacks[1]

THE PREVIOUS CHAPTER ADDRESSED why it is so important that Jews be concerned about Israel and respectfully and lovingly speak out when they think Israel's policies are counterproductive. This chapter considers why a just, comprehensive, sustainable, mutual-ly-agreed-upon resolution of Middle East conflicts is essential and will have many benefits for Israel, the U.S., and even the entire world.

Let me first make it clear that I am fully aware of past intransigence in the Arab world. I know that hatred of Jews and Holocaust denial are taught in many Muslim schools, and that some governments and violent groups like Hamas refuse to acknowledge Israel's right to exist. The many

---

1. Jonathan Sacks, *The Dignity of Difference: How to Avoid the Clash of Civilizations* (London/New York: Continuum, revised edition, 2003), 189, 190.

outrageous acts of terrorism by Palestinians must be condemned and steps to prevent further acts of terror must continue. However, since I am a Jew speaking primarily to fellow Jews, I want to focus on what I believe we, as Jews, should be doing to work for peace. Instead of each side demonizing the other, we need to seek common ground and ways to overcome obstacles to peace.

AN IMPORTANT ISRAELI PEACE GROUP: OZ V'SHALOM/NETIVOT SHALOM

Rather than offer only my own opinions as an American Jew on peace issues in Israel, I will base my analysis largely on the views of the Israeli Orthodox peace group Oz V'Shalom/Netivot Shalom and the views of retired Israeli security and military experts.

The phrase *oz v'shalom* literally means strength and peace, and that makes a very important point. Pursuing peace is not an indication of weakness. Israel can and must remain strong while, at the same time, seeking peaceful solutions to conflicts. Oz v'Shalom was founded in 1975 to present an alternative, more moderate expression of religious Zionism. They later merged with Netivot Shalom (Paths of Peace), which was formed after the 1982 war in Lebanon, in which a disproportionate number of religious students who combined their military duty with studies at *Hesder* yeshivas were killed. This, in turn, caused their teachers and others to question the direction that Zionism was going and take a stronger stance for peace.

The name Oz v'Shalom was taken from Psalm 29:11: "God will grant His people strength (*oz*); God will bless His people with peace (*shalom*)." The name Netivot Shalom was taken from Proverbs 3:17: "[The Torah's] ways are pleasant, and all her paths (*netivot*) are peace (*shalom*)." The two organizations combined, because both are Orthodox groups committed to promoting the ideals of justice, tolerance, and pluralism – concepts central to Jewish tradition and law. For the sake of brevity, I shall refer to them collectively as Netivot Shalom. While the group is no longer active, I think it is important to consider their views as an Orthodox Israeli group that promotes reconciliation and peace based on Jewish values.

This movement originally began with a group of Orthodox Jewish academics that were alarmed by the growing militarism and intolerance they saw in much of the religious Zionist community. They became aware that religious fundamentalism was gaining hold throughout the region on both the Arab and Jewish sides and represented a major threat to coexistence. They believed that any effective counter argument in the religious community must also be based on authentic Jewish tradition. They were convinced that the established religious Zionist camp had drifted away from the values that had been its initial foundation. Unfortunately, this tendency has only increased since the 1970s.

As a religious Zionist peace organization, Netivot Shalom is in a unique position to counter fundamentalist and extremist political arguments that they believe have placed the value of possessing the Land of Israel ahead of other vital Torah values, such as human life, justice, and peace – concerns that have always been central to Jewish law and tradition.

Because they are committed to Jewish tradition and law, while at the same time supporting peace, equality, and co-existence, Netivot Shalom is able to enter into a dialogue with both the secular left and the religious right. They seek to effect a fundamental change within the entire national religious community and throughout Israeli society by endeavoring in the words of their mission statement to:

- Demonstrate support for the peace process on the basis of political reality and justice.
- Enhance Jewish unity and pluralism among Israel's religious and secular communities.
- Promote coexistence and support for equality for Israel's Arab minority.
- Advocate political rights for Palestinians and work toward the establishment of a Palestinian state.

Netivot Shalom argues that the Jewish people's special relationship towards the Land of Israel should not override the preservation of Jewish lives (as well as others). They view the pursuit of peace as a central religious value and believe that Jews have a religious obligation as a nation to seek and pursue peace. They believe that Jewish law clearly requires us to establish a fair and just society, and that attempting to achieve co-existence between Jews and Arabs is not merely an option, but an imperative.

Netivot Shalom sees the pursuit of peace as a political necessity, a religious duty, and an ethical obligation. They understand political reality and the necessity to require territorial compromise as part of any plan to achieve lasting peace between Israel and the Arabs. The State of Israel's survival and success take precedence over the desire to maintain control over *Eretz Yisrael Hashleimah* (Greater Israel), including the West Bank (the historical *Yehudah* and *Shomron,* or Judah and Samaria). Therefore, they advocate making the painful concession of parts of the Land of Israel so that the State of Israel might live in peace with her neighbors. They believe that a peace settlement based on territorial compromise is necessary to realize the values of religious Zionism, which are the preservation of the Jewish character of Israeli society and the maintenance of the highest ethical standards. And they stress that their daily lives and the political life of Israel must be guided by the biblical verse "And you shall do what is right and good in the eyes of God" (Deuteronomy 6:18) and the Talmudic principle *mipnei darchei shalom* (for the sake of peace).

Netivot Shalom believes that lasting peace can only be achieved when the basic needs and aspirations of both peoples are met, with each side acting in consideration of the ideals and constraints of the other. They quote Rabbi Joseph B. Soloveitchik, a leading modern Orthodox rabbinic authority of the 20th century:

> Saving the life of a single Israeli young man takes precedence over the entire Torah. The Jewish law regarding saving lives must be taken into account when dealing with politics. There are now many who call for giving up not an inch of the land of Israel, who think not, that for our intransigence we may pay a dear price in human lives. The notion that the Messiah must come at the high cost of human blood opposes the breath and spirit of Jewish law. . . . In matters of territories, politics, *and* saving lives, the recognized experts are the army and the Israeli government. If they find that it is possible to give up territories without endangering lives in the community or the state's very existence, then they [the secular authorities] must be listened to.[2]

Netivot Shalom also points out that continuing to rule over a nationally conscious Arab population is a threat to the internal welfare and ethical character of Israel. They stress that if Israel continues the way she has been going, she will soon be faced with the choice of either annexing the West Bank permanently and giving its inhabitants full citizenship (which would result in an Arab majority and destroy Israel's Jewish character), or continuing to oppress an entire population as second-class citizens

---

2. *Maariv,* Rosh Hashanah, 1975, quoted by David Bedein, "Genesis of an Israeli Religious Left," New Outlook, January 1976, 39.

and being considered an apartheid state (which would destroy Israel's ethical character). Neither of these is a viable option. Both would be the end of Israel as a Jewish, democratic, honorable nation (as some Israelis have also warned).

So, while acknowledging that it takes two sides to make peace, Netivot Shalom believes that Israel is responsible for forging and advancing a vision of a Jewish state and for acting in pursuit of that vision. They see the choice as between:

- A Jewish state governed by Biblical values, just laws, and reason – *or* a garrison state characterized by chauvinism, institutionalized injustice, and xenophobia.
- A democratic society, flourishing within smaller borders, in which the Arab minority enjoys full human dignity and civil rights – *or* all of *Eretz Yisrael* (the land of Israel) at the price of repressing the political freedom of millions of Palestinian Arabs;
- Mutual recognition and co-existence between Israelis and Palestinians – *or* escalating destruction and loss of life.[3]

As Netivot Shalom outlines these stark choices, it becomes clear that it is long past time that we move beyond the current impasse and start using our wisdom and resources to seek a long-lasting solution that will be of enormous benefit for Israel, the Jewish people, the Palestinian people, and all of humanity. While, as previously indicated, Netivot Shalom is no longer active, its essential message of peace and justice is needed more than ever before.

In a Netivot Shalom 1986 English Language Series article, "Religious Zionism Today," author Janet Aviad argues that peace groups have difficulty attracting followers because:

- The voice of moderation and rationality is always dim next to the voice of emotionalism and extremism.
- The voice that introduces ambiguities and complications is always dim next to the voice of self-certainty and clarity.
- A movement that critiques society and the religious establishment in the name of transcendent values is far less appealing than one which identifies the sacred with a specific social order.

---

3. Oz V'Shalom poster.

- A movement that speaks in the name of universal ethical values and the rights of others is far less comfortable than one that asserts the superior status and rights of the "group" or nation.

In a follow-up article in that series, "Education and Ideology in Jewish Education Today," Lawrence Kaplan, a then Professor of Jewish Studies at McGill University, argued that it is Jewish education that is at fault. He stated that the Jewish component of education in many yeshivas today is "overlaid with a coating of Messianic, nationalist Zionism" and is essentially "fundamentalist, authoritarian, and particularistic in character, having a narrow, if intense, range of concerns, and basically unconcerned with general universal, social, ethical, and humanistic issues." Due to the increasing shift of Orthodox Jews to the right, this is likely more true today.

WHY PEACE IS SO IMPORTANT FOR ISRAEL

Peace in the Middle East is critically necessary for Israel's future, and Jewish communities should make the pursuit of peace one of our highest priorities. Some reasons include:

Time is not on Israel's side. As stressed by Netivot Shalom and other Israelis, if there is not a two-state solution relatively soon, Israel will face a situation in the future where Arabs are a majority or close to a majority of the population of Israel and the West Bank. Israel would then face the very difficult choice of either giving the West Bank Arabs voting rights, which would mean the end of Israel as a Jewish state, or not doing so and being looked on by much of the world as an apartheid state. Of course, neither of these choices would be good for Israel.

The unstable situation and the widespread hatred and violence in the Middle East could result in a wider war with devastating consequences for Israel and many other nations. Another war in the area could be especially destructive for Israel, since Hamas and Hezbollah have been stockpiling more missiles and other increasingly lethal weapons. Furthermore, the record wildfire near Haifa in early December 2010 should provide a warning of the potential grave dangers to Israel if her forest areas were set afire in a war by enemy missiles, especially at a time when these areas are often very dry from lack of rain.

In January 2011, Colonel Dan Zusman, who is in charge of defending about 1.5 million Israelis in the Tel Aviv area, said on IDF (Israeli Defense Forces) radio that "missiles and rockets from all fronts will reach Tel Aviv in the next round. . . . We are talking about dozens of missiles of different kinds that will hit Tel Aviv and, therefore, the estimate is that there will be hundreds of dead, destruction of buildings, and destruction of infrastructure."[4]

Unfortunately, since then the situation has become worse and every major Israeli city may be threatened in a future war, God forbid, not only those on the northern and southern borders, and very frighteningly, it is estimated that there are now 200,000 missiles and rockets targeting Israel.[5]

Failure to resolve the Israeli/Palestinian conflict is making Israel diplomatically isolated. In 2012, the UN General Assembly approved the de-facto recognition of a Palestinian state, with 138 votes in favor and only nine votes against, with 41 abstentions. On December 16, 2014, the European parliament passed a resolution in favor of Palestinian recognition.[6] While the resolution is only symbolic, it stated that the European Parliament "supports in principle the recognition of Palestinian statehood and the two-state solution, and believes these should go hand in hand with the development of peace talks, which should be advanced." Similar resolutions previously passed by the British, French, Irish and Portuguese parliaments requested that their respective governments recognize a Palestinian state immediately.

Israel's increasing isolation is indicated by a cover article in the May 22, 2015 *Jewish Voice* (NY), "Israel Targeted for International Isolation by the EU, Vatican and FIFA." The article discussed efforts by a group of influential former European leaders to have the European Union (EU) step up its efforts in support of a Palestinian state and to consider promoting a deadline for the negotiation of a two state solution; the recent Vatican recognition of a two-state solution; and efforts by the Palestinian

---

4. Gil Ronen, "'Hundreds of Civilian Deaths in Next War,' Says IDF" *Arutz Sheva*, January 12, 2011.

5. Yaakov Lippin, "[Israeli Homeland Defense Minister Gilad] Erdan: Enemies have 200,000 rockets and missiles pointed at Israel," *Jerusalem Post*, October 9, 2013.

6. Barak Ravid, "European Parliament passes motion in favor of Palestine recognition," *Haaretz*, December 17, 2014.

Football Association to have FIFA (Federation Internationale de Football Association), world soccer's governing body, suspend Israel, which would prevent Israel from participating in international soccer competitions. Fortunately the appeal to the FIFA was withdrawn, but future such efforts are likely if current conditions are not changed.

In addition, the campaign to "boycott, divest from, and sanction" Israel (BDS) is growing in many U.S. campuses and among groups in Europe. While I am, as indicated above, a strong supporter of a two-state solution, I oppose the BDS campaign, because many of its supporters oppose Israel's existence or support a one state solution, which would mean the end of Israel as a Jewish state or as a democratic state. However, support for BDS is likely to grow as long as the world sees Israel as an occupier.

Along with many Israeli security experts, I believe that the best way to reduce Israel's increasing isolation is through a settlement of her conflict with the Palestinians and surrounding Arab nations, followed by cooperative efforts to improve economic, environmental, and social conditions in the area.

Although there are many causes of anti-Semitism, and it is never justified, one major source for anti-Semitism today is the ongoing Israeli/Palestinian-Arab conflict. When Palestinians daily experience or see on television other Palestinians being detained at security checkpoints –sometimes rudely – and other examples of what they regard as humiliation, it builds resentment against all Israelis and Jews in general. There was a significant increase in anti-Semitism during and shortly after the Israeli wars in Gaza in January 2009 and during the summer of 2014. Although, unfortunately, anti-Semitism will never be completely eliminated, a just, comprehensive, sustainable settlement of the present disputes could be a major factor in reducing it. Also, when Muslims worldwide see pictures on their TV screens that emphasize negative aspects of Israel's occupation, it makes terrorism and future conflicts more likely, which will negatively affect not only Israel but Jews throughout the world. An end to the occupation would mean an end to broadcasting these types of images.

Of course, there is never an excuse for anti-Semitism, and, as discussed in chapter 5, Israel is doing many positive things, including humanitarian work in Nepal after the country was struck with volcanoes and providing medical help even to her enemies. Unfortunately, there will be some anti-Semitism no matter what Israel does, but properly resolving the conflicts between Israel and Palestinian and the Arab nations should be considered in terms of reducing anti-Semitism, among other reasons indicated in this chapter.[7]

Israel needs a comprehensive, sustainable, secure peace to effectively address her major economic, social, and environmental problems. Israel has a large and growing poverty gap. According to a flyer, "Fighting Poverty in Israel," from the anti-poverty and anti-hunger group Meir Panim, which operates 14 free restaurants throughout Israel and delivers meals daily to the elderly and homebound, "over 1.75 million Israeli citizens suffer from hunger; two of five Israeli children live below the poverty line; over 817,200 children face the daily challenge of hunger; and 186,700 of Israel's elderly citizens are completely destitute."

The educational and healthcare systems have suffered in recent years because so much of the Israeli budget necessarily goes to security. High school class sizes are increasing to as many as 40 students in some cases. As university budgets are slashed, many departments, especially in the humanities, have been closed. Many Israeli scholars have sought jobs in other countries because of decreases in funding for education and research, creating a serious "brain drain." Israel's healthcare system faces a major crisis as government subsidizes health maintenance organizations, and hospitals are unable to pay doctors adequate wages. For five months in 2011, Israeli doctors were on a partial strike, performing only emergency surgery.

Israel badly needs peace in order to address its many domestic problems. Almost a fifth of Israel's budget goes to defense and this is likely to increase as new weapon systems are introduced in response to security threats.[8] Meanwhile, social services are often being reduced, and the number of middle-class Israelis has significantly decreased.

In July and August of 2011 there were about a dozen major demonstrations in Tel Aviv and ten other Israeli cities, protesting the high costs of

7. Raphael Magarik,"Do Jewish Actions Ever Cause Anti-Semitism," *Forward*, September 24, 2014; MJ Rosenberg, "Sorry, Jewish Organizations, the Cause of Spike in Antipathy Toward Jews is Israel's Behavior," MJ Rosenberg on Everything, September 18, 2014.

8. Moti Bassok, "Israel shells out almost a fifth of national budget on defense, figures show," *Haaretz*, February 14, 2013.

housing and food and low wages. An estimated 150,000 Israelis took to the streets of Tel Aviv and other Israeli cities on the evening of July 30, 2011, protesting the high cost of living.[9] This is about two percent of Israel's population, which would be the equivalent of about six million Americans, to give perspective on the size of the protests. Later demonstrations kept getting bigger, culminating with an estimated 450,000 Israelis demonstrating on September 3, 2011 in Tel Aviv and many other Israeli cities.[10]

The record wildfire in December 2010 made Israelis aware of how woefully unprepared the country was to fight fires.[11] Many requests over the years for more money and resources for firefighting have been turned down, largely because so much money had to be allocated for security concerns. While politicians knew of the serious deficiencies of the firefighting service in Israel, a succession of government agencies and ministers had failed to deal with the situation because they were necessarily focused on Israel's security.

Israel needs peace in order to effectively address an impending climate crisis and many other environmental threats. Some climate experts are saying that climate change could spin out of control with disastrous effects within a few years, unless drastic changes are soon made. If this crisis is not properly responded to, nothing else will matter. It is essential that the world focus its attention on saving the global environment, but this will be more difficult if there is continued instability and violence in the Middle East. Of course, this is also true of other world trouble spots.

Israel is especially threatened by climate change. The Israeli Union for Environmental Defense projects that, unless major changes that reduce greenhouse emissions soon occur, Israel will experience major temperature increases, an average decrease in rainfall of 20 to 30 percent, severe storms, increased desertification, an inundation of the coastal plain where most Israelis live by a rising Mediterranean Sea, along with other negative effects from climate change. On May 27, 2015, the temperature in

---

9. Ilan Lior, "150 protesters take to streets around the country, calling for reform of welfare state," *Haaretz*, July 31, 2011.

10. "Israel Protests: 450,000 Hit The Streets In Country's Largest Demonstrations," *The Huffington Post*, November 5, 2011.

11. Donald Macintyre, "Criticism mounts over Israel's 'unpreparedness' for wildfire," *The Independent*," December 6, 2010.

Tel Aviv reached 108 degrees Fahrenheit, and it was also over 100 degrees Fahrenheit in much of Israel for a few days about a week later, with one tourist falling to her death from Masada after becoming dehydrated. So, it is essential that Israel find peace so that she can devote greater attention to responding to climate change. This is discussed more in Chapter 11.

Israel faces many other environmental problems that are not being adequately addressed, largely because so much attention and resources are devoted to security concerns. Far more people die from air pollution in Israel than from terrorism and traffic accidents combined. Some Israeli rivers are badly polluted. There is a shortage of open space. Less than 10 percent of Israel's garbage is recycled. The flow in the Jordan River is less than a tenth of its normal flow, and most of it near its entrance to the Dead Sea is sewage. Since the Jordan River is the main source of replenishment for the Dead Sea, the Dead Sea is rapidly shrinking, with resulting nearby sinkholes that threaten the tourist industry in the area. Once again, a resolution of Middle East conflicts would enable Israel to respond more effectively to these problems.

Benefits for Israel, if peace is finally reached, would potentially include open borders, an end to boycotts, international cooperation, and free movement of persons, products, and services across borders – all of which could lead to major economic growth. Peace would reduce the need for military expenditures in all the countries involved in the conflict. Billions of dollars would become available for economic development to improve the quality of life for everyone. Peace would open transportation connections, air travel, maritime relations, and better telecommunications. More outside investments would be attracted, leading to more jobs and greater prosperity.

Because of the great stress on security issues, Israel's progressive forces have been considerably weakened. When people are primarily concerned about terrorism and other security measures, it is hard for a politician who is concerned about the environment, poverty, education, and other social issues to get a receptive hearing. HaYeruka, a political party led by leading Israeli environmentalists Alon Tal and Eren Ben Yemini that stressed a greater emphasis on environmental and social issues, received less than one percent of the vote in the 2008 Israeli national elections. This was so discouraging that there has been no separate 'green' party in later elections.

In a column in the *Jerusalem Post*, Larry Derfner wrote that when he tries to explain Israel to Americans, he asks them to imagine 80 percent of their fellow citizens being Republicans.[12] In 2015 Israel elected the most right-wing government in her history.

Threats to Israel's security rightly occupy Jews' attention but they also divert attention from other issues of great importance. When I try to engage Jews on the need to apply Jewish values to the solution of current global threats, I am often told, "All I care about is Israel." Many U.S. Jews support Republican politicians because they think they are better for Israel, agreeing with their very hawkish Republican positions, while ignoring their very conservative positions on the environment, climate change, social security, taxes, job creation, and other issues.

None of these negatives matter, as long as politicians are perceived as being "good for Israel," which generally means supporting Israeli right-wing politicians. Jews have a special mission to be a "light unto the nations" (Isaiah 49:6), but it is very difficult when so much attention and resources must be given to combating terrorism and to maintaining a strong military force.

Failure to achieve a settlement of the Israeli/Palestinian conflict damages Israel's image worldwide. A poll commissioned by the BBC in December 2010 and January 2011 asked over 28,000 people in 27 countries around the world: "Please tell me if you think each of the following countries is having a mainly positive or mainly negative influence in the world."[13] For Israel, the results were 21% positive and 49% negative. Of the 27 countries involved in the survey, a majority of people in 22 countries saw Israel in a negative light.

A 2013 BBC poll[14] showed the following: The U.S. was the only country

---

12. Larry Derfner, "To Be Israeli Today," *Jerusalem Post*, January 13, 2010.

13. Israel's popularity climbs in annual BBC poll, but overall global impression is still negative, *Haaretz* archive, March 9, 2011.

14. "America is the Only Country with a Favorable View of Israel," *Washington Post blog*, July 25, 2014.

with a majority (just 51%) with a mostly favorable view of Israel. The average for the world with a mostly favorable view of Israel was just 20%, and many countries had very low percentages of their people with mostly favorable views of Israel: Japan (3), Spain (4), Germany (8), United Kingdom (14), and Greece (15).

Of course, much of the negative views about Israel are due to misleading and false media reports, but a just settlement of her conflicts would greatly improve Israel's image.

Israel's long struggle to maintain security is making her less tolerant of dissent. One important example of this is the hearings that were held in the Knesset in 2011 to determine if the U.S.-based organization J Street could be considered a pro-Israel organization. Many groups, including the Anti-Defamation League and the American Jewish Committee, condemned the hearings, with some comparing it to the McCarthy witchhunts in the United States. Naomi Chazan, former president of the New Israel Fund and a former Knesset member, stated:

> Let us be clear about what is happening here. Proponents of a narrow, demagogic, ultra-nationalist, pro-settlement, anti-peace point of view have decided that every other point of view is illegitimate. They believe that only they can define what it means to love and support Israel and what is best for its future. In so doing, they undermine Israel's standing as a liberal democracy, alienate its most stalwart supporters in the Jewish world, and sadly contribute to its de-legitimization in the international arena.[15]

Rabbi Michael Melchior, Former Minister of Social and Diaspora Affairs and leader of the dovish religious party Meimad, stated:

> A large portion of the Jewish world, mainly the non-Orthodox, is drifting away from Israel and I find it very disturbing. We mustn't push them away but bring them closer to us. They are allowed to object to legislation and our views. J Street is within the family.[16]

---

15. Sabithulla Khan, "Middle East Peace Talks 2010: Investigating the role of lobbying and advocacy groups in Washington, D.C. as spoilers," academia.edu, Spring 2011.
16. "Current & Former Knesset Members, Jewish Leaders Strongly Defend J Street in

There have been several other examples of a shift in Israel toward curbing freedom of thought and actions, including the following reported in a *New York Times* article, "How Israel Silences Dissent:"[17]

- On July 12, 2014, four days after the latest Gaza war, hundreds of Israelis gathered in Tel Aviv to protest Israeli policies with regard to Gaza and to call for an end to the Israeli occupation of the West Bank. They chanted, "Jews and Arabs refuse to be enemies." The protesters were attacked by a group of Israeli extremist Jews chanting "Death to leftists" and "Deaths to Arabs." While several protesters required medical attention from being beaten, the police made no arrests.
- A similar event occurred a week later in Haifa, with the deputy mayor and his son being among the victims this time.
- In July 2014, Gila Almagor, a veteran Israeli actress received threats that she would be murdered on stage after she told a reporter about feeling ashamed after learning of the kidnapping and burning alive of the 16-year-old Palestinian, Abu Khedeir.
- The popular comedian Orna Banai was fired from her position as a spokesperson for an Israeli cruise ship company after she expressed sorrow in an interview about the killing of Palestinian women and children during the Gaza War.
- Haaretz hired bodyguards to protect its columnist Gideon Levy because he received threats after he wrote an article critical of Israeli pilots.

Because of these and other examples of intolerance by the Israeli government, one of Israel's leading authors David Grossman stated:[18]

> The danger is that if such a process continues and if our isolation in the world increases – Israel will become nothing more than a militant, fundamentalist and inward-looking sect on the margins of history. . . . The [Culture] Minister's highest interest needs to be contact with reality, and [to allow] criticism to be as deep and wide and varied as possible.
> Sometimes we need to also include what makes us hurt. The principle of absolute freedom to express one's opinion is such a strong

Unprecedented Committee Debate," J Street Blog, March 23, 2011.

17. Mairav Zonszein, "How Israel Silences Dissent," *NY Times*, September 26, 2014.
18. Gil Itzkovich, "David Grossman: Culture minister turning Israel into a militant, fundamentalist sect," *Haaretz*, June 15, 2015.

element in the life of society, and we are in a constant process of its erosion and even abhorring it. We are pursuing a narrow, literal "justice" that is more than anything self-righteousness. In such a place, as [Israeli poet] Yehuda Amichai said, no flowers or culture will grow.

Knowing of all the positive things Israel is doing, it pains me to report the above. But I think it is necessary that Jews be aware of what is happening in order to help shift Israel back to a more democratic, tolerant path.

Recently this intolerance has spread to the U.S. where some disruptive groups tried to prevent the progressive coalition – T'ruah, New Israel Fund, Americans for Peace Now, and Partners for Progressive Israel – from marching in the 2015 Celebrate Israel Parade. They were permitted to march, but, as in the past, near the very beginning before the part of the parade that was televised.

Another example is the booing and jeering of Orthodox Jewish Jacob (Jack) Lew –Secretary of the Treasury, former Obama Chief of Staff, a long time strong supporter of Israel and other Jewish causes including the struggle for freedom for Soviet Jews during the 1970s – as he defended the Obama administration's positions on Israel and preventing Iran from developing a nuclear weapon, at a forum sponsored by the Jerusalem Post in Manhattan on June 7, 2015.

If a resolution of the Israeli/Palestinian conflict can be found, it would serve as a model for other trouble spots in the world. At a time when military conflicts are becoming increasingly destructive and when so many human needs are unmet, as nations spend large percentages of their wealth on weapons, it is essential that there be a reduction in wars and violence. If Israelis and Palestinians – two peoples who have been at war for decades – can make peace, it could demonstrate that peace is possible everywhere.

PROSPECTS FOR MIDDLE EAST PEACE

Based on the many reasons given above, it is essential that there be a comprehensive, sustainable, and just resolution of the Israeli/Palestinian conflict. Of course this depends on actions and compromises by the Palestinians as well as by Israelis. Friends of Israel can win many debates, by pointing out negative things that the Palestinians have done in the past, and Palestinians feel that they can do the same about Israel. However, the important thing now is not to harp on past negatives and reasons why it is hard to negotiate with the other side, but to find common ground and solutions.

A key question I often ask with regard to Israel's future is, "How will Israel avert renewed violence and increased diplomatic isolation, effectively respond to her environmental, economic, and other domestic problems, and remain both a Jewish and a democratic state, without a proper resolution of her conflict with the Palestinians and the surrounding Arab nations?" I have raised the question often in recent years in personal conversations, in comments posted after online articles, and in letters to editors. Unfortunately, in October 2015, violence broke out in Israel again, causing many Israelis to curb their travels for fear of being attacked by Palestinians.

Nobody has been able to disagree with my assumptions or effectively respond to my question. However, two responses that I often received were to the effect of "Yes, but what can we do – we have no partner for peace," and "Yes, but as bad as that would be, giving back land as part of a peace agreement would be even worse." These responses were often combined with statements like "Arabs can't be trusted," and/or "the Palestinians won't be satisfied until they have all the land."

Prospects for peace are certainly not good now (as of January 2016), but we should recall that opinions about peace prospects can change overnight, which happened when Egyptian President Anwar Sadat came to Israel in 1977 and spoke at the Knesset. Currently, there is an increase in Palestinian terror attacks, anti-Israel rhetoric and support for violence against Israelis, support for BDS, and isolation of Israel. Also, it is unlikely that any successor to Palestinian Authority President Mahmoud Abbas would be as cooperative in security efforts and resisting a return to armed struggle. If hatred and fear continue to escalate among Israeli and Palestinians, conditions for both peoples will become increasingly difficult, and possibly intolerable. For these reasons, and the many others indicated previously, it is essential that Israel make resolving her conflict with the Palestinians a priority.

Over the years, many former Israeli prime ministers who were initially hawkish came to the conclusion that Israel must make painful territorial compromises in order to seek a peaceful resolution of the Israeli/Palestinian conflict. They include Yitzhak Rabin, Ariel Sharon, and Ehud Olmert.

In January 2006, Olmert said: "The choice is between allowing Jews to live in all parts of the land of Israel and living in a state with a Jewish majority [which] mandates giving up parts of the Land of Israel. We cannot continue to control parts of the territories where most of the Palestinians live."[19] Former Prime Minister Ariel Sharon told the Likud Party in May 2003, "The idea that it is possible to keep 3.5 million Palestinians under occupation is bad for Israel, bad for the Palestinians, and bad for the Israeli economy."[20] Former Prime Minister Yitzhak Rabin made the following statements:[21]

- "I enter negotiations with Chairman Arafat, the leader of the PLO, the representative of the Palestinian people, with the purpose to have coexistence between our two entities, Israel as a Jewish state and Palestinian state, entity, next to us, living in peace."
- "I would like Israel to be a Jewish state, and therefore not to annex over 2 million Palestinians who live in the West Bank and the Gaza Strip to Israel, which will make Israel a bi-national state."
- "I believe that it is my responsibility as the prime minister of Israel to do whatever can be done to exploit the unique opportunities that lie ahead of us to move towards peace."

In 2013, an Israeli Academy Award-nominated documentary, *The Gatekeepers*, provided valuable insights on Israel's security situation. What

---

19. Greg Myre, "Israel's Acting Leader Backs Creation of Palestinian State," *NY Times.* January 24, 2006.
20. Bickerton, Ian J., *The Arab-Israel Conflict: A History*, Google Books, 2009, 195.
21. BrainyQuote, http://www.brainyquote.com/quotes/authors/y/yitzhak_rabin.h tml#qiL3Xx40T3LkXws

made it special is that its Israeli director, Dror Moreh, interviewed all of the then-living retired heads of the Shin Bet, Israel's security service, and they responded with great candor about their experiences combating terrorism and striving to help maintain Israel's security. These six men know much about the Israeli/Palestinian conflict from personal experience, so their opinions should be thoughtfully considered.

The strategic experts are unanimously critical of Israel's continued occupation of the West Bank and feel that Israel should be doing more to help resolve the Israeli/Palestinian conflict in order to provide Israel with a decent future. Here are a few quotations from some of the former Shin Bet directors who appeared in the documentary:[22]

- Yaakov Peri: "I know about plenty of junctures since 1967 when in my view . . . we should have reached an agreement and ran away from there." In discussing his growing tired of pulling suspects from their beds in the middle of the night and watching the anguish of their wives and children: "These are not easy moments. They get etched deep [in your psyche]. And when you retire from the agency, you become a bit of a lefty."
- Avraham Shalom, on concluding that Israeli policy had become primarily about punishing the Palestinians: "We became cruel . . . to the occupied population in the guise of fighting terrorism."
- Amit Ayalon: "The tragedy . . . [is] that we win every battle, but we lose the war."

There are other examples of key Israeli security experts and others coming to conclusions similar to the retired Shin Bet directors. According to the Israeli national Security Project,

> The roster of former Israeli security officials who support the two-state solution to the Israeli-Palestinian conflict is long and varied. It ranges from those on the left to those on the right to those without any partisan affiliation. It includes senior political figures, such as former presidents, prime ministers, and defense ministers; seasoned bureaucrats; and apolitical experts, such as heads of think tanks. It includes some of the highest decorated soldiers the state of Israel has known, as well

---

22. Dan Ephron, "The Gatekeepers: Shin Bet Chiefs Air Peace Views in Documentary," *Newsweek*, February 5, 2013.

as civilians who have served in the highest capacities within Israel's intelligence agencies.[23]

OUTLINE OF STEPS TOWARD A PEACE AGREEMENT

Gershon Baskin is a long-time peace activist in Israel and founder and former Israeli CEO of the Israel/Palestine Center for Research and Information (IPCRI), a joint Israeli-Palestinian public policy research think-tank on Middle East conflict issues. The group proposes policy options to decision makers about the peace process. Baskin is also a weekly columnist for the *Jerusalem Post* and was an elected member of the leadership of the Green Movement political party, *HaYeruka*. In his July 5, 2010 *Jerusalem Post* article, "Encountering Peace: And We Shall Dwell in Peace," Baskin discussed key points on the potential for peace that are still relevant:[24]

- The basics of an agreement are well understood for what is "the most researched conflict in the history of conflicts, and there are more detailed plans on how to resolve even the minutest of details in this conflict than any other." Every possible issue in the conflict has been explored in depth by Israeli and Palestinian negotiating teams.
- Until now, the peace process has been a failure, and time is running out, as current options may no longer be available in the near future.
- A majority of Israelis and Palestinians say that they want peace and are ready to make painful compromises, but they both also feel that there is no partner on the other side.
- Failure to make peace would be catastrophic for both Israel and the Palestinians, since "the survival of the Jewish people on our land, of the Zionist enterprise in its entirety, is based on our ability to extricate ourselves from the occupation of the Palestinian people and to make peace on the basis of two states for two peoples."
- Since there is a lack of trust on both sides, based on a long history in which many agreements have been broken, there must be a reliable third party who will monitor implementation and verify that all aspects

23. "Two States for a Strong Israel," Israel National Security Project, http://www.isr aelnsp.org/the-experts.html
24. Gershon Baskin, "Encountering Peace and we will dwell in peace," Jerusalem Post, July 5, 2010.

of all agreements are being fully implemented. The reliable third party must be able to act immediately with full transparency when there are breaches, "to call the parties to task, to demand explanations, and to insist on implementation."

- It is essential that President Obama become actively and directly involved and that intense, direct negotiations mediated by a leading American mediator be held, to reach an agreement that both sides can live with and that leaders on both sides will support enthusiastically.
- Prime Minister Netanyahu must, in effect, look Israelis in the eye and describe to them the necessary conditions for a peace agreement, including that the Palestinian state will include about 96% of the West Bank with the Palestinians given land inside Israel in exchange for the 4% percent of the West Bank that Israel will annex as part of the agreement, and that Jerusalem will be the capital of both countries. Because of mutually agreeable land swaps, about 80% of the settlers in the West Bank and East Jerusalem will remain in place as part of Israel.
- President Abbas must also look into the eyes of his people and tell them that they will not be able to return to their lost homes inside Israel, but that they have the potential to build a model state using the latest technologies, create the first successful, working democracy in the Arab world, and have the best school system in the region.

OTHER CONSIDERATIONS

Some other considerations about a possible resolution of the Israeli/Palestinian conflict include:

- Several polls have shown that most Israelis, American Jews, and Palestinians favor a two-state solution. The problem is that both sides feel that they have no partner in efforts to obtaining peace. So confidence-building measures from both sides are essential.
- On the evening of June 4, 2011, an estimated 20,000 Israelis marched through the streets of Central Tel Aviv under the banner "Israel says yes to a Palestinian state." Organizers argued that the establishment of a Palestinian state would serve vital Israeli interests.
- The terrorist group Hamas, whose charter favors the elimination of Israel, has stated several times that it would abide by a negotiated settlement obtained by the Palestinian Authority if it was also supported

in a referendum of Palestinians.[25] Of course, no matter what promises are given, steps to insure Israeli security must be taken.

CONCLUSION

In conclusion, there is an important choice that Israel and its supporters must now face, between (1) continuation of the status quo, in which case violence, diplomatic isolation, and current socio-economic problems will continue and likely worsen, and Israel may face the difficult choice of remaining a Jewish state or a democratic state, or (2) recognizing that the alternative to such a bleak and depressing future is to make seeking peace Israel's highest priority.

The achievement of peace between Israel and the Palestinians and Arab states will not be easy, but working toward it is essential to a decent future for Israel and puts into practice essential Jewish values and mandates: to seek and pursue peace (Psalms 34:14), to turn enemies into friends (*Avot d'Rebbe Natan* 23:1), to work cooperatively for justice (Deuteronomy 16:20), and to preserve God's world (Genesis 2:15). Fortunately, there are signs of movement among some Palestinians who have recognized that terrorism is counterproductive to their cause and have started to build the infrastructure and economic and security conditions that can form the basis of a future Palestinian state.

Among the many blessings a just Mideast peace would bring is that it would enable Israel to strive to completely fulfill her true moral mission as a model of justice, compassion, and, most important, *shalom*. Then the vision of Isaiah can be fulfilled: "It shall come to pass in the latter day ... that out of Zion shall go forth Torah, and the word of the Lord from Jerusalem" (Isaiah 2:2–3).

---

25. Reuters, "Hamas vows to honor Palestinian referendum on peace with Israel," *Haaretz*, December 1, 2010.

Chapter 8

Jewish Values and U.S. Foreign Policy

$\mathcal{E}$very gun that is made, every warship launched, every rocket fired signifies, in the final sense, a theft from those who hunger and are not fed, those who are cold and are not clothed.   – Dwight D. Eisenhower

$\mathcal{A}$nd the work of righteousness shall be peace; And the effect of righteousness, quietness and confidence forever.

       – Isaiah 32:17

$\mathcal{M}$ankind must put an end to war or war will put an end to mankind.   – John F. Kennedy

WITH THE UNITED STATES spending almost as much money on the military as all the other major powers combined, still feeling negative effects from our wars in Iraq and Afghanistan, and struggling against terrorism, it seems appropriate to consider an alternate U.S. foreign policy, one consistent with basic Jewish values. As Lester Brown, former President of Earth Policy Institute, points out in the preface to his book, *World On The Edge: How to Prevent Environmental and Economic Collapse*, there is a pressing need to "redefine security for the twenty-first century: The [primary] threats to our future now are not from armed aggression, but rather climate change, population growth, water shortages, poverty, rising food prices, and failing states."

ARE RELIGIOUS JEWS MORE AGGRESSIVE THAN OTHER JEWS?

Although there are Orthodox Jewish peace activists, such as the members of Oz v"Shalom/Netivot Shalom discussed in Chapter 7, I have found many religious Jews to be especially antagonistic toward Muslims and Arabs. I have heard some say that Israel should just destroy the Palestinians or drive them out of Israel and the territories altogether. Several Orthodox Jews have told me that the United States should just bomb Muslim countries back to the Stone Age one by one, since "the only thing Muslims understand is force." In addition to the moral callousness of such positions, these Jews ignore the effects that unprovoked and massive violence committed by the United States or Israel would have on world opinion. We would become pariah states. Furthermore, such actions might trigger a severe recession or a depression due to threats to oil supplies, and would greatly increase prospects for anti-Semitism, anti-Americanism, instability, terrorism, and war.

A 2006 study found that Jews who attend synagogue services at least once a week were twice as likely to support the war in Iraq and to define themselves as politically conservative as Jews who seldom or never go to synagogue.[1] Of course I am not advocating that Jews go to synagogue less often. Rather, I am suggesting that they apply the rich Jewish teachings on peace and justice, some of which were discussed in Chapter 3.

Some of the reasons for this hawkishness are quite understandable. Because the Soviet Union brutally oppressed Jews for decades, many Jews supported tough U.S. policies toward the USSR and escalation of the arms race, even after we and the Soviet Union had the nuclear capacities to destroy each other (and, indeed, the entire world) hundreds of times over. Also, because enemies have surrounded Israel since the moment of her birth in 1948, Jews have supported major arms expenditures by Israel and by the United States, Israel's main and sometimes only ally. But are these policies still viable today?

AN ANALYSIS OF PRESENT UNITED STATES FOREIGN POLICY

Stalemates and quagmires that developed during the United States' wars in Vietnam, Iraq, and Afghanistan, as well as Israel's wars in Lebanon and Gaza, suggest that overwhelming conventional forces cannot effectively respond to terrorism and guerilla wars. Other approaches must be found.

---

1. Ori Nir, "U.S. poll: Synagogue-goers more likely to be politically conservative," *Haaretz*, February 7, 2005.

The United States' invasion of Iraq and the chaotic and ill-planned efforts at "nation-building" that followed have been frustrating and ineffective at the expense of America's influence, security, and economy.

It was a initially thought to be a great thing for the people of Iraq, and for democracy in the Arab world in general, that the mass-murderer and tyrant Saddam Hussein was overthrown. But in many ways, the cure has been worse than the disease. The American public was misled into thinking that Saddam had or was building weapons of mass destruction, although U.N. inspectors on the ground were not finding any evidence of this – making the Iraq war very unpopular and, many believe, unnecessary. The Iraqi infrastructure was badly damaged (water, health, education, electricity) and disaffected Sunni military personnel weren't rehabilitated, but sent home jobless. Depleted Uranium used heavily by the U.S. in Iraq has caused skyrocketing cancer rates, miscarriages, and severe birth defects among the Iraqi people. By taking our attention away from the war in Afghanistan by invading Iraq, we minimized the chances of quickly finding Osama Bin Laden, winning the war there, and greatly weakening the Taliban. Now the instability in the area in and around Iraq, largely due to US intervention, led to the formation of the brutal terror group ISIS, according to military and security experts.

Thousands of U.S. and allied soldiers have been killed in Iraq and Afghanistan, and many more have been wounded and traumatized. Many soldiers served four or more tours of duty, and the ability of the United States to meet other military threats has been greatly diminished. Hundreds of thousands of Iraqi and Afghan Muslims have been killed, with many more wounded and/or made homeless. This has increased hostility toward the U.S. and has given propaganda victories to terrorists. People in the area are aware that cancer and birth defect rates have soared and that their air, water, and soil have been and will remain poisoned for many years

All the above has been at a staggering financial cost. Imagine what could have been done with the estimated three-trillion dollars that the Iraq war will end up costing the U.S. when all the expenses, including expensive medical and rehabilitative care for many thousands of wounded and traumatized soldiers, are taken into account. That money could have been far better spent to make the United States more secure, to rebuild our infrastructure, to reduce unemployment and poverty, and to respond to many other pressing societal needs. Instead, many teachers, police officers, firefighters, sanitation workers, and others, were laid off, and important programs were cut back for budgetary reasons.[2] Taking all this into account, the U.S. invasion of Iraq is arguably one of the biggest blunders in U.S. military history.

SHOULD THE U.S. OR ISRAEL ATTACK IRAN?

When it comes to Iran and its efforts to develop nuclear weapons, a common response from congregants in my Orthodox synagogue and others in the Orthodox Jewish community is that we should long since have bombed them or be preparing to do so soon. Although I agree with the strong consensus that it is very important that Iran not develop nuclear weapons, I also believe we should consider the many negative consequences an attack on Iran would likely have.

A comprehensive case against such an attack by Israel on Iran's nuclear facilities is in a study by Abdullah Toukan and Anthony Cordesman of the Center for Strategic and International Studies in Washington.[3] Some of their important conclusions are:

- There is no guarantee of success. Limited aerial resources would permit Israel to target only three sites among Iran's many nuclear development centers. Pinpoint accuracy would be needed to penetrate deeply buried, thick reinforced concrete and impact underground facilities. Therefore, there is no assurance that a strike against Iran would finish off its nuclear program or even slow it down for more than a few years.

- An Israeli attack would likely spur Iran to continue and possibly accelerate their nuclear program, in an effort to obtain a reliable deterrence against future attacks. So attacking them would almost guarantee that they would become a nuclear power at some point.

- Israel could lose large numbers of planes and lives during an attack. Since Iran has built an extensive aerial-defense system, it would be difficult for Israeli planes to reach their targets safely.

- Israeli aircraft would need to be refueled both en route to and when returning from Iran. The IAF (Israeli Air Force) would have difficulty

---

2. Dean Baker, "The Economic Impact of the Iraq War and Higher Military Spending," Center for Economic Policy and Research, May 2007.

3. Abdullah Toukan and Anthony H. Cordesman, "Study on a Possible Israeli Strike on Iran's Nuclear Development Facilities," Center for Strategic and International Studies, March 16, 2009.

finding an area above which the tankers could cruise without being detected and possibly attacked.

- An ecological disaster and many deaths from released radiation could occur, affecting surrounding nations besides Iran, thereby further increasing hatred of Israel and provoking military and terrorist responses. Pollution does not respect borders. Radiation from the Fukishima nuclear plant is affecting the west coast of the U.S.

- Iran would likely launch retaliatory attacks against Israel, American military forces in Iraq, and Western interests in the region. These attacks might include ballistic missiles – some with biological, chemical, and radiological warheads – targeting Israel's civilian and military centers. Iran possesses missiles whose range covers all of Israel.

- Iran would likely use Hamas and Hezbollah to launch rocket attacks and suicide bombers against Israel. Recent events have demonstrated Hezbollah's vastly expanded rocket capability and Hamas' ability to fire missiles from the Gaza Strip. During the second Lebanon War, Hezbollah launched 4,000 rockets from South Lebanon, which nearly paralyzed northern Israel for a month. Their supply has since been replenished and enhanced; they and Israel's other enemies had an estimated 200,000 rockets and missile targeted at Israel in 2013.[4]

- An Israeli strike on Iran would further increase instability in the Middle East. The Iranians would likely use proxies to stir up trouble in many areas.

- The Iranians would also likely try to disrupt the flow of oil from the Persian Gulf to the West by blocking the Gulf of Hormuz. Oil prices would soar due to the unstable conditions and possible disruptions. Steps to get the U.S. economy back on track would be set back, with even worse economic conditions resulting.

- United States relations with Arab allied nations would likely suffer if we attacked Iran or were perceived to have given Israel a green light or cooperated with Israel in any other way. Although recent Wikileaks materials show that some Arab leaders hope that the U.S. will attack Iran, Muslim populations would likely demand that there be retaliations against the U.S. and Israel.

---

4. Yaakov Lappin, "[Israeli Homeland Defense Minister Gilad] Erdan: Enemies have 200,000 rockets and missiles pointed at Israel," *Jerusalem Post*, October 9, 2013

- There would likely be a sharp increase in terrorism against Jews world-wide.

The above points are applicable to a US strike on Iran as well.[5]

In summary, there is no guarantee that an Israeli (or United States) strike on Iranian nuclear facilities would be successful, and there are many possible harmful effects of such an attack. It is crucial that Iran not be permitted to develop nuclear weapons and thereby precipitate a nuclear arms race in the Middle East, but military methods cannot accomplish that, and even if it could, the side effects would be extremely negative as indicated above. It is more effective to deploy serious economic sanctions along with diplomatic isolation and punishment.

Iran must be convinced that any nuclear attack on Israel or any other country will result in immediate devastation of Iranian cities, while co-operating with the west and the international community could lead to many economic and diplomatic benefits for them.

Along with most people, I hope and pray that Iran does not acquire a nuclear capacity, and I support strong sanctions and other approaches that may get Iran to change its strategy. However, we also should remember that for many years the U.S. and the former Soviet Union built many thousands of nuclear weapons and kept them on trigger alert with a strategy of "mutually assured destruction" that threatened the entire world. Fortunately, neither side was crazy enough to use these weapons, but we came close when the Soviet Union brought nuclear weapons into Cuba, and we threatened to attack Soviet ships that were trying to end a blockade of Cuba. While the present Iranian regime is certainly evil, with some of its leaders denying that the Holocaust occurred, it would be suicidal for them to attack Israel with nuclear weapons.

The world would, of course, be far better off without a nuclear-armed Iran. But we should remember the deep-seated Iranian resentment of the CIA-supported 1953 coup, which ejected an elected Iranian government and installed the Shah, and the subsequent U.S. aid, which provided the Shah with the weapons to suppress and torture his opponents.[6] Iran also

---

5. Noah Shactman, "U.S. Attack on Iran Would Take Hundreds of planes, Ships, and Missiles," *Cows*, September 7, 2012.
6. Saeed Kamali Dehghan amd Richard Norton-Taylor, "CIA Admits role in 1953 Iranian coup," *The Guardian*, August 19, 2013.

recognizes that if Iraq had actually possessed nuclear weapons, the U.S. would likely never have invaded that country – hence their desire to have such weapons today in the belief that it will deter a U.S. attack.

I very much hope that the recent nuclear deal, signed by Iran and the United States, Russia, China, England, France, and Germany will be successful in preventing Iran from getting a nuclear weapon. It was strongly opposed by Israeli PM Netanyahu, most Israelis, and all congressional Republicans, but they proposed no feasible alternative. There was widespread support for the agreement from many U.S. and Israeli strategic, military, and nuclear experts, including some Nobel prize winners, former Republican Secretary of State, Colin Powell, former directors of Mossad and Shin Bet, the Israeli Nuclear Advisory Committee, the vast majority of world leaders who stated a position, the vast majority of former diplomats who took a position, 42 of the 46 Democratic and Independent U.S. senators, eight of the ten Jewish senators, a majority of American Jews (according to polls), and at least 26 former leaders of major Jewish organizations, including Thomas Dine who served as AIPAC's executive director for 13 years and three past chairmen of the Conference of Presidents of Major Jewish Organizations. Of course, any compromise agreement will not give each side all that they want, but many experts believe that the agreement provides excellent inspection conditions and provides the best chance of preventing Iran from developing a nuclear weapon. Iran has already significantly reduced their nuclear capability, removing 98% of its enriched nuclear material and disabling most of its centrifuges and one nuclear reactor.

TOWARD A MORE RATIONAL U.S. FOREIGN POLICY

We live in a very dangerous world today, one with threats of a different nature and magnitude than those that past generations faced. Major battlefield conflicts are less likely, but there are greater threats of battles with enemies hiding among a large civilian population. The U.S. wars in Vietnam, Iraq, and Afghanistan, Israeli wars in Gaza and Lebanon, and the Soviet war in Afghanistan show how difficult it is to win guerilla wars. Terrorism is another significant danger, one that is elusive and hard to prevent or fight with conventional methods. Attempts to oppose terrorism can have unexpected effects and blowback. So now seems to be a good time to consider a different U.S. foreign policy, one that will be consistent with Jewish values and can also increase the security of the U.S., Israel, and all of the world's people.

REDUCING TERRORISM

One problem in developing a thoughtful and balanced foreign policy is that, as indicated previously, most people see the world in terms of black and white, good versus evil, us against them. They prefer to demonize people and groups who are not like them and to score debating points, rather than looking at situations from various perspectives in order to seek greater understanding, common ground, and solutions.

As we will discuss in chapter 10, many Americans believe that a significant number of Muslims are evil and are plotting to take over the world. Many also assume that the U.S. is blameless, that our actions have nothing to do with hatred of the U.S, and we therefore do not need to rethink anything or change.

Difficult as it may be, if we wish to reduce threats of terrorism, we should consider whether American actions are at least partially responsible for the antagonism toward the United States and the West, and whether or not this contributes in part to the growth of terrorism. The United States does many wonderful things across the globe, such as providing much aid when tsunamis, hurricanes, earthquakes, volcanoes, and other disasters strike other nations. But we have also done many things that lead others to view the U.S. harshly as an imperial power, concerned primarily about our economic interests. Hence it is very important to try to change the image of the U.S.

In 2004, a task force commissioned by then Defense Secretary Donald Rumsfeld to study the causes of terrorism concluded that "Muslims do not hate our freedom, but rather they hate our policies," specifically "American direct intervention in the Muslim world," and what they regard as our "one-sided support in favor of Israel," support for Islamic tyrannies in several countries including Egypt and Saudi Arabia, and, most of all, "the American occupation of Iraq and Afghanistan."[7] Another comprehensive study by Robert Pape, a political science professor at the University of Chicago and former Air Force lecturer, concluded that the prime cause of suicide bombings is not hatred of our freedoms or inherent violence in

---

7. Glenn Greenwald "They hate us for our occupations," *Solon*, October 12, 2010.

Islamic culture, nor it is a desire to establish worldwide *sharia* rule. Rather, it is our "foreign military occupations."[8] Drawing on data from a six-year study of suicide terrorist attacks around the world that was partially funded by the Defense Department's Defense Threat Reduction Agency, Pape and his research team found that the common cause of most suicide terrorism around the world since 1980 is military occupation. Reporting on his findings, Pape stated: "We have lots of evidence now that when you put the foreign military presence in, it triggers suicide terrorism campaigns . . . and that when the foreign forces leave it takes away almost 100% of the terrorist campaign."[9]

These and other reports describe how Muslims are angered when foreign militaries bomb, invade, and occupy their countries, and when Western powers interfere in their internal affairs, sometimes overthrowing or covertly manipulating their governments. Historically, nations have always objected to being invaded, occupied, and bombed by an occupying power. So we should not be surprised that people resent us doing the same. U.S. military actions in Iraq and Afghanistan were arguably counterproductive to reducing terrorism, because we created additional angry people who may consider turning to terrorism as revenge for what they consider our unjust and harmful actions in their country.

Here are some recent examples of terrorists in the U.S. claiming that they killed Americans not because they thought we were weak or that they hated our values, but because they were angry about our policies: Dzokhar Tsarnaev, one of the Boston marathon bombers, claimed that it was revenge for U.S. wars in Iraq and Afghanistan that inspired his attack on one of the U.S.'s largest sporting events. Other terrorists like Fort Hood shooter Nidal Hassan, Times Square bomber Faisal Shahzad, and "underwear bomber" Umar Abdulmutallab all said they did what they did to retaliate against policies of our government, which have caused the deaths and displacement of millions of Muslims worldwide.

The above analysis is very different from the conventional wisdom in the U.S., that we are hated because of our democracy, so I did an Internet search to see what else I could find about the issue. Among the many additional articles connecting U.S. military actions to increased terrorism was one that I found in *the Guardian* of April 24, 2013, "The same motive

---

8. Ibid.
9. Ibid.

for anti-US 'terrorism' is cited over and over." The article pointed out that in all the cases of Muslim terrorism, the terrorists "emphatically all say the same thing: that they were motivated by the continuous, horrific violence brought by the US and its allies to the Muslim world - violence which routinely kills and oppresses innocent men, women and children." Long before the U.S. invasions of Iraq and Afghanistan, there has been a long U.S. history of interventions abroad to further our interests. Major General Smedley D. Butler described in a 1933 talk how he rose through the ranks of the Marine Corps by "being a high class muscle man for big business, for Wall Street and for the bankers ... a racketeer for capitalism." He was rewarded with honors, medals and promotions because, as he continues:

> I helped make Mexico, especially Tampico, safe for American oil interests in 1914. I helped make Haiti and Cuba a decent place for the National City Bank boys to collect revenues in. I helped in the raping of half a dozen Central American republics for the benefits of Wall Street. The record of racketeering is long. I helped purify Nicaragua for the international banking house of Brown Brothers in 1909 ... I brought light to the Dominican Republic for American sugar interests in 1916. In China I helped to see to it that Standard Oil went its way unmolested.[10]

Ralph McGehee, who served in the CIA from 1952 to 1977, gives a similar analysis in the introduction to his 1983 book *Deadly Deceits: My 25 Years in the CIA.*

> My view, backed by 25 years of experience is, quite simply, that the CIA is the covert action arm of the presidency. Most of its money, manpower and energy go into covert operations that ... include backing dictators and overthrowing democratically elected governments. . . . The CIA uses disinformation, much of it aimed at the U.S. people to mold opinion. . . . The U.S. installs foreign leaders, arms their armies, and empowers their police to help those leaders repress an angry, defiant people. . . . The CIA-empowered leaders represent only a small fraction

---

10. Common Sense (November, 1935), American Empire (New York: MacMillan Co.), 1970, 150.

who kill, torture and impoverish their own people to maintain their position of privilege.

The Rev. Martin Luther King, Jr. was also very critical of U.S. foreign policy. He left behind a strong anti-imperialist message that sharply questioned the very nature of the "American Empire."[11] When still a graduate student, King wrote of threats from the "False God of Nationalism," which he considered a kind of pseudo-religion. To King, "my country right or wrong" was the watchword of this religion. Its preachers, absolutely convinced of its supremacy, were determined to persecute anyone who questioned its tenets.

In later years, King was sharply critical of the U.S. war in Vietnam, in spite of the great backlash he knew he would receive for that criticism, even from some fellow civil rights leaders. He stated that the U.S. was the "largest purveyor of violence in the world."[12] He recognized the great cost of the war in terms of increased poverty and cuts to basic services, and stated that "the bombs that are falling in Vietnam explode at home"[13] in American cities. A primary force propelling U.S. policy has been, and remains to be, the protection of U.S. corporate interests, regardless of the undemocratic nature or negative human rights record of the groups and governments with which we have allied ourselves. As mentioned previously, the U.S. government in August 1953 helped undermine the democratically elected Iranian government of Mohammad Mosadegh and installed the Shah in power. The Shah subsequently used widespread repression and torture in a dictatorship that lasted until the 1979 Islamic revolution, which also has produced tyranny, quashing demonstrations, violating civil liberties, and rigging elections to stay in power.

The U.S. has also supported dictatorships in the Philippines, Haiti, Nicaragua, El Salvador, Chile, Spain, Portugal, and many other countries. We have even backed dictators like Saddam Hussein and terrorists like Osama bin Laden when it was in our interest. Both Democratic and

---

11. Be Scofield, "Wikileaks, Dr. King, and 'War Psychosis,'" *Tikkun Daily,* Decmber 6, 2010.

12. "Beyond Vietnam," Talk by Rev. Dr. Martin Luther King, Riverside Church, NYC, April 4, 1967, http://mlk-kpp01.stanford.edu/index.php/encyclopedia/documentsen try/doc_beyond_vietnam/

13. *Ibid.*

Republican administrations have supported repressive Arab regimes, with increasingly counterproductive results. This makes the U.S. appear hypocritical and lose credibility with Arab publics and has provided an important recruiting tool for Al Qaeda and ISIS.

Given the above and other examples in U.S. history, it is not surprising that some people do not look on the United States as kindly as most Americans do. I believe that part of the battle against terror has to include changing the way America acts worldwide, which would help reshape how the world views us. Anti-Americanism costs the United States cooperation in dealing with such global problems as terrorism, climate change, nuclear proliferation, HIV/AIDS, disease epidemics, and potential security crises. This analysis is especially timely and important today as recent acts of terrorism by ISIS and ISIS-influenced terrorists have made homeland security a major concern in the U.S., with Republican presidential candidates urging major military efforts to destroy ISIS and extensive efforts to suppress rights of Muslims, efforts that could provide major recruiting tools for ISIS, increasing prospects for future terrorism. I believe that a far better response would be for the U.S. to admit that our past and some current anti-democratic foreign policy efforts have contributed to terrorism against us, apologize for them, and vow to make positive changes. We should also work to reduce societal problems that can be a catalyst for terrorism, as discussed in the next section.

TOWARD A "MARSHALL PLAN" FOR THE WORLD:
TO RESCUE THE PLANET, RECONSTRUCT OUR
WORLD, LIFT UP THE POOR AROUND THE GLOBE,
AND IMPROVE RELATIONS BETWEEN NATIONS

Creative new ideas are needed to improve conditions for the world's many displaced and desperately hungry people, improve relations between peoples and nations, and decrease the prospects for terrorism and war. One possible approach is for the United States, along with other developed nations, including Israel, to lead a global campaign to greatly reduce poverty, hunger, illiteracy, illness, pollution, and climate change. This might be done by applying on a worldwide scale the successful model of the Marshall Plan, suggested and led by General George Marshall after World War II. Marshall recognized that if Europe was left in a state of social and economic devastation, the resulting discontent could lead to an expansion of communism and/or another war, as it did after World War I. His plan was designed to help prevent this.

Under the Marshall Plan, the United States rebuilt post-World War II Europe, rescuing millions from starvation and reconstructing entire cities and countries, thereby winning friends and allies; reducing strife, revolution, and violence; and even creating customers and markets for U.S. industries. A similar plan on a more global scale has been proposed by Rabbi Michael Lerner and the interfaith Network of Spiritual Progressives (NSP).[14] Their plan seeks a new strategy for the U.S., one based on "generosity, not domination, in its foreign policy." To help end centuries of war and violence and attempts to dominate others, they are calling for "a fundamentally new approach that emphasizes that generosity and genuine caring for others can be a much more effective and morally coherent approach to human security, peace, and development." They point out that a new paradigm is needed today, a "Strategy of Generosity," that aims to "reestablish trust and hope among the peoples of the world" in order to reduce world poverty and save the global environment from climate change and the many additional current environmental threats.

The Network of Spiritual Progressives aims to shift a foreign policy based on self-interest to one that considers "what best serves all the people on this planet and best serves the survival of the planet itself." They argue that because of the interconnectedness of all people on the planet, "the best interests of America and the best interests of our children and grandchildren are best served by considering the best interests of everyone else, and the best interests of the planet," rather than to frame things in terms of narrow self-interest. They believe that the plan will only work if it is supported for the right reasons, with the "Strategy of Generosity" at the core, and global common good as the primary goal.

Such a worldwide Marshall Plan might be a tough sell to the wealthier countries that would have to provide the funding. On the other hand, we are currently spending hundreds of billions of dollars on defense with the old paradigm, which is no longer working. Our current course is an unsustainable one, which will in all probability lead to greatly increased

14. "The Global Marshall Plan," Network of Spiritual Progressives, http://www.spiri tualprogressives.org/article.php/gmp_one

famines, wars, and chaos. Essentials of the Marshall plan developed by the Network of Spiritual Progressives include:[15]

- Providing enough funding (perhaps one to two percent of the gross domestic product of the richer nations) to greatly reduce global poverty, homelessness, hunger, illiteracy, disease, and environmental degradation, and to provide dignity and hope to billions of desperate people.
- Creating an unbiased, international nongovernmental mechanism for receiving and properly distributing the funds.
- Funding the plan in a way that is "environmentally sensitive, respectful of native cultures, safeguarded against corruption, protected from manipulation to serve corporate profit motives or the interests of elites, and empowering of the people in each region."
- Governing the funding agency or mechanism "by a board of ethicists, religious leaders, poets, writers, social theorists, philosophers, economists, scientists, and social change activists, all of whom have demonstrated that they give higher priority to the well-being of others than to the well-being of corporations or wealthy elites."

Creating a Marshall Plan for the world may seem utopian, but it might be the most practical and reasonable idea to deal with the grave crises we face today. In the words of the title of a book by Buckminster Fuller, we confront a choice between *Utopia or Oblivion*. We can continue on the present path, based on greed, nationalism, domination, hatred, and bigotry, with increasingly worsening economic, ecological, and social conditions, as well as continued instability, terrorism, and war, or we can strive for a more generous, tolerant, just, peaceful, humane, and environmentally sustainable world. The choice between a far better future and a far worse future is in our hands, and because the stakes are very great, we must not fail.

Even if we never accomplish a complete Marshall Plan for the planet, we should explore ways in which the U.S. and other governments, along with millions of individuals joining together in non-governmental organizations, can significantly increase economic and humanitarian aid in specific areas of need, and make it more effective long-term. Imagine, for example, what the effect might be if the U.S. and Israel were to include, as

---

15. *Ibid.*

part of a plan to resolve the Israeli-Palestinian conflict, an offer to devote a percentage of the money now spent on the military and domestic security toward improving economic conditions for Palestinians and others in the Middle East. This would bring much more stability, cooperation, and unity than increased spending on blockades, weapons, and defense.

PREVENTING "CLIMATE WARS"

Another threat to the security of the U.S. and other nations that is becoming an increasing concern is what some military experts are calling "climate wars." In 2014, 16 former U.S. three- and four-star generals and admirals warned that climate change is a leading national-security threat, calling it a potential "catalyst for conflict."[16] The military experts argued that, unless properly addressed, climate change will have an impact on "military readiness, strain base resilience both at home and abroad, and may limit our ability to respond to future demands." They are concerned that major heat waves, droughts, severe storms, flooding from rising seas and storm surges, wildfires, and other consequences of climate change will result in waves of climate refugees, failed states, and increased potential for instability, violence, terrorism, and war.

There is some evidence that climate change-caused major droughts helped spark recent civil wars in Darfur[17] and Syria.[18] Syria experienced a very severe drought between 2006 and 2011, which caused widespread crop failures, resulting in many farmers leaving the land for the cities at a time when many refugees fleeing the violence in Iraq were pouring into Syria. This caused frustration, tension, and anger, which eventually exploded into a civil war that was exploited by jihadists and fanatics, including ISIS. Hence, the climate-induced drought, along with the negative effects of the U.S. invasion of Iraq, is having widespread repercussions.

The effects of climate change in Darfur and Syria are especially frightening when one considers that climate-change-caused-drought and

---

16. Andrew Johnson, "Retired Generals, Admirals Warn Climate Change is a 'National Security Issue,'" *National Review*, May 14, 2014.

17. Julian Berger 'Darfur conflict heralds era of wars triggered by climate change, UN warns," *The Guardian*, June 23, 2007.

18. Mark Fischetti, "Climate Change Hastened Syria's Civil War," *Scientific American*, March 2, 2015.

desertification is causing chaos in many other countries in the Middle East and Central and North Africa, potentially causing social revolutions or civil wars. This poses major security threats to Israel and the West, with drought-induced food scarcities leaving populations angry, frustrated, and vulnerable to radical messages. Drought, famine, and violence are also causing major migrations, increasing the potential for further chaos, instability, and violence.

Much of the Middle East is already a semi-arid or hyper-arid area, and military experts believe that the likelihood that the area will become even hotter and drier due to climate change make future instability, violence and war more likely there.[19] Hence the urgency of reducing climate change. There is currently (December 2015) much understandable concern about terrorism in the U.S. after recent major ISIS-inspired terrorism attacks in Paris and San Bernardino, California, but there seems to be little understanding by the many people who are urging major military responses and the prevention of fleeing Syrian refugees to enter the U.S. that climate change can greatly increase the prospects for future terrorism due to a great increase in desperate refugees fleeing the effects of climate change in a much more unstable, violent world.

DENIAL MAY PREVENT PROPER RESPONSES TO CLIMATE THREATS

Largely due to the major disinformation campaigns by the oil, coal, and other industries that are gaining greatly from the status quo (as brilliantly discussed in *Climate Cover-Up* by James Hoggan), many people do not regard climate change as a threat or accept that human activities are a significant factor.

Many Jews, especially in the Orthodox community, are in denial about climate change. Instead of considering the major scientific consensus as indicated by the thousands of peer-reviewed articles and the consensus of scientific academies worldwide, they are more influenced by the views of *Fox News* and other conservative media sources that ignore or downplay climate threats. Most Jews and others, as we will discuss in Chapter 13,

---

19. Ruth Schuster, "Mideast climate change: Hotter, drier, and more dangerous," *Haaretz*, February 11, 2015.

seldom consider the major impact of animal-based agriculture on climate change.

In my synagogue, when I try to stress the urgency of actions to combat climate change, including the importance of dietary changes to reduce greenhouse gas emissions, I am often told that I should be more concerned about terrorism, Iran getting a nuclear weapon, and Israel's security. Of course these are critical concerns, and they have been discussed previously in this book. But finding a way to avert the impending climate catastrophe that climate scientists are increasingly warning us about, along with its potential consequences of instability, terrorism, and war, must also become a societal imperative, and Jews should be playing a leading role in increasing awareness of these threats.

In summary, present U.S. foreign policies likely will lead to continued, and possibly increased, instability, terrorism, and war. They should be replaced by policies designed to bring people together and change the image of the U.S., including applying a global Marshall Plan, and by making a major effort to reduce climate change.

Chapter 9

An Economic System Consistent
with Jewish Values

$\mathcal{T}$ he pursuit of profit has led to the condition where the great treasures of natural resources are accumulated in the hands of the few individuals who, because of further profits, have brought to tens of millions of human beings pain, hunger, and want. Does this not show clearly the wickedness of the present capitalist order, which is in glaring contradiction to the religious ethical tendencies of Judaism? . . . The fight for Socialism is the fight for human liberation . . . moral rebirth and not mere economic reconstruction. The fight for Socialism . . . must be firstly a fight for values, higher spiritual values, infinite values.

– Rabbi Abraham B. Bick[1]

WITH MANY PEOPLE FRUSTRATED by the failure of our current economic system to meet their needs, major and increasing gaps between the wealthy and the poor, high unemployment and underemployment in many countries, decaying infrastructures, and other economic problems, this seems to be a good time to consider what economic arrangement and conditions would be most compatible with basic Jewish values. One can also make a strong case that climate change and many other current environmental threats as well as hunger, poverty, resource scarcities, and other social problems

---

1. Statement of Rabbi Abraham B. Bick, a disciple of Rabbi Abraham Isaac Hakohen Kook, and a fighter for religious, ethical socialism in the early twentieth century, quoted in a thesis *Religious Ethical Socialism: The Origins and Philosophy of the Jewish Religious Labor Movement*, by Max Bressler, Hebrew Union College, New York, Class of 1941.

are caused to a large extent by the desire of huge corporations and wealthy individuals to maximize their profits, without concern for the impact on people and the planet.

Socialism (and by this I mean "democratic socialism") is being considered much more seriously these days than most people realize. A Pew Research Center poll released on May 4th, 2010,[2] showed these surprising statistics:

- 29% of Americans say they have a positive reaction to the word "socialism."
- Among those younger than 30, identical percentages react positively to "socialism" and "capitalism" (43% each).
- 37% of the total population has a "negative reaction" to the word "capitalism."

Perhaps these numbers will grow because of Pope Francis' denunciation of capitalism during his visit to Paraguay on July 11, 2015, claiming that it is a major cause of social injustice and climate change. The Pope called, in effect, for a social revolution because of the failure of global capitalism to provide equity, fairness, and dignified livelihoods for poor people.[3]

As further indication of the increased support for socialism, Senator Bernie Sanders, a self-proclaimed "democratic socialist," is seeking the Democratic Party nomination for president, with an emphasis on working toward an economic system that works for all Americans, rather than a few billionaires. His campaign talks have been attracting huge crowds, greater than for any other candidate, and his support has been growing. A further indication of the campaign's success is that on December 21, 2015, it broke the fundraising record for most contributions at this point in a presidential campaign with over 2.3 million donations. Polls indicate that Sanders' positions on income inequality, taxing the wealthiest Americans, rebuilding the U.S. infrastructure, climate change, and other issues are supported by a majority of Americans.

This current widespread disillusionment with our current economic set-up – full of corruption, favoritism, exploitation, chronic unemployment

---

2. "Socialism Not So Negative, Capitalism, Not So Positive" Pew Research Center report, May 4, 2010.
3. Jim Yardley and Binyamin Appelbaum, "In Fiery Speeches, Francis Excoriates Global Capitalism," *New York Times*, July 11, 2015.

and under-employment, ecological destruction, poverty, manipulation of money and trading to benefit the few and the best connected, and rampant crony capitalism – results from many sources. These include bailouts of risk-taking banks, corporate scandals, foreclosures, devastating medical emergencies, and environmental disasters.

WHAT DO I MEAN BY SOCIALISM?

I want to clarify that by "socialism," I do *not* mean Soviet-style communism or government control of all our businesses or personal assets. Private enterprise has value, if it is properly used and regulated. The Torah clearly provides for personal ownership of land, businesses, and moveable property, and the Talmud discusses this in great detail. What is being considered here is the responsibility of the community to take care of the more vulnerable members of society and to share resources more equitably.

In many European democracies there is a political party called the "Social Democrats" or something similar that combines democratic principles with certain socialist ideas such as universal health care and public ownership of mineral resources and utilities. Modern social democratic parties – which may be called "social democratic" (as in Germany), "labor" (as in Britain and Israel), or even "socialist" (as in France) – departed long ago from the idea of a mostly state-run or state-owned economy. They also obey the rules of democratic elections by winning, sharing, or losing power depending upon the majority or plurality will of their country's electorate.

Of course, I am not proposing an anti-democratic revolution, but rather I would like to see extensive reforms that would safeguard the rights and living standards of the poor and middle classes. Nor is it my purpose to confiscate the legal earnings of the wealthy. I support electing politicians who will pass laws to curb predatory practices by corporations and their elite managers and shareholders by means of curbing the influence of money in our elections, and expanding the regulatory powers of government in the interest of consumers, employees, and average tax payers. I also support protecting the right of workers to unionize and bargain collectively (a right increasingly under attack nowadays). It could also be valuable to have expanded public involvement in certain areas, such as health care, but this is a matter of public policy analysis that goes beyond the scope of this book.

This gives an idea of what I mean – but it's important to not get hung up on labels. Instead of saying "socialism," perhaps we should speak of "Torah-based economics." As with everything in this book, I am seeking to help return Judaism to Torah-based values, rather than assimilating things from the surrounding culture that may or may not be in tune with Judaism. So what I mean by "socialism" is really a "cooperative economy" based on human solidarity and kinship. The practices of modern capitalism are a prime cause of ecological damage, poverty, hunger, resource scarcities, and war. For global sustainability, it is necessary that it be replaced by a more just and humane system, based on cooperation and empathy, rather than on excessive competitiveness.

In summary, I believe that the system most consistent with Jewish values is one of economic democracy: Democratic Socialism – or, as it is sometimes called nowadays, Social Democracy – somewhat modified in consonance with Jewish teachings, so that it might be considered as Torah-based economics.

BUT WHAT, EXACTLY, DOES THIS MEAN?

First, let's clearly indicate what it does *not* mean. As explained above, it is certainly not the type of system of the former Soviet Union; it is not undemocratic and certainly not oppressive; it does not involve a small elite who make the major decisions and control most of the wealth and power; it does not mean that you are told where to work, what to buy, where to live, what opinions to hold; it does not mean that you have no personal possessions and cannot own a home or a car.

Formulating a detailed program for Democratic Socialism is beyond the scope of this book. But some key features (all consistent with Jewish values) would include:

- High priority and value given to human life and well-being rather than money and possessions.
- People treated as ends not means (consistent with the Torah teaching that people are created in God's image), demonstrating respect for their dignity, ability, and potential.
- Social ownership and democratic control of the major economic resources (such as oil, coal, natural gas, and other major resources) for the benefit of everyone. This does not mean that every business would be taken over by the workers. It does mean that the important economic

institutions of the country would be controlled by the people, directly or through elected representatives, rather than by private corporations that rarely consider the interests of common people.

- A more equitable distribution of income, wealth, and services.
- A broader distribution of power, with workers participating in decisions that affect them.
- Progressive taxes designed to reduce inequality, rather than to magnify it.

I am uncertain about how this will come about, but if enough people recognize how harmful capitalism is, for individuals and the environment, hopefully a democratic way will be found. It is important to recognize that there is much in American life that is already socialistic – Medicare, Medicaid, social security, unemployment insurance, police and fire services, and the library system, for example.

While not a socialist, Theodore Herzl believed that a revolutionary enterprise like Zionism could not succeed based solely on the capitalist market model. In his book *Altneuland*, he pictured the future Land of Israel as a social welfare society, positioned between socialism and capitalism where natural resources – mineral wealth, land, and water – would be publicly controlled; most industry and agriculture would be run cooperatively, while individuals would still be involved in retail trade; society would provide all citizens with health, welfare, and education; and everyone would have to do two years of national service to staff social service institutions.

It is not enough merely to change the methods of production and distribution, and to establish more democratic decision-making. It is also essential to try to responsibly change people's outlook and behavior. And that is exactly what Judaism tries to do: to transform the human being into a more compassionate, spiritual self who cares more about others. The Talmud even defines mercy and compassion as the essence of being a Jew. "Whoever is merciful to his fellow human beings is certainly of the children of our father Abraham, and whosoever is not merciful to his fellow human beings is certainly not of the children of our father Abraham" (*Bezah* 32b). One purpose of educational and religious institutions would be to try to bring out the compassionate, empathetic, and sharing nature of people.

WHY SHOULD SOCIALISM BE CONSIDERED TODAY?

Many people may ask, "Why should I consider socialism? I'm doing well under capitalism. I have a good job and a home and am able to purchase what I need for my family. And I have the freedom to do what I want, work where I want, travel where I want." But are things really all that good for you and others?

Stop and think about it: Are there areas near your home where you and your family are afraid to go, especially at night? Is your transportation system as good as it could be? Do you recognize that many Americans fear losing a job, not having enough money for retirement, and that their children will not have it as well as they do? Are you concerned about threats from climate change, pollution, acid rain, and toxic wastes? Do you feel that our government is doing enough to make sure that foods are adequately inspected? Are you concerned about cutbacks in social services as the wealthiest Americans and multinational corporations get continued tax breaks? Do you ever consider that our wellbeing is built upon the exploitation of other people? Do you think people can really learn ethical, religious values in a society whose mottos often are "What's in it for me?" and "Do unto others before they do unto me"?

Considering that the United States consumes a huge amount of the world's resources, is this fair to the rest of the world? The psalmist (24:1) says that "the Earth is the Lord's," not "The Earth belongs to humans to exploit as they wish." Shouldn't we be concerned with the well-being of the world's people?

An economic transformation is badly overdue. Although there have been recent improvements, unemployment and underemployment are still too high. Our climate is dangerously chaotic. The safety of our food, water, medicines, toys, and breathable air is threatened. Toxic pollution flows from massive feedlots and creates dead spots in our seas. Our forests tumble. Our financial system is rocked by fraud and abuse, but the banks continue their perilous policies and go on awarding enormous bonuses to those who, in effect, robbed us all. Too many politicians seem to be for sale, as we appear to have "the best Congress that money can buy." Corporations reap record profits but hoard their cash rather than investing in hiring.

HOW CAPITALISM OFTEN VIOLATES JEWISH VALUES

Judaism does not recommend one type of economic system. However, its principles of social conduct are clear. The Torah is opposed to exploitation and to concentration of wealth in the hands of a few, with the resultant impoverishment of the many. The Torah desires that people should be able to work and enjoy the fruits of their labor, but some elements of modern capitalism are inconsistent with basic Jewish values of justice, compassion, consideration for the poor, concern for the dignity of every person, and love for our fellow humans:

- While Jewish values are epitomized in the visions of prophets, many capitalists dream mainly of profits. Many things are done in a capitalistic society not because they are just, righteous, or kind, but because they are profitable.

- While Judaism teaches "love thy neighbor as thyself," under capitalism the motto seems to be, as Rabbi Abraham Joshua Heschel expressed it, "suspect thy neighbor as thyself." Our society and economy often train people to be selfish and antagonistic, not cooperative and sharing.

- While Judaism teaches that each person is created in God's image and hence is of infinite worth, under capitalism people are often treated primarily as consumers. Advertisers do not attempt to educate people or to increase their sensitivity, but rather to appeal to their greed, vanity, insecurity, and competitiveness.

- While Judaism teaches that life is sacred and that we must make all possible efforts to save lives, under capitalism lives are often endangered to increase profits. The owners and operators of unregulated or poorly regulated gun shops, strip mines and underground mines, asthma-causing and mercury-spewing factories and power plants, and all kinds of dangerous and deadly products spend millions on propaganda and lobbying to evade their just responsibility. In recent years, there have been numerous recalls of dangerous products manufactured in countries where there are little or no safety regulations (such as China).

- While Judaism stresses *tzedek, tzedek tirdof* ("justice, justice shall you pursue"), and that God is sanctified through acts of justice, society is filled with injustice. There are great income gaps in the U.S. and Israel, two of the most unequal societies on earth, and the gaps have been widening in recent years. While a small minority of the world's people lead lives devoted to wasteful consumption, millions of God's children lack adequate food, water, shelter, health care, sanitary facilities, and education.

- While Judaism mandates that we practice compassion for animals and avoid inflicting unnecessary pain on them, in our capitalistic system animals are often treated like mere commodities to maximize profits.
- While Judaism asserts that each person is "his brother's (and sister's) keeper" and that "we must be kind to the stranger, for we were strangers in the land of Egypt," under modern capitalism each person is primarily out for himself and his family. Primary attitudes include: "Me first," "Cut services for others," "Let 'George' do it," and "Where's mine?"
- While Judaism proclaims a jubilee every fifty years, when wealth is redistributed and property is returned to its original owners, under capitalism there are very large and increasing gaps in people's wealth. The wealthiest 400 Americans have more wealth than the poorest 150 million Americans! Due to the tremendous power that wealth provides, these gaps are likely to continue growing, increasing the potential for unrest and violence.
- While Judaism teaches that God is the Creator of all people and that one person (Adam) was created to teach our common ancestry and thus that there should be no prejudice against people because of race, religion, nationality, or gender, there is widespread discrimination in our society. Some people have to fight each other for the scraps from the tables of the truly comfortable and well connected.

We have a moral duty to ask ourselves can modern capitalism (especially in its most isolating, harsh, and unfeeling versions) be reconciled with Judaism? Can a system that emphasizes the pursuit of personal financial gain with little concern for the needs and welfare of others be consistent with Jewish values? Under today's corporate-dominated form of capitalism we have what philosopher Richard Lichtman calls "the alienation of economic activity from moral concern." Can Jews accept this separation of economic from moral concerns when we affirm a Creator whose laws and concern extend to every person and all forms of life?

The Talmud teaches that when we die and go before the Heavenly Court, the first thing we will be asked is "Were you honest in your business dealings?" (*Shabbat* 31a). Not "Do you believe in God?" or "Did you keep kosher?" or "Did you observe Passover?" but *how did you behave in the marketplace?* The business world is the hardest place to be honest, so if you are honest there, the likelihood is you are an upstanding person in other areas as well.

Many of the world's people today face economic conditions similar to those indicated in the following passage from the book of Job (24:5–11):

> Lonely as wild asses in the wilderness
> They go forth to their labor;
> They must hunt the desert for sustenance,
> There is no harvest for the homeless.
> They must harvest fields that are not theirs . . .
> Naked must they pass the night for lack of clothes.
> They have no covering from the cold.
> They are drenched by the downpour of the mountains,
> They must embrace the base rock for want of shelter.
> They must go naked, without garments;
> Hungry, they must carry the sheaves.
> Shut in by walls, they must press the oil;
> Thirsty, they must press the winepress.

Under a profit-based system where each person seeks personal gain first and foremost above all else, the following words of Jeremiah are all too relevant today:

> Run to and fro through the streets . . .
> Look and take note!
> Search her squares to see if you can find a man,
> One who does justice and seeks truth; . . .
> But they all alike had broken the yoke,
> They had burst the bonds . . .
> From the least to the greatest of them,
> Everyone is greedy for unjust gain;
> And from prophet to priest everyone deals falsely . . .
> There is nothing but oppression within her.
>
> (Jeremiah 5:1,5; 6:13; 8:10; 6:6)

The Prophets were well aware of the injustices that come with corruption and greed. Many modern rabbis are also aware of this connection. The fact that Jewish ethical teachings are inconsistent with an insufficiently regulated profit-based system was explicitly stated in a pronouncement of the Rabbinical Assembly of America (rabbis of the Conservative movement) in 1934, in the midst of the Great Depression. Considering that we are currently still trying to emerge from the severest recession since then, I think their statement merits our attention:

> In all of Jewish ethical tradition, it is assumed as axiomatic that men must live for each other, that mutual aid and human cooperation are indispensable both for peace in society and for moral excellence in the individual. Judaism has always asserted the brotherhood of human beings. If this concept has any meaning for life at all, it insists that men must live cooperatively for the common good.
>
> We therefore hold an individualistic, profit-inspired economy to be in direct conflict with the ideals of religion. We maintain that our present system based, as it is, on acquisitiveness and selfish competition, is in practice a denial of human brotherhood. It exalts the aggrandizement of the individual above the interests of the group, it emphasizes the competitive rather than the co-operative elements in human character. It means that our social order is based on the theorem of "Every man for himself" rather than on the ideal of mutual aid . . .
>
> We hold that only a cooperative economy, only one that has for its objective the enrichment of all rather than profit for a few – only such an economy can be moral, can elevate man, and can function successfully.

SOCIALIST/COOPERATIVE CONCEPTS IN JEWISH HISTORY AND TRADITION

When the Jews wandered in the wilderness after the Exodus from Egypt, and in the early years after settling in the land of Israel, the people were strongly egalitarian; there was no hierarchy of kings or rulers. Decisions were reached democratically by the assemblage of one man from each family or tribe. And there was essentially communal ownership of the wealth-producing property. The rights to pasture lands and water were vested in the tribe as a unit, and private property was minimal. Later, in the days of Samuel, when the people clamored for a king in order to be like the surrounding nations, God told Samuel to warn the people about what would happen with such centralization of wealth and power:

This will be the practice of the king who will rule over you: He will take your sons and appoint them as his charioteers and horsemen, and they will have to run before his chariot . . . or they will have to plow his fields and make his weapons and equipment for his chariots. He will take your daughters as perfumers and bakers; he will seize your choice fields, vineyards, and olive groves and give them to his courtiers . . . He will take a tenth part of your flocks and you will become his slaves. The day will come when you will cry out because of the king whom you yourselves have chosen; and the Lord will not answer you on that day.

(Samuel I 8:11–18)

If we substitute "international corporations" for "kings" we can see a kind of similar exploitation today. We see CEOs (the corporate kings) making huge salaries and garnering millions of dollars in bonuses each year, while at the same time they lay off workers in the name of making even greater profits. The disparity between a CEO's income and the average worker's salary is far greater than ever before. Is this really what God wants?

Division of property was initially part of the Torah's plan to insure social equality. Originally, land was distributed among the Israelite tribes, using the principle that "to the more [larger tribe] you shall give the greater inheritance, and to the fewer [smaller tribe] you shall give the lesser inheritance" (Numbers 26:54). This first distribution of land was on the basis of social need, not individual power or privilege.

To avoid conditions whereby, due to bad fortune, a family might be compelled to sell or mortgage its land and thereby suffer for generations, a complete redistribution of land every 50 years was provided for in the Jubilee law: "In the year of the Jubilee, you shall return every man unto his possession" (Leviticus 25:13). This law protecting property rights in ancient Israel was designed to insure social equality. Therefore, the Torah's concept of property rights was very different from that of modern capitalism, which tends to lead to great concentrations of wealth perpetuated generation after generation, while poverty also persists from one generation to another.

A literal Jubilee Year would be impossible to carry out today, and everyone's property cannot be confiscated and redistributed every 50 years. But we can still learn the basic principle behind this amazing law. It is not socially responsible to allow vast amounts of wealth to accumulate in the hands of the few while allowing others to suffer in abject poverty for generations.

The underlying message and meaning of the Jubilee Year, as with other "commandments dependent on the land," such as the laws related to leaving the gleanings of the harvest and the corners of the field for the poor, is the principle that "the Earth is the Lord's" (Psalm 24:1). In proclaiming the Jubilee Year, the Torah states the logic behind this periodic revolution in property rights: "For the land is mine; for you are strangers and settlers with me" (Leviticus 25:23).

In the Torah a person's rights to property are not those of an outright owner, but rather of a steward who is a co-partner with God in preserving and protecting the earth and seeing that its resources are used for the benefit of everyone. As Rabbi Eleazer of Bertothas says, "Give unto God of what is God's, seeing that you and what you have are God's" (*Pirkei Avot* 3:8). King David expresses a similar idea: "For all things come of You [God] and out of Your own have we given You" (Chronicles I 29:14).

The Sabbatical Year included the cancellation of financial debts in order to limit inequality and excessive accumulation of capital. The Torah's prohibition on taking interest for loans served the same goal. Both of these arrangements were later bypassed for pragmatic reasons, but the basic idea behind them is that property should be used for one's own (simple) living and for the common good, not for the enormous accumulation of wealth. With the income gap in the U.S. very large and growing, the concept of a Jubilee year in which wealth would be redistributed is intriguing (if impractical). Here are a few examples of the growing income and wealth gaps in the US:[4] while the wealthiest 1% of Americans own 40% of the nation's wealth, the bottom 80% own only 7%. That top 1% possesses more wealth than the poorest 90%. The average employee has to work over a month to make as much as the average CEO makes in one hour. This has resulted in an increasingly economically squeezed U.S. middle class.

Yet, most of the very rich want more and more, and they seem unconcerned about damaging the existing political and social order to get it. During the 2014 U.S. midterm elections, billionaires poured hundreds of millions of dollars of secret money into the campaign, helping to elect dozens of conservative Republican members of Congress. Having made

---

4. "Wealth Inequality in the United States," Wikipedia Encyclopedia, https://en.wik ipedia.org/wiki/Wealth_inequality_in_the_United_States

their investment, they expect their congressional "employees" to produce, so they will be able to increase their wealth. The Koch brothers plan to spend nearly a billion dollars in 2016 in support of conservative candidates. Republicans in Congress seem to be on board as they overwhelmingly support continued tax breaks for the wealthy and for major corporations, while opposing continued unemployment benefits for the long-term unemployed and supporting major cuts in many programs that benefit the middle class and the poor.

The Jewish view that private property rights are not absolute but are subjected to proper regulation and civic authority and must be guided by the common good, and that property should not be wasted or exploited in damaging ways, but rather used sustainably, is exemplified by the many *mitzvot* obliging Jewish farmers to share with the poor:

- A corner of each field (*Pe'ah*) had to be left unharnessed; it was the property of the poor (Leviticus 19; 9–10).
- If less than three ears of corn were dropped during the harvest (*Leket*), they were not to be gleaned, but were to be left for the poor (Leviticus 19: 9- 10).
- A sheaf forgotten by the farmer (*Shik'khah*) could not be retrieved but must be left for the poor (Deuteronomy 24: 19–21).
- Every third year, a part of the tithe of the harvest (*Ma'aser Ani*) had to be set aside for the poor (Deuteronomy 14:28).
- Prior to every Purim, *matanot l'evyonim,* a special donation for the poor, is collected.
- Before Passover, there are large campaigns for *ma'ot chittim,* donations to enable poor people to purchase matzah, wine, and other Passover needs.

These principles not only help the poor, they also help the landowner by teaching him to "let go" and say "*dayenu* (enough), I did not create this bounty; it ultimately belongs to God." The same is true of any business, not just agriculture.

Shabbat, and the holidays that require Jews not to work, might just be the first labor law, mandating a day of rest for everyone. This was revolutionary at the time of the Torah, and is not trivial today when many work places require employees to be available 24/7, with technology making this possible anywhere, anytime. The long and difficult campaign for an eight-hour workday is becoming relevant again where in some areas (from agriculture to high-tech and law) people work from the early morning to late night. The biblical idea that all people (and animals) deserve a day of rest each week, and days for worship and communal celebrations, is under attack in our society.

Another important point to consider is the open hostility of the Jewish tradition toward the arrogantly rich and their "conspicuous consumption," when the desired state is modest, limited, self-restrained living. The prophet Amos rails against such extravagance at the expense of others:

> Woe to those who are at ease in Zion,
> And to those who feel secure on the mountains of Samaria . . .
> Woe to those who lie upon beds of ivory,
> And stretch themselves upon their couches,
> And eat lambs from the flock,
> And calves from the midst of the stall;
> Who sing idle songs to the sound of the harp . . .
> Who drink wine in bowls,
> And anoint themselves in the finest oils,
> But are not grieved on the ruin of Joseph!   (Amos 6:4–6)

The last line tells us that it is not the enjoyment of good food and wine per se that the prophet denounces; rather, it is because "those who are at ease in Zion" were "not grieved at the ruin of [the tribes of] Joseph" that had been conquered and decimated by the invading Assyrians. Amos felt it was a terrible sin to indulge in such luxuries while one's fellow Jews had been killed or exiled, and had not even the barest necessities of life. As the modern saying goes, we should "live simply so that others may simply live."

An element of the Ten Commandments, "You shall not steal," along with the subsequent prohibition of coveting, are reminders not to make material gain the purpose of our lives. Even when we do not actually steal, we are in a way stealing from the poor when we are overindulgent and wasteful, or when we exploit the resources of Third World countries in order to increase our own country's power and wealth, or when we stand idly by the starvation and degradation of others when we could do something to help.

Since, as the Torah clearly states, everything belongs to God, the Jewish principle that the rich are obligated to assist the poor, preferably by helping them find work or providing them with a living wage, derives from God's ownership. The Hebrew word *tzedakah* means both charity and justice. Why? Because Judaism considers charity to be an act of justice. The Torah teaches that people in need have a right to dignity and succor, to food, clothing, and shelter that has a claim on those who are more fortunate. According to Jewish law, it is unjust for Jews to not give charity to those in need. This can be contrasted with those political conservatives in the secular world, who want to cut taxes for the rich and maintain loopholes for corporations, while making draconian cuts in programs of food, shelter, and medical care for the indigent. This goes against Jewish principles.

In addition to laws about charity, the Torah also provides instruction in honest business practices:

> You shall do no wrong in judgment, in measures of length, of weight, or in quantity. Just balances, just weights, a just *ephah* [the standard dry measure] and a just *hin* [a measure for liquids], shall you have. I am the Lord your God, who brought you out of the land of Egypt.
>
> (Leviticus 19: 35, 36)

The rabbis of the Talmud gave concrete expression to the many Torah and prophetic teachings regarding justice and righteousness. They indicate in detail what is proper when conducting business. Rabbinic literature translates prophetic ideals into specific laws for the marketplace concerning duties of employers to employees and of workers to their employers, as well as suppliers to customers: fair prices; the avoidance of false weights and measures; proper business contracts; and fair methods of competition. For example, wages for day laborers must be given on the day that work is done, not delayed, in order to preserve the dignity and provide for the basic needs of poor workers (Deuteronomy 24:10–15). This principle applies to some extent even today, where field workers harvesting produce often live hand-to-mouth, and cannot wait for weeks to be paid.

The sages were also very harsh towards attempts to take away a person's livelihood by unfair competition (*Sanhedrin* 81a). Their overall view of business ethics can be summarized by the verses "And you shall do that which is right and good in the sight of the Lord" (Deuteronomy 6:18), and "better is a little with righteousness than great revenues with injustice" (Proverbs 16:8).

The Talmudic sages were also very strict about their personal ethical standards, as the following story illustrates:

Reb Saphra had wine to sell. A customer came in to buy wine at a time when Reb Saphra was saying the *Shema* prayer [which cannot be interrupted by conversation]. The customer said, "Will you sell me the wine for such and such an amount?" When Reb Saphra did not respond, the customer thought he was not satisfied with the price and raised his bid. When Reb Saphra had finished his prayer, he said, "I decided in my heart to sell the wine to you at the first price you mentioned; therefore I cannot accept your higher bid."   (*Sheil'tot, Parshat Vayechi*)

Consistent with Torah principles, the Talmud, though firmly recognizing personal property rights, did not consider such rights to be unlimited. They often restricted them, even eliminating them in some instances for the common good. For example, the *halachah* (Jewish law) prohibits profit related to "fraudulent misrepresentation" (*Baba Metzia* 49b). It opposes monopolization of basic necessities and bans hoarding for the purpose of increasing prices (*Baba Batra* 90b). The Talmud prohibits the export of articles of food to foreign countries if this would increase the domestic price of these articles (*Baba Batra* 90b). For the common good, the rabbis even justify the confiscation of private property in some cases (*Yebamot* 89b; *Gittin* 36b).

A good example of this is a case in the Talmud concerning a well of water essential to people in a village. The rabbis concluded that the title to the well should not be maintained in trust by any one individual or small group, but by the entire community, so as to be open and accessible to all without cost.[5] Judaism points toward communal possession and control of those social enterprises that are essential to life. The earth's vast resources should be developed for the welfare of every person, and not for the enrichment of the few.

During the U.S. banking crisis in 2008, the credit unions – which are member-owned cooperatives, not "banks" in the usual sense – did not experience the same economic collapse as did the corporate banks. Credit union members elect their officials and do not have CEOs drawing enormous salaries. They also have a say in how their money is being invested. Credit unions are, in the most positive sense, collective, even socialist institutions.

---

5. Sidney E. Goldstein discusses this in *The Synagogue and Social Ethics* (New York: Block Pubs. 1955), 337.

Interestingly, both the Reform and Conservative rabbinical groups have passed resolutions supporting this principle of public ownership. In 1934, (in the midst of the Great Depression), the Social Justice Commission of the Central Conference of American Rabbis (Reform) stated that for society's safety, basic social enterprises should not be left in the control of private groups, which consider private profit ahead of community service. They advocated the nationalization of banking, power plants, housing, and transportation and communication systems.[6] In that same year, the Rabbinical Assembly (of Conservative rabbis) also stated that some social enterprises, such as banking and credit, power, transportation, and communication, were so essential to community welfare that they must be publicly owned.[7]

In the late 1800s and early 1900s, many Jews were actively involved in revolutionary socialist and trade union movements in Europe and the U.S. in reaction to the exploitative conditions of the time. They felt that the salvation of the Jewish people could only come about as part of the salvation of humanity. Morris Hillquit, a Jewish labor movement leader in New York in the early years of the twentieth century, gave a typical view:

> I am a socialist because I cannot be anything else. I cannot accept the ugly world of capitalism, with its brutal struggles and needless suffering, its archaic and irrational economic structure, its cruel social contrasts, its moral callousness and spiritual degradation.[8]

There are also many Hasidic stories about how great rabbis chose to live simply in order to give more to others. This does not mean we should live in abject poverty. In fact, Jewish law forbids giving away all or most of one's possessions, lest one become a burden on the community. But we can and should ask ourselves if our current lifestyles could be more in harmony with the world around us. As the Jewish community in America has become more affluent, we seem to be forgetting many of the Torah's communitarian and compassionate principles.

Whether we call it "social democracy" or "Torah-based economics," the message is the same. Based on such Jewish values as justice, compassion,

---

6. *Ibid,* 338

7. *Ibid,* 338, 339

8. Irving Howe and Kenneth Libo, eds. *How We Lived* (New York: Signet, 1981), 190.

and concern for the poor, Jews should be in the forefront of efforts to establish an economic system that can provide dignity and basic necessities to every person. Jews should work for a more cooperative system consistent with Torah teachings: elevating individuals through religious ethical education, forming worker's cooperatives like Israel's *kibbutzim* and *moshavim*, and striving for peaceful and harmonious progress that will benefit all of humanity.

Chapter 10

How Should Jews Respond to Radical Islamists and to Bias and Hatred Toward Muslims?

*W*hoever saves the life of another, surely he saves the lives of all humanity.   –Qur'an, Surah al-Ma'aidah 32

*W*hoever saves a single human life is considered as having saved an entire world.

–TALMUD YERUSHALMI, SANHEDRIN 4:9

*T*he face of terror is not the true faith of Islam. That's not what Islam is all about. Islam is peace. These terrorists don't represent peace. They represent evil and war.

When we think of Islam we think of a faith that brings comfort to a billion people around the world. Billions of people find comfort and solace and peace. And that's made brothers and sisters out of every race.

America counts millions of Muslims amongst our citizens, and Muslims make an incredibly valuable contribution to our country. Muslims are doctors, lawyers, and law professors, members of the military, entrepreneurs, shopkeepers, moms, and dads. And they need to be treated with respect. In our anger and emotion, our fellow Americans must treat each other with respect.

–PRESIDENT GEORGE W. BUSH,

SHORTLY AFTER SEPTEMBER 11[1]

---

1. "Islam is Peace, Says President," The White House, September 17, 2001, http://geor gewbush-whitehouse.archives.gov/news/releases/2001/09/20010917-11.html

W HEN I STARTED WORKING on the first edition of this book a dozen or so years ago, if someone had suggested that I would need to include a chapter on prejudice toward Muslims and terrorism on the part of some Muslims, I would have thought that he or she was crazy. The term "Islamophobia" didn't even exist back then. But years after September 11, 2001, it is now an important issue to consider.[2]

On May 3, 2015 two Muslim terrorists were killed while trying to kill many people attending an exhibit of cartoons about the Prophet Mohammed sponsored by anti-Muslim activist Pamela Geller, and security forces in the U.S. went on high alert concerned about other possible terrorist attacks inspired by Islamic terrorist groups. How to effectively respond to radical Islamists and reduce the potential for future terrorist attacks and how to respond to people like Pamela Geller, who exploit and worsen the situation, will be considered in this chapter.

In December 2015, after ISIS-related terror acts in Lebanon, Paris, and San Bernardino, California, and their destruction of a Russian passenger plane with over 200 people aboard, people in the U.S. and other western countries are very fearful of additional terrorism. This has become a major part of the presidential primary discussions with a Republican debate on December 15, 2015 devoted entirely to national security, including how to respond to terrorism. Republican presidential candidates have advocated drastic steps against Muslims, including shutting down mosques, requiring Muslims to register in a data base, shutting down any place that Muslims gather, permitting only refugees who are Christians to enter the U.S., and preventing desperate Muslim refugees fleeing the Syrian civil war – who were vetted for 18 to 24 months – from entering the U.S. They have also advocated a major increase in military actions against ISIS, although there have been many airstrikes for months already.

The demonization of Muslims by the politicians and others has resulted in a rash of attacks against Muslims and mosques. A December 20, 2015 NBC News report, "Hate Attacks Against Muslims in the U.S. Spike After Recent Acts of Terror [by Muslims]," indicated that there were 38 incidents

---

2. My thanks to Rabbi Yonassan Gershom for suggesting this chapter, and for his many hours of research and editorial input in developing it. I am also grateful to Karima Bushnell, a Muslim multicultural educator in Minneapolis, for reviewing the material and making valuable suggestions.

of anti-Muslim violence since the terrorists acts in Paris on November 13, with 18 of them occurring since the terrorist act in San Bernardino on December 2. These violent attacks against Muslims are providing a major recruiting tool for ISIS in that it reinforces their argument that the West is incompatible with Islam and hostile to Muslims who live there.

I want to make it clear at the start that I, of course, condemn all acts of terrorism, no matter who carries them out, no matter the rationale. This certainly includes the horrendous crimes by Muslim terrorists on September 11, 2001 and the incredibly cruel acts of ISIS, including their shooting down of a passenger plane and horrible terrorist acts in Lebanon and Paris in November 2015. I, along with many others, including Muslims, also greatly deplore discrimination and degradation in some Muslim countries directed toward Jews, women, homosexuals, freethinkers, "heretics," Christians, and minority Muslim sects. However, it is also important to recognize the positive, religious, and ethical values within Islam, the contributions that many Muslims have made and are making to American society and the world, and the need to find common ground and solutions – lest extremists gain more credibility and support. It is also essential to condemn the major increase in terrorist acts of violence against American Muslims and mosques that have recently occurred as Muslims are demonized by some politicians and others. The world cannot afford a "clash of civilizations," involving over 1.6 billion Muslims, nor can it afford the erosion of civil liberties and damage to the social fabric which would result from treating every Muslim as a potential terrorist. Certainly we should recognize the threats from radical Islamists but we should consider carefully how we respond to them, as I do at the end of this chapter.

WHY ANTAGONISM TOWARD MUSLIMS SHOULD BE ADDRESSED

The ways we respond to Muslims crystallizes the choice we have today between a future world based on hatred, bigotry, intolerance, militarism, and selfishness and one based on understanding, compassion, tolerance, kindness, and the seeking of common ground and cooperation. Many politicians and media commentators try to exploit fear and hatred in order to advance their careers and their agendas (which too frequently succeeds), especially after September 11 and other terrorist attacks. Demonizing

Muslims and propagating a message that Islam is dangerously spreading also shifts the public's attention away from important issues, including economic difficulties, climate change, disease, mass species extinction, world hunger, lack of clean water, deforestation, poisoning and depletion of fish stocks in the world's oceans, human population increases, and other current threats to humanity. So it is necessary to understand and consider how to overcome the current widespread ignorance, insensitivity, hatred, and bigotry, in order to pursue a better world, especially at a time when the world's attention should be on responding to other important issues, including the ones mentioned above. To combat conservative politicians who are using fear and bigotry to gain power, we need progressive, forward thinking leaders.

When considering American society and demagogues' attempts to blame and marginalize Muslims, it is instructive to recall that the verse which recurs most often (36 times) in the Hebrew Scriptures is a variation of "Be kind to the stranger, for you were strangers in the land of Egypt." An intolerant world is not conducive to Jewish well-being.

The need to reduce Islamophobia was even more apparent after considering the killing spree in Norway by Anders Behring Breivik on July 22, 2011. The confessed terrorist was greatly influenced by people who had warned for years about "Islamic threats." His 1,500-page manifesto was filled with quotations from them. This document, which was posted on the Internet, showed his great interest in debates in the United States about Islam and efforts to prevent Muslims from building mosques. These distorted views of Islam led him to murder 70 innocent teenagers at a Norwegian summer camp, in the mistaken belief that their liberal views were enabling radical Islamists to take over the world.

Horrified at what hatred, bigotry, and the extensive demonization of Muslims can lead to, I became even more determined to investigate the realities, dispel the myths, and seek common ground to potentially increase tolerance, understanding, and harmony, while also seeking ways to reduce Islamic radicalism that led to the formation of the brutal terrorist group ISIS. In an article in *The Washington Post* on July 29, 2011, "Norwegian attacks stem from a new ideological hate," Abraham H. Foxman, former national director of the Anti-Defamation League, condemned the increasing hatred of Muslims in the United States and Europe that contributed to the terrorism in Norway. He concluded:

In America, the polarization, vitriol and fear engendered by anti-Islamic activists must be replaced by reasoned and civil debate. We must rally the voices of reason to overcome the voices of intolerance before it is too late.[3]

HISTORICAL EXAMPLES OF DISCRIMINATION AGAINST RELIGIOUS GROUPS

Discrimination against religious groups is not a new phenomenon. Demagogues have always used prejudice to whip up the masses. Pharaoh used an argument about Jews that was similar to what we hear about Muslims today: they are getting too numerous and might join with our enemies (Exodus 1:9–10). Abraham Lincoln's opponents told poor Southern Baptist whites that he was a Catholic. John F. Kennedy was a Catholic, so his opponents evoked the fear that the Pope would soon rule over America. Some of FDR's enemies said he was Jewish and called him "Jewsevelt." Nazi propaganda referred to him as "*der Jude Rosenfeld.*" Now an amazing number of suggestible Americans believe that President Obama is a Muslim and/or that he was not born in the United States – despite overwhelming evidence to the contrary.

Jews, of all people, should be aware of the dangers of scapegoating an entire ethnic or religious group for society's ills. After all, Hitler rose to power by blaming the Jews for Germany's problems during the Great Depression. Santayana's famous statement that "those who do not learn from history are condemned to repeat it" takes on a very ominous meaning in this context. In the 1600s Peter Stuyvesant, founder of New Amsterdam (later to become New York City), tried to expel the first Jews who arrived in Manhattan. However, the Dutch West India Company said that Jews could stay, so Stuyvesant relented, but forbade the Jews to build a synagogue anywhere in Manhattan. The first Jewish synagogue in New York was not permitted until 1730.

Contrast this with Benjamin Franklin who, although not a Jew (he was a Quaker), donated his own money toward building Mikveh Israel, the first synagogue in Philadelphia, in 1788. Or consider George Washington, who wrote in a letter to the Hebrew Congregation of Newport, Rhode

---

3. Abraham H. Foxman, "Norway attacks stem from ideological hate," *The Washington Post*, July 29, 2011.

Island, on August 17, 1790, "May the children of the stock of Abraham who dwell in this land continue to merit and enjoy the good will of the other inhabitants – while every one shall sit in safety under his own vine and fig tree and there shall be none to make him afraid."

Discussions of whether or not a Muslim community center, including a mosque, should be built two blocks from Ground Zero, the site of the former World Trade Center which was destroyed by Muslim fanatics on September 11, 2001, dominated the news for some time right before the 2010 mid-term election, overwhelming far more important issues. The intensity of this controversy has died down, but it is still representative of conflicts that will likely continue for years to come between anti-Muslim bigots and those trying to expand the mosaic of loyal discourse, so it will be discussed in this chapter for lessons that can be learned. The community center had a small-scale opening with an exhibit of photographs on September 21, 2011, but it is still years and millions of dollars away from completion.

Of course the sensitivities of those who lost loved ones on September 11 must be taken into account in any planning for the area. But those survivors have a wide range of views on the "mosque," and they, like everyone else, have been subjected to massive misinformation and distortions. There have also been strong oppositions to other mosques proposed in locations far from Ground Zero. So clearly this controversy is not a one-time event, but rather a growing tendency toward intolerance.

Many people opposed the Muslim center project because they believe that all Muslims are evil or potentially evil, constantly plotting terrorism, and other negative things. Republican and Tea Party politicians, including Sarah Palin, Newt Gingrich, and conservative commentators such as Rush Limbaugh, Sean Hannity, and Glenn Beck, as well as much of the coverage on *Fox News,* reinforced these views as a way to increase their power, build their audiences, reinforce people's prejudices, and advance their ambitions. Polls showed that many Americans believe these conservatives' propaganda, and are questioning whether there is a place in America for their Muslim neighbors. Some factors that opponents of the proposed center should consider include:

- It was fanatics, almost all of them Saudis, not typical Muslims and certainly not American Muslims, who destroyed the World Trade Center.
- Hostility toward all Muslims is exactly what the terrorists want. The Taliban used the Ground Zero controversy to recruit more followers.
- Muslims also died at the Trade Center, and their families still mourn for them.
- Muslims were among the first responders on September 11.
- In addition to a mosque, the proposed community center would have a memorial to the victims of September 11, a swimming pool, a library, a 500-seat auditorium, meeting rooms, classrooms, a cafeteria, and other facilities available to both Muslims and non-Muslims.
- Muslims have lived peacefully in the United States since the mid-1800s, playing constructive roles and contributing to the multilayered fabric of American life.
- There were also Christians and Jews involved in the planning for the proposed center, including Rabbi Joy Levitt of the Manhattan JCC, who was an unofficial advisor for the project. The proposed project is modeled after the 92nd Street Y in Manhattan, which is a Jewish institution, but is used by people of many religions and communities, including Muslims. A major goal of the future center is to promote interfaith understanding and tolerance.

In some ways it would be better if the proposed Muslim center were built further from Ground Zero, which might avoid much of the controversy and hurt. But with better tolerance and open-mindedness on the part of the American public, the proposed Muslim community center could have produced greater harmony, understanding, and healing. Instead, it was turned into an opportunity for divisiveness, largely by political opportunists and conservative commentators.

Some critics have inaccurately called the mosque a triumphalist edifice and a victory monument for terrorism, while some have complained that it would "tower over" Ground Zero. But anyone who has been to lower Manhattan knows that a building more than two blocks away, even if it is thirteen stories high, is not going to tower over anything. It won't even be visible from Ground Zero.

The initial name of the proposed center, Cordoba House, was chosen to evoke the interfaith tolerance that once existed among Christians, Jews, and Muslims in Cordoba, Spain during the 8th-12th centuries – a historical reference that was apparently lost on most Americans. Maimonides, who was court physician to the Sultan of Turkey and one of the greatest scholars in Jewish history, was born in Cordoba. There is even a famous statue honoring him there. But opponents of the project have wrongly claimed the name is a reference to the Muslim conquest of Christian Spain and a call to "Islamicize" America – an accusation disturbingly similar to the Inquisition's fear that secret Jews were "Judaizing" Christianity. Because of this misguided opposition, the project's name was changed to the rather meaningless "Park 51," based on the address of the site.

SUPPORT FOR THE CONSTRUCTION OF THE MUSLIM CENTER

Some people recognized the great potential of the center, and the damage that would be done if the constitutional right of Muslims to build it was thwarted. For example, in an event on August 3, 2010 at which clergy members of several religions (including Judaism) gathered to support the project, then New York City Mayor Michael Bloomberg said:

> Let us not forget that Muslims were among those murdered on 9/11, and that our Muslim neighbors grieved with us as New Yorkers and as Americans. We would betray our values and play into our enemies' hands if we were to treat Muslims differently than anyone else. In fact, to cave to popular sentiment would be to hand a victory to the terrorists, and we should not stand for that.[4]

With anti-Muslim feelings growing, it would be well to consider the words of President Bush that are included at the start of this chapter.

Although most Republicans and other Conservatives were strong supporters of our 43rd president, somehow these words do not seem to have much influence on their views about Muslim Americans. President Obama was following in George Bush's footsteps (as well as George Washington's as cited earlier) when he, too, affirmed the principle of religious freedom by stating that Muslims have the right to build their community center where they want – for which, sadly, he was strongly criticized.

---

4. Press release: "Mayor Bloomberg Discusses the Landmarks Preservation Commission Vote on 45–47 Park Place," News from the Blue Room, August 3, 2010.

Jewish Support for the Construction
of the Muslim Center

How should Jews react to situations like the Muslim Center controversy? Such events provide golden opportunities to work together with our Muslim neighbors and to combat prejudice. This, in turn, might help create closer relations between Jews and Muslims.

Fortunately, some Jewish groups have responded very positively in support of the construction of the Muslim Center. Imam Feisal Abdul Rauf thanked American Jewish supporters in August 2010:

> I express my heartfelt appreciation for the gestures of goodwill and support from our Jewish friends and colleagues. Your support is a reflection of the great history of mutual cooperation and understanding that Jewish and Muslim civilizations have shared in the past, and remains a testament to the enduring success of our continuing dialogue and dedication to upholding religious freedom, tolerance, and cooperation among us all as Americans.[5]

The imam was referring to, among other examples, the demonstrations supporting the Islamic center by Rabbi Arthur Waskow, director of the Shalom Center, and by the progressive group J Street, which presented over 10,000 signatures backing the center. Rabbi Waskow stated that the center would enable people to learn about Islam and recognize that much of what people believe about that religion is a myth. J Street spokesman Isaac Luria stated at a J Street demonstration in August 2010 in support of the Muslim center:

> As American Jews, as minorities here in this country, we know – from our experience elsewhere – that standing up for minority rights is incredibly important. If anybody in this country is threatened, if his or her rights are taken away, that means all of us are at risk. So we're here standing up strong for religious freedom.
>
> We believe that this Islamic cultural center is an important addition to the city. What they are doing is absolutely within their right. It's

5. Natasha Mozgovaya, "'Ground Zero mosque' imam thanks U.S. Jews for support, *Haaretz*, August 4, 2010.

going to be modeled after the 92nd Street Y here in our city, a cultural institution.

This was a critical moment for the American Jewish community. Would we line up with religious freedom? Or would we side with bigotry and Islamophobia?[6]

Daisy Khan, executive director of the American Society for Muslim Advancement, one of the initiators of the effort to construct the Muslim Center, and the wife of Imam Rauf, told a Rabbis for Human Rights conference that I attended in New York on December 7, 2010 that many Jews offered practical and morale-boosting advice and she and her husband "could not have done this without your support."[7]

RECENT EXAMPLES OF DISCRIMINATION AGAINST MUSLIMS

The argument that only the location of the Center was objected to – and not the Center itself – is belied by the many other examples of anti-Muslim feeling and public actions throughout the United States. This includes opposition to the construction of mosques in Brooklyn, Staten Island, and several states that are hundreds, and in some cases thousands, of miles from Ground Zero, including California, Wisconsin, and Tennessee.

Opponents of mosques have sometimes been hostile and aggressive. In some cases, they have brought dogs to intimidate Muslims while they were holding prayer services – an insult as serious as bringing a pig into a synagogue. Some opponents spray-painted "Not Welcome" on a construction sign announcing construction of a mosque in Tennessee, and later tore the sign apart. A fire was also set at that mosque.

One example of fear mongering and Muslim-bashing occurred in the midterm 2010 election in Oklahoma. After a major scare campaign, 70% of voters in Oklahoma approved a state Constitutional amendment making it illegal for a state judge to base any court decision on Islamic religious law (*sharia*), or to consider any form of international law. This was a completely manufactured problem, since the issue has never come up in the state's courts.

---

6. Reid Pilliant, "J Street: Mosque like 92nd Street Y," *Observer*, August 3, 2010.

7. Steve Lipman, "Rabbis For Human Rights Host Cordoba House Founder," *The Jewish Week*, December 7, 2010.

Anti-Islam activists and some cynical politicians apparently persuaded some voters that Islamic law was a threat in Oklahoma. However, *sharia* is no more a threat to the U.S. court systems than is Jewish *halachic* law or Catholic canon law. Nevertheless, a major part of the political campaign was based on Islam-bashing. Muslim leaders in Oklahoma reported increased levels of hate mail.

In an August 10, 2011 op-ed article for the *Jewish Telegraphic Agency* (JTA), Abraham Foxman, national director of the Anti-Defamation League, criticized efforts by American politicians, including some Republican presidential candidates, to claim that *sharia* might infiltrate into the American court system. He stated:

> But the anti-*sharia* bills are more than a matter of unnecessary public policy. These measures are, at their core, predicated on prejudice and ignorance. They constitute a form of camouflaged bigotry that enables their proponents to advance an idea that finds fault with the Muslim faith and paints all Muslim Americans as foreigners and anti-American crusaders.
>
> If the hysteria over *sharia* law continues to percolate through our political and social discourse, there is bound to be unintended consequences.[8]

More recently, an online article in *Huffington Post Political*, "Muslim Americans Widely Seen as Victims of Discrimination," reported that 73% of Americans believe that American Muslims face a fair amount or a great deal of discrimination. Negative feelings about Muslims reached a fever pitch after the radical Muslim group ISIS destroyed a Russian plane and murdered many innocent people in Beirut and Paris in acts of terror during November 2015. This caused Republican presidential candidates to advocate drastic steps against Muslims, including shutting down mosques and requiring Muslims to register in a data base, shutting down any place that Muslims gather, permitting only refugees who are Christians, and preventing desperate refugees fleeing the Syrian civil war from entering the U.S.

---

8. Abraham H. Foxman, "Shout Down the Sharia Myth Makers," Anti Defamation League Op-Ed, August 10, 2011.

POTENTIAL EFFECTS OF ANTI-SHARIA LAWS ON *HALACHAH*

Efforts by conservative lawmakers across the United States to outlaw *sharia* law have Jewish organizations concerned that *halachah* (Jewish laws and legal authority) could be next. "The laws are not identical, but as a general rule bans on *sharia* could be interpreted broadly to prevent two Jewish litigants from going to a *beit din* (Jewish court)," said Abba Cohen, the Washington director of the Orthodox organization Agudath Israel of America.[9] "That would be a terrible infringement on our religious freedom." He added that laws protecting religious behavior in the workplace – such as wearing head coverings or taking holy days off – could also be affected.[10]

These threats led Agudath Israel and the Orthodox Union to sign on to an American Jewish Committee-initiated letter to state legislatures in the spring of 2011, urging them to reject anti-*sharia* laws.[11] Other groups supporting the AJC letter include the American Civil Liberties Union, the Baptist Joint Committee for Religious Liberty, and Americans United for Separation of Church and State, an indication of the widespread opposition to the legislation targeting Islamic law. Several Jewish groups, including the Orthodox Union, Agudath Israel, and the Union for Reform Judaism, are also urging their constituent synagogues to oppose anti-*sharia* laws in states where they are being considered.

DISINFORMATION CAMPAIGNS AGAINST MUSLIMS

There is widespread disinformation against Muslims and Islam, and people generally do not bother to examine the truth of these accusations. I once received an email from a friend stating that traffic at Madison Avenue and 42nd Street in Manhattan is stopped every Friday afternoon, so that Muslims can gather and pray. Several photos of Muslims bowing down in prayer and covering an entire street accompanied and reinforced the message. I would certainly understand anger at Muslims if the report

---

9. Ron Kampeas, "Anti-Sharia Laws Stir Concerns that Halachah Could be Next," *Jewish Week*, April 30, 2011.
10. *Ibid.*
11. *Ibid.*

of alleged disruptions every Friday at one of the busiest locations in Manhattan were true. However, I found it very hard to believe that such a thing was actually happening in my city without my ever having heard about it, and without any coverage on local media, not even on Fox News and other Conservative media sources. So I did a quick Internet search. It turns out that this is not a weekly event, but that *once a year* the Muslim Foundation of America organizes a Muslim Day Parade that includes a gathering of Muslims for their noon prayer.[12] The Muslim parade event has been held every year since 1985.

Criticizing the event is like attacking the St. Patrick's Day Parade or the annual Salute to Israel Parade that blocks traffic on many New York City streets once a year. The same thing happens all across America on the Fourth of July and on other occasions. Another incorrect email message that I received indicated that "Muslim parents demanded the abolition of pork in all the school canteens of a Montreal suburb." A quick Internet search revealed that this is also false.

Jews have also often been the victims of false information. For many years, Jews have had to contend with anti-Semitic writers who claim to "unmask" the Talmud by making lists of every negative quote they can find, usually taken out of context and poorly translated. A person reading these lists without any prior knowledge of Judaism and Jewish religious practices would probably think it is the cruelest and most hateful religion on the planet. Now the same thing is happening to Islam, with biased enemies of Islam collecting everything negative ever said by any Muslim anywhere, while including none of the positive teachings. These lists are deliberate distortions, which is why one should be suspicious of websites claiming to "unmask" Islam. We should keep in mind Mark Twain's statement a century before the Internet, "A lie can travel halfway around the world while the truth is putting on its shoes."

Perhaps the most extreme case of misinformation about Muslims is Donald Trump's repeated assertions that thousands of Muslims in Jersey City cheered as the World Trade Center collapsed, a claim without any factual basis.

---

12. "Muslims Praying Every Friday in Streets of New York Protest Message," *Hoax-Slayer*, http://www.hoax-slayer.com/muslim-fridays-new-york.shtml

Muslims have been singled out for suspicion and mistreatment. One example occurred on May 6, 2011 when two imams dressed in Muslim attire were removed just before takeoff from an Atlantic Southeast Airlines flight, because some passengers felt uncomfortable with the pair being on the flight.[13] This occurred even though the imams had both successfully passed through two security checks. Ironically, the two imams were traveling to attend a conference about prejudice against Muslims.

Many Americans' ideas about Muslims are based on misconceptions and misunderstandings. Many people believe that while not all Muslims are terrorists, all, or at least the vast majority, of terrorists are Muslims. It turns out that this is far from true. Please consider the following very surprising statistics about terrorism acts in the U.S. and Europe from an analysis in The Daily Beast in 2015:[14]

- Less than 2% of the terrorist attacks in the past five years in the U.S. and Europe were carried out by Muslims; the vast majority were carried out by separatist groups. For example, in 2013 only two of 152 terrorist acts were religiously motivated, while 84 were based on ethno-religious or separatist beliefs, such as France's FLNC, which advocates that the island of Corsica should become an independent nation.

- According to an FBI study, 94% of terrorist acts in the U.S. between 1980 and 2005 were committed by non-Muslims.

- A 2014 University of North Carolina study found that since the 9/11 attacks, 37 Americans died due to Muslim terrorism, while 190,000 Americans were murdered in gang fights, school shootings, domestic violence, and other forms of homicide.

- The reason many people have the mistaken belief that most terrorist acts are due to Muslims is that the media, especially Fox News, give far more attention to terrorist acts by Muslims than other terrorist acts.

---

13. "Airline bailouts, security lapses, and false alarms," http://www.akdart.com/airl ine7.html
14. Dean Obeidallah, "Are All Terrorists Muslims? Not Even Close," *The Daily Beast*, January 14, 2015.

A front page article in the June 24, 2015 *International New York Times* reported that since September 11, 2001, white supremacists, antigovernment fanatics, and other non-Muslin extremists killed nearly twice as many people as radical Muslims.[15] The article mentioned a study that concluded "Law enforcement agencies around the country have told us the threat from Muslim extremists is not as great as the threat from right-wing extremists."

This view was reinforced by an article at Thinkprogress.org on November 30, 2015 with the title, "You Are More Than 7 Times As Likely To Be Killed By A Right-Wing Extremist [in the U.S.] Than By Muslim Terrorists." This is so far from the conventional wisdom in the U.S., largely because of the focus of the media and messages from conservative politicians, that I did an Internet search to find out more. Among the articles I found that reinforced the above analysis are: "Non-Muslims Carried Out More than 90% of All Terrorist Attacks" and "All Terrorists are Muslims . . . Except the 94% that Aren't."

Of course there are evil and extremist forces among Muslims, including the Taliban, Al Qaeda, and ISIS, that have carried out horrible acts of terror, and we must be vigilant in guarding against future terroristic acts. The incredibly barbaric actions of ISIS, including beheading captives or burning them to death must be condemned completely. This has been the reaction of the vast majority of the world's people, including Muslims, as indicated by the swift response by the Jordanian government when one of their soldiers was burned alive by ISIS, executing two ISIS captives they were holding, with the widespread approval of the Jordanian people.

There have been many examples of the mistreatment of Jews and other minorities in Muslim countries. While evil and terrorism will never be completely eradicated from the world until the Messiah comes, I believe that, as discussed in Chapter 8, a U.S.-led global Marshall Plan to significantly reduce poverty, hunger, illiteracy, disease, pollution, and other societal ills, has the potential to improve the image of the United States and reduce instability, violence, and terrorism.

Generally people who have actually met and spoken with average Muslims are far less prejudiced against them than those who have not. When you sit down with members of another religion and listen to what

---

15. Scott Shane, "Homegrown Radicals More Deadly Than Jihadists in U.S.," *International New York Times*, June 24, 2015.

they really believe, you often find it is not what you thought. Islam forbids suicide and the killing of innocent people. A "jihad" that targets innocent people is, by definition, not a real jihad.[16] Most Muslims stress that suicide bombings and other terrorist acts are a wicked perversion of their religion. However, as documented by the Southern Poverty Law Center, many anti-Muslim groups were started as a reaction to 9/11.

A number of factors seem to be ominously converging to lead to the scapegoating of American Muslims. First, there was the attack on September 11, 2001, carried out by Saudi fanatics, but widely misperceived as representative of all Muslims everywhere. Then there were the unwinnable and seemingly un-endable wars in Iraq and Afghanistan, which are Muslim countries, as well as continued terrorist attacks around the world, many by Muslim extremists. Plus we have a recovering but still shaky economy that has left many Americans concerned about their futures and that of their children, many students and others with serious debts, and many middle class people economically challenged. All of this leaves many people feeling that the U.S. society has gone profoundly astray, with conditions heading in a negative direction. Add these factors together, and people are looking for someone to blame.

IS BIAS AGAINST MUSLIMS HURTING U.S. STRATEGIC INTERESTS?

Opponents of the proposed Muslim center and other Muslim projects are potentially harming U.S. security and endangering American troops by making it more difficult to "win the hearts and minds" of Muslims in Iraq, Afghanistan, and other Muslim countries where U.S. forces are deployed. They are also potentially increasing chances of terrorism by confirming the message of Muslim extremists that the U.S. is at war with Islam. In addition, they are undermining the messages of religious tolerance and cultural pluralism upon which the United States was founded, and which we have been trying to propagate in the world.

How can we convince other countries to grant religious freedom

---

16. According to Breslov Hasid Lee (Tzvi) Weissman's blog, *Jihadi Jew*: "The root meaning of Jihad is to 'struggle,' to strive against one's own negativity in the pursuit of spiritual mastery and submission to the One true God." This struggle is known in Islam as "The Greater Jihad" – the conquest of oneself.

to Christians, Jews, Baha'is, and other minorities if we are not doing it ourselves? It is indeed ironic that some of the strongest voices calling for a more "patriotic" America are actually working to undermine the First Amendment and our cherished American liberties.

The Taliban seized onto the "Ground Zero mosque" controversy as a tool for recruitment to the point that they are happy that this Manhattan Muslim cultural center has not been built, because that provides better propaganda for their cause. In August 2010, Taliban spokesman Zabihullah Mujahid told *Newsweek:*

> By preventing this mosque from being built, America is doing us a big favor. It's providing us with more recruits, donations, and popular support.... We talk about how America tortures with water boarding, about the cruel confinement of Muslims in wire cages in Guantanamo, about the killing of innocent women and children in air attacks – and now America gives us another gift with its street protests to prevent a mosque from being built in New York.... The more mosques you stop, the more jihads we will get.[17]

Brian Fishman, a research fellow at the Combating Terrorism Center at the United States Military Academy at West Point and also at the New American Foundation in Washington, said, "When you've got folks who are looking for the worst in Islam and are promoting that as the entire religion of 1.5 or 1.6 billion people, then you only empower the real extremists."[18]

In Gainesville, Florida, Christian minister Terry Jones, leader of a tiny congregation of about 30 people, threatened to hold a "Burn a Qur'an Day" on September 11, 2010. This sparked worldwide protest from Muslims (including violent riots in some places) and non-Muslims alike. Once again, this echoes history, when book-burnings, disputations, and bans of holy works were directed at Jews. Pastor Jones backed down and called off the event at the last minute, apparently in reaction to negative attention and protests. No Qur'ans were burned then, but the damage had been done, increasing ill will toward America throughout the Muslim world.

---

17. Sami Yousafzou, "Taliban Using Mosque Controversy to Recruit," *Newsweek,* August 30, 2010.
18. Laurie Goodstein, "Drawing U.S. Crowds With Anti-Islam Message," *The New York Times,* March 7, 2011.

On September 12, Pastor Jones went to New York to meet with Imam Rauf about the proposed Muslim project. Then, implying that the imam had given him a private commitment that he would abandon the project, Jones did a complete U-turn and stated that he would never again threaten to burn a Qur'an, nor would he try to hurt any other religion.

Despite that statement, Pastor Jones reversed himself again, and did conduct a Qur'an burning in March 2011, after holding a "trial" of the Qur'an and finding it "guilty." When this became known in early April, despite years of efforts to improve U.S. relations with Afghanistan, thousands of Afghans rioted, shouting anti-American slogans, overrunning a UN compound, and killing at least twenty people, including seven UN workers. Rather than be repentant for the terrible results of his arrogant and grossly insensitive action (which top American government and military officials had personally pleaded him to forgo), Pastor Jones indicated that he next planned to hold a "trial" about the life of Mohammad. Jones is a "Christian" in the same sense that "Muslim terrorists" are "Muslims," people who misuse their religion to whip up anger and hatred as a vehicle to gain personal power or publicity, utterly ignoring their religion's basic teachings.

A recent example of Islamophobia fueling recruitment of Muslims to terrorist groups occurred in January 2016 when Al-Shebab, a Somali terrorist group linked to al-Qaeda, come out with a new recruiting video, with Donald Trump playing a starring role because of his proposal to ban all Muslims from entering the U.S.

POSITIVE MUSLIM TEACHINGS

As in the sacred writings of all religions, there are destructive and troubling teachings in the Islamic scriptures, and people who want to speak negatively about Islam spread them widely. But there are far more Muslim teachings that reflect a broadminded religion of compassion and tolerance. A few examples:

- "Oh, humanity! We [God] created you from a single (pair) of a male and a female, and made you into nations and tribes that you may know each other. Truly, the noblest of you in the sight of Allah is the best in conduct" (Qur'an 49:13).
- "It may be that God will grant love (and friendship) between you and those whom you now hold as enemies, for Allah has power over all

things. And Allah is Oft Forgiving and Merciful" (Qur'an 60:7).

- "Allah loves those who are just" (Qur'an 60:8).
- "Nor can goodness and evil be equal. Repel (evil) with what is better: then will he between you and whom there was hatred become as it were your friend and intimate" (Qur'an 41:34).

Of course, as with other religious people, Muslims do not always live up to the highest values of their religion. Nevertheless, the above quotes are a sample of positive teachings that Muslims strive for.

MUSLIM OUTREACH FOR SOLIDARITY AND DIALOGUE

Since at least 2007, some elements in the global Muslim community have reached out to non-Muslims, calling for solidarity and dialogue. On October 11, 2007, a 29 page letter, titled "A Common Word Between Us and You" and signed by 138 Muslim religious leaders and scholars worldwide, was sent to Christian leaders. Citing the Qur'an, Christian Scriptures, and the Torah, the letter is an invitation to work together for harmony and peace.[19] It represents an effort to show that moderate Muslims are willing to actively oppose violence and to demonstrate that Islam is a peaceful religion. The letter concludes: "Without peace and justice between our two communities, there can be no meaningful peace in the world."

On February 25, 2008, the same Muslim scholars and clerics sent to the Jewish community "A Call to Peace, Dialogue, and Understanding Between Muslims and Jews."[20] This clear attempt to establish mutual respect between our communities and to improve Jewish-Muslim relations stressed commonalities between Judaism and Islam and urged an end to dehumanizing prejudices and stereotypes.

Another example of Muslim efforts to establish better relations with other religions and groups occurred in July 2015 when a number of Muslim groups raised tens of thousands of dollars to help rebuild Christian churches that were burned down in the weeks after nine black worshippers

---

19. "138 Muslim Scholars Issue Open Letter to Christian Religious Leaders," *A Common Word*, http://www.acommonword.com/138-muslim-scholars-issue-open-letter-to-christian-religious-leaders/

20. "An Open Letter: A Call to Peace, Dialogue and Understanding Between Muslims and Jews," Berkeley Center for Religion, Peace, and World Affairs, February 25, 2008.

were murdered at a Bible study session at Mother Emanuel AME Church in Charleston, South Carolina. A statement by the organizers of the fund raising initiative included:

> ALL houses of worship are sanctuaries – a place where all should feel safe, a place we can seek refuge when the world is too much to bear. . . . We want for others what we want for ourselves: the right to worship without intimidation, the right to safety, and the right to property.[21]

In addition, Muslims and Jews have been working together to rebuild the Christian churches that were destroyed by arson after the killings at the Charleston church. Explaining why Jews and Muslims were at the forefront of efforts to rebuild the churches, Rabbi Susan Talve said, "We believe that the church is the heart and soul of a community."[22]

   It is to be hoped that such endeavors to establish reconciliation and open exchange will continue and expand. Some recent examples of Jewish/Muslim cooperation are given in the next section.

JOINT JEWISH-MUSLIM EFFORTS TO COUNTER PREJUDICE

Muslim and Jewish groups have been attempting to work together to combat bias and antagonisms that focus on prejudices against both groups. In the spring of 2011, the World Jewish Congress, the Foundation for Ethnic Understanding, the Muslim Jewish Conference, the World Council of Muslims for Interfaith Relations, and the European Jewish Congress co-sponsored a month-long initiative to speak out against the rise of far-right extremist groups throughout Europe. They ran a series of educational events in May 2011, culminating in Brussels on May 30, when top Jewish and Muslim leaders presented a joint declaration to European Commission President José Manuel Barroso, stating:

> We resolve to work together to counter efforts to demonize or marginalize either of our communities. Bigotry against any Jew or any Muslim

---

21. Lindsay Bever, "Muslims raise nearly $45,000 to rebuild burned-down black churches," *Washington Post.* July 9, 2015, July 12, 2015.
22. "Jews and Muslims Work to Rebuild Arson-hit Black Churches," *Haaretz*, July 12, 2015.

is an attack on all Muslims and all Jews. We are united in our belief in the dignity of all peoples ... We recognize that the issues of identity, integration, multiculturalism and immigration are complex ones that need to be addressed properly and in consultation with the minority communities in Europe. However, there must be no tolerance for the demonization of an entire faith.[23]

Rabbi Marc Schneier, president of the Foundation for Ethnic Understanding, an organization dedicated to promoting unity and understanding among ethnic groups, said in a talk to the World Jewish Congress in May 2011, "Our purpose is to make clear that Jews and Muslims will be there for each other if either is being unfairly attacked and will stand united in support of principles of democracy and pluralism that will ensure a decent future for all Europeans."[24]

Rabbi Shmuly Boteach, a conservative who ran unsuccessfully for Congress as a Republican, wrote on this subject in his May 25, 2011 blog (while at the same time condemning Muslim extremists):

I am a Rabbi and a Jew who has forever fought Islamophobia and has repeatedly written and preached in front of tens of thousands of Jews and Christians that Islam is a great world religion that took Jews in when they were kicked out of Catholic Spain and Portugal. I am constantly inspired by everyday Muslims I meet in the US who observe Halal [dietary laws], fast on Ramadan, and take their religion seriously.[25]

More recently, an article posted in the July 23, 2014 *Jewish Journal*, "Choose Life: Jews and Muslims working for peace together in Israel," discussed a center, called Shorashim, involving West Bank Jewish settlers and Palestinians, based between Bethlehem and Gush Etzion, that coordinates nonviolence training and interfaith dialogue for Israeli and Palestinian families, children, women, and local leaders. The center includes a summer camp, cultural exchanges and language learning.

---

23. Shlomo Shamir, "Jewish and Muslim leaders join forces to combat xenophobia," *Haaretz*, May 13, 2011.

24. *Ibid.*

25. Marcia Schaffer and Marian Evashevski, "Muslims in Europe: A curriculum resource for teachers," http://www.unc.edu/euce/resources/mich_muslims_in_europe.pdf

HOW TO RESPOND TO ISIS AND
OTHER MUSLIM TERRORISTS

While combating Islamophobia is important, it is also essential to recognize the great threats from ISIS and other radical Muslims. ISIS's brutal beheadings and burning innocent people alive cannot be ignored, nor can their territorial gains and success in attracting misguided people to their ranks. And of course their bringing down a Russian passenger plane and their mass killings in Lebanon and Paris in November 2015 and in San Bernardino, California in December 2015 were properly widely condemned. How best to respond? First let us consider what many believe to be counterproductive approaches.

In May 2015, anti-Muslim activist Pamela Geller's name was in the news for organizing, along with her group the American Freedom Defense Initiative, a contest involving cartoons depicting the prophet Mohammad. While most Muslims ignored the event, although they find any cartoon depiction of Mohammad very offensive, two Muslim terrorists were fortunately killed by a local police officer before they were able to carry out their plans to kill many people at the site of the cartoon contest. Previously Geller had been active opposing the building of the Muslim Center in lower Manhattan discussed earlier by putting ads on buses and subway cars with inflammatory messages about Muslims, such as, "In any war between the civilized man and the savage, support the civilized man; Support Israel; Defeat Jihad."

Geller and her supporters defend her provocative actions as examples of free speech. Of course free speech is an important democratic principle that should be defended and it should never be responded to with violence. Fortunately, the vast majority of Muslims are peaceful and recognize that responding to insults with violence is not consistent with Islam, but much media attention is devoted to the few violent responses, such as the one by the two Muslims at the cartoon conference site.

Free speech should certainly be defended, but using it is not always wise. Why hold provocative events and press hot buttons that separate people and make violence more likely?

Another wrong approach is that of Republican presidential candidates demonizing Muslims in response to very cruel terrorist attacks by ISIS in November and December 2015. As indicated previously, the candidates have advocated drastic steps against Muslims, including requiring Muslims to register in a data base, shutting down mosques and other places that Muslims gather, permitting only refugees who are Christians to enter the U.S., and preventing desperate, thoroughly vetted refugees fleeing the Syrian civil war from entering the U.S. Leading Republican candidate Donald Trump has even advocated that no Muslims be permitted to enter the U.S. until "our country's representatives can figure out what is going on." These proposals and other statements that demonize Muslims have resulted in a great increase of violent acts against Muslims and mosques. This threatens to reduce the great help that Muslims have provided in preventing acts of terror. It also provides a very valuable recruiting tool for ISIS, which wants nothing more than to be able to argue that America and the West are at war with Islam, and that U.S. and other western countries are invading Muslim countries.

How then should we respond to ISIS and other radical Islamists? Unless we find an effective approach, they will likely continue gaining recruits and territory, and the Middle East will face increasing instability, violence, terrorism, and war, with great suffering for the people in the region.

I do not claim to have a magic answer that will immediately end terrorism. While supplying forces in the area that are battling ISIS with military equipment, advice, and training is part of the answer, it is unlikely to be sufficient. We should recognize lessons from the disastrous results of the U.S. invasion of Iraq, and also that drone strikes may create more terrorists than they destroy when innocents as well as militants are killed.

I believe it is important to have a respectful dialogue on the issues, and therefore I offer the suggestions below for consideration, all of which are based on points previously made in this book. Of course I am completely open to considering other suggestions.

- We should seek common ground with moderate Muslims and solutions rather than using provocative, insulting statements and events. When politicians imply that all or most Muslims are potential terrorists or that there is a "clash of civilizations," it is counterproductive.
- We should encourage building alliances and holding joint events involving Jews, Christians, and Muslims, like the ones discussed previously in Chapter 5.
- As indicated in Chapter 8, the U.S., along with other developed nations, should strive to create a global Marshall Plan to reduce poverty, hunger, illiteracy, and other social ills. This would help improve the

image of the U.S., and establish a new paradigm of support and co-operation that brings people together, rather than increasing distrust, hatred, competitiveness, and potential violence. It would also reduce the ability of ISIS and other radical groups to recruit people to commit acts of terror, sometimes by being willing to give up their lives in suicide attacks.

- We should stress that the horrible acts of ISIS are not consistent with the teachings of Islam.
- We should make reducing climate change a major priority. As indicated previously, severe droughts that were caused or worsened by climate change were major causes of civil wars in Sudan and Syria. Military experts fear that climate change will be a multiplier effect for violence, terrorism, and war, since it will cause tens of millions of hungry, thirsty, desperate refugees to flee from droughts, wildfires, storms, floods, and other effects of climate change. Many of the countries that are prime potential sources for terrorism are in the Middle East, an area that is semi-arid or worse, and which is likely to become drier and hotter due to climate change.
- With the help and support of the U.S. and other nations, Israel should increase efforts to obtain a peaceful resolution with the Palestinians and surrounding Arab nations. As indicated in chapter 7, this would have many benefits for Israel and would also reduce the ability of radical Muslim groups to recruit additional terrorists. Of course, as indicated previously, any Palestinian state would have to be demilitarized and additional measures should be taken to assure the security of all parties to the agreement. To increase the chances of obtaining a sustainable resolution, the U.S. and other developed nations should make loans, grants, and other contributions to improve economic conditions for the region's people, so they recognize that they have a chance for far better lives, rather than the continued violence that has plagued the region for so long.
- President Obama should make a major address at the U.N. indicating that the U.S. recognizes the need for new approaches based on coop-eration, and that we recognize we have often acted incorrectly in the past by undermining a democratically elected government in Iran and then backing the forces of oppression in that country, and backing other dictators in support of U.S. interests. He should stress that the entire world is threatened by climate change, and the world can no longer

afford to waste time, people, and resources on battles but must focus on averting a climate catastrophe and other environmental disasters.

Utopian? Naïve? Perhaps. But what could be more naive than thinking the world can continue on its present path without a disastrous outcome? I believe that steps like the ones above must be tried, lest terrorism puts an end to a decent future world before we put an end to terrorism.

Chapter 11

Should Jews Be Environmental Activists?

*A*nd the Lord God took the man [Adam] and put him
into the Garden of Eden to work it and to guard it.

– GENESIS 2:15

*T*he earth was not created as a gift to you. You have
been given to the earth, to treat it with respectful consideration, as God's earth, and everything on it [must be
seen] as God's creation, and [animals recognized as] your
fellow creatures — to be respected, loved, and helped
to attain their purpose according to God's will . . .

– RABBI SAMSON RAPHAEL HIRSCH[1]

THE WORLD IS APPROACHING an unprecedented climate catastrophe, major food, water, and energy scarcities, and is also
severely threatened by many other environmental problems.
Yet in spite of Judaism's many powerful teachings on environmental
stewardship, the religious Jewish community (along with most other
communities) is not adequately responding to today's environmental
crises. This failure of the religious Jewish community to sufficiently address these environmental threats is one major reason that I believe my
religion has been stolen.

While there are a number of Jewish groups – including the Coalition
on the Environment and Jewish Life (COEJL) and Canfei Nesharim – the
Jewish community as a whole is far from sufficiently involved. It is urgent

---

1. Rabbi Samson Raphael Hirsch, *The Nineteen Letters* (Nanuet, NY: Feldheim Pub-
lishers, 1969), Letter 4.

that Jews play our mandated role to be a "light unto the nations," and apply our eternal teachings in response to the many environmental threats that face our planet in this generation.

WHAT MUST GOD THINK ABOUT CURRENT ENVIRONMENTAL CONDITIONS?

When God created the world, He was able to say, "It is very good" (Genesis 1:31). Everything was in harmony as God had planned: the waters were clean, the air was pure, and the animals and humans lived in harmony. But what must God think about the world today? Please consider:

- The rain God provides to nourish our crops is often acid rain, darkened by the many pollutants spewed into the air by smokestacks and tailpipes.
- The endless diversity of species of plants and animals that God created are becoming extinct at an alarming rate in tropical rainforests and other threatened habitats, before we have even begun to study and catalog most of them.
- The abundant fertile soil God provided is quickly being depleted and eroded; the climatic conditions that God designed to meet our needs are threatened by global warming.

OUR MODERN TEN "PLAGUES"

Today's environmental threats bring to mind the Biblical ten plagues in the book of Exodus. Is it a coincidence that we read this story in the synagogue during the weeks leading up to the environmental holiday of Tu B'Shvat, or is God giving us a warning here? The list of today's Ten Plagues might include:

- **The rapid melting (due to global warming) of polar ice caps** and sheets of permafrost and mountain glaciers, which could soon precipitate a disastrously sudden recalibration of the earth's climate for humans and other creatures. We are in the process of creating a potential catastrophe comparable to the biblical flood.
- **A permanent increase both in severe droughts (due to the drying effect of heat where water is scarce) and severe floods** (due to the evaporative effect where water is plentiful), straining humanity to the limits of our ability to cope and survive.

- **Extreme deforestation** (about half of the world's rainforests have already been destroyed), decimating one of the world's most valuable providers of natural goods and services and, by slashing the planet's ability to sequester carbon, further exacerbating climate change and all its consequences.
- **Severe heat waves**, with each of the last five decades being warmer than the previous one, and record temperatures being recorded in many areas.
- **Rapid loss of thousands of species** faster than during any previous time in history.
- **Widespread soil erosion** and nutrient depletion, reducing fertility, increasing desertification, and severely compromising humanity's ability to feed itself.
- **The serious pollution** and, in some cases, "killing" of fresh water bodies by runoff contamination with pesticides, inorganic fertilizers, and animal wastes from factory farms, as well as by fallout from smokestack and tailpipe air pollution.
- **An epidemic of heart disease**, many types of cancer, and other chronic degenerative diseases, largely due to gluttonous consumption of animal products and junk foods, sedentary lifestyles, and a glut of toxic environmental chemicals.
- **Increasingly widespread and severe wildfires**, because of warmer temperatures and the resultant dryer environment in many areas.
- **Increasing hunger and famine** as global demand for food increases due to rising population, increased affluence leading to rising demand for animal products, and increasing use of biofuels. This is along with decreased food production due to shrinking glaciers and aquifers, droughts, floods, heat waves, and other damaging effects of climate change, and the loss of farm land to urban sprawl.

While the Egyptians in the time of Moses were subjected to only one plague at a time, the modern plagues threaten us all at once. The Jews in Goshen were spared most of the biblical plagues, while every person on earth is imperiled by these modern plagues. And it is we ourselves who are the causes of these modern plagues, though it is future generations who will be most severely afflicted. Instead of an ancient Pharaoh's heart being hardened, our own hearts today have been hardened by the greed, materialism, waste, and lack of recognition of our precarious relationship with nature that are at the root of the current environmental threats. God provided the Biblical plagues to free the Israelites from oppression. Had Pharaoh heeded the warning of the first plague, and simply let the people go, there would have been no need for the other nine plagues. Unfortunately, he did not. Today we must learn from this lesson, and heed the many environmental warnings we are getting almost daily. We must apply God's teachings in order to save humanity and our precious but endangered planet, before we are destroyed because of our own hard-heartedness.

JEWISH TEACHINGS ON THE ENVIRONMENT

Let us consider some of Judaism's powerful teachings about how we should be treating the environment. Some Jews (as well as members of other biblically-based religions) argue that humankind has been given a license to exploit the earth and its creatures, because God gave us "dominion over the fish of the sea, and over the fowl of the air, and over every living thing that creeps upon the earth" (Genesis 1:28). However, the Talmudic sages interpret that "dominion" as one of *guardianship or stewardship,* serving as co-workers with God in caring for and improving the world, and *not* as a right to conquer and exploit animals and the earth (*Shabbat* 10a, *Sanhedrin* 7). The fact that people's dominion over animals is a limited one is indicated by God's first (and completely vegan) dietary regime in Genesis 1:29, and also the statement in Genesis 2:15 that humans are to work the earth and *guard it* charges us with responsibility for the land and all the creatures on it.

Rabbi Abraham Isaac Hakohen Kook, the first Chief Rabbi of pre-state Israel, stated that "dominion" does not mean the arbitrary power of a tyrannical ruler who whimsically and cruelly governs in order to satisfy his personal desires.[2] He observes such a repulsive form of servitude that could not be forever sealed in the world of God, whose "tender mercies are over all His works" (Psalm 145:9).[3]

---

2. Rabbi Abraham Isaac Hakohen Kook, *A Vision of Vegetarianism and Peace,* Section 2; Also see J. Green, "Chalutzim of the Messiah —The Religious Vegetarian Concept as Expounded by Rabbi Kook," (lecture given in Johannesburg, South Africa), 2.
3. *Ibid.*

JEWS ARE TO BE CO-WORKERS WITH GOD
IN PRESERVING THE ENVIRONMENT

The Talmudic sages assert that the assigned role of the Jewish people is to enhance the world as partners of God in the work of creation (*Shabbat* 10a; *Sanhedrin* 7).They express great concern about preserving the environment and preventing pollution, and they state three clear principles that can still be applied today:

- "It is forbidden to live in a town which has no garden or greenery" (*Mishnah Kiddushin* 4:12, *Kiddushin* 66d).
- Threshing floors must be placed far enough from a town so that it will not be dirtied by chaff carried by winds (*Mishnah Baba Batra* 2:8).
- Tanneries must be kept at least 50 cubits (a cubit is about half a meter or 20 inches) from a town and may be placed only on the east side of a town, so that odors and pollution will be carried away from the town by the prevailing winds from the west (*Mishnah Baba Batra* 2:8, 9).

These three specific rules lead to a general principle that industries should be regulated in such a way that they do not spoil the environment. Dust and air pollution must be controlled, and green spaces must be provided for the health and enjoyment of the people and animals living there.

THE EARTH IS THE LORD'S

Judaism asserts that there is one God who created the entire earth as a unity, in ecological balance; that everything is connected to everything else, and, in turn, everything is connected to – and belongs – to the One God. These lines from Psalm 104 perhaps best express this idea:

> ... You [God] are the One Who sends forth springs into brooks, that they may run between mountains,
> To give drink to every animal of the fields, the creatures of the forest quench their thirst.
> Beside them dwell the fowl of the heavens ...
> You water the mountains from Your upper chambers ...
> You cause the grass to spring up for the cattle, and herb, for the service of humans, to bring forth bread from the earth ...

How manifold are your works, O Lord! In wisdom You have made them all; the earth is full of Your property . . .

There is an apparent contradiction between two other verses in Psalms: "The earth is the Lord's" (Psalms 24:1) and "The heavens are the heavens of God, but God has given the earth to human beings" (Psalms 115:16). Jewish sages reconcile this apparent discrepancy in the following way: Before a person says a *bracha* (a blessing), before one acknowledges God's ownership of the land and its products, then "the earth is the Lord's." After a person has said a *bracha*, acknowledging God's ownership and that we are stewards assigned to ensure that God's works are properly used and shared, *then* "the earth He has given to human beings" (*Mishnah Berachot* 30:5).

Property is a sacred trust given by God; it must be used to fulfill God's purposes. No person has absolute or exclusive control over his or her possessions. The concept that people have custodial care of the earth, as opposed to ownership, is illustrated by this ancient Jewish story:

Two men were fighting over a piece of land. Each claimed ownership and bolstered his claim with apparent proof. To resolve their differences, they agreed to put the case before a rabbi. The rabbi listened but could come to no decision because both seemed to be right. Finally he said, "Since I cannot decide to whom this land belongs, let us ask the land." He put his ear to the ground and, after a moment, straightened up. "Gentlemen, the land says it belongs to neither of you, but that *you* belong to *it.*"[4]

Even the produce of the field does not belong solely to the person who farms the land. The poor are entitled to a portion:

And when you reap the harvest of your land, you shall not wholly reap the corner of your field, neither shall you gather the gleaning of your harvest. And you shall not glean your vineyard, neither shall you gather the fallen fruit of your vineyard; you shall leave them for the poor and for the stranger; I am the Lord, your God.   (Leviticus 19: 9 -10)

---

4. Jewish folk wisdom. Rabbi Shlomo Riskin in "Biblical Ecology, A Jewish View," a television documentary, directed by Mitchell Chalek and Jonathan Rosen, told this story.

These portions set aside for the poor were not voluntary contributions based on kindness. They were, in essence, a regular Divine assessment. Because God is the real owner of the land, God claims a share of the bounty that He has provided, which is to be left for the poor.

As a reminder that "the earth is the Lord's," the land must be permitted to rest and lie fallow every seven years (the Sabbatical year):

> Six years you shall sow your land, and gather in the increase thereof, but the seventh year you shall let it rest and lay fallow, so that the poor of your people may eat; and what they leave, the animals of the field shall eat. In like manner you shall deal with your vineyard, and with your olive yard. (Exodus 23: 10, 11)

The Sabbatical year also has ecological benefits. The land is given a chance to rest and renew its fertility.

JEWS ARE NOT TO WASTE OR UNNECESSARILY DESTROY ANYTHING OF VALUE

The prohibition against wanton destruction or wastage of any useful resource that God has given us, called *bal tashchit* ("you shall not destroy") in Jewish law, is based on the following Torah statement:

> When you besiege a city a long time, in making war against it to take it, you shall not destroy (*lo tashchit*) the trees thereof by wielding an ax against them; for you may eat off them. You shall not cut them down; for is the tree of the field a human being, that it should be besieged by you? Only the trees of which you know that they are not trees for food, those you may destroy and cut down, that you may build bulwarks against the city that makes war with you, until it falls. (Deuteronomy 20:19, 20)

This Torah prohibition is very specific. Taken in its most literal sense, it prohibits only the destruction of fruit trees during wartime. However, the Talmudic sages and the Jewish Oral Tradition greatly expanded the types of objects, methods of destruction, and situations covered by *bal tashchit*:

> Whoever breaks vessels, or tears garments, or destroys a building, or clogs a well, or does away with food in a destructive manner violates the prohibition of *bal tashchit*.   (*Kiddushin* 32a)

Later rabbinic rulings extended the prohibition of waste or destruction to everything of potential use, whether created by God or altered by people (*Sefer Ha-Chinukh*, 530). Talmudic rulings on *bal tashchit* also prohibit the unnecessary killing of animals (*Hullin* 7b) and the eating of extravagant foods when one can be nourished and satisfied by simpler ones (*Shabbat* 140b). In other words, *bal tashchit* prohibits the destruction, complete or incomplete, direct or indirect, of all things that are of potential benefit to people and the world.

The following Talmudic statements illustrate the seriousness with which the rabbis considered the violation of *bal tashchit*:

- The sage Rabbi Hanina attributed the early death of his son to the fact that the boy had unnecessarily chopped down a fig tree (*Baba Kamma* 91b).
- Jews should be taught very young that it is a sin to waste even small amounts of food (*Berachot* 52b).
- Rav Zutra taught: "One who covers an oil lamp or uncovers a naphtha lamp transgresses the prohibition of *bal tashchit*." (*Shabbat* 67b). Both actions mentioned would cause a faster (hence wasteful) consumption of the fuel.

Maimonides spells out these specific details:

> It is forbidden to cut down fruit-bearing trees outside a besieged city, nor may a water channel be deflected from them so that they wither ... Not only one who cuts down trees, but also one who smashes household goods, tears clothes, demolishes a building, stops up a spring, or destroys articles of food with destructive intent transgresses the command "you must not destroy."
>
> (Maimonides, *Mishneh Torah*, Laws of Kings and Wars 6:8, 10)

The *Sefer Ha-Chinukh*, a thirteenth century text which discusses the 613 *mitzvot* (commandments) in detail, indicates that the underlying purpose of *bal tashchit* is to help one to learn to act like the righteous, who are repelled by and meticulously avoid all waste and destruction:

The purpose of this mitzvah [*bal tashchit*] is to teach us to love that which is good and worthwhile and to cling to it, so that good becomes a part of us and we avoid all that is evil and destructive. This is the way of the righteous and those who improve society, who love peace and rejoice in the good in people and bring them close to Torah: that nothing, not even a mustard seed, should be lost to the world, that they should regret any loss or destruction that they see, and if possible they will prevent any destruction that they can. Not so are the wicked, who are like demons, who rejoice in destruction of the world, and they destroy themselves. (*Sefer Ha-Chinukh*, 529)

Rabbi Samson Raphael Hirsch, the leading Orthodox rabbi of nineteenth century Germany, viewed *bal tashchit* as the most basic Jewish principle of all: to acknowledge the sovereignty of God and the limitations on our own will and ego. When we preserve the world around us, we act with the understanding that God owns everything. However, when we destroy, we are, in effect, worshipping the idols of our own desires, living only for self-gratification without keeping God in mind. By observing *bal tashchit*, we restore our harmony not only with the world around us, but also with God's will, which we place before our own. Rabbi Hirsch also taught that "destruction" includes using more things (or things of greater value) than is necessary to obtain one's aim.[5] The following *Midrash* is related to this concept:

Two men entered a shop. One ate coarse bread and vegetables, while the other ate fine bread, fat meat, and drank old wine. The one who ate fine food suffered harm, while the one who had coarse food escaped harm. Observe how simply animals live and how healthy they are as a result. (Ecclesiastes *Rabbah* 1:18)

HOW SERIOUS IS CLIMATE CHANGE?

There is an overwhelming consensus among climate experts that climate change is real, that it poses a major threat to humanity, and that human activities are the primary cause.[6] This is the view of science academies

---

5. Ibid.
6. "Scientific consensus on Global Warming," Union of Concerned Scientists report,

worldwide and 97% of climate experts. Especially significant is that 99.9% of the thousands of refereed papers in respected science journals that address climate change agree. Some climate experts believe that we are close to a tipping point, when climate change will spin out of control, producing a climate catastrophe.

The 2014 Fifth Assessment Report (AR5) of the Intergovernmental Panel on Climate Change (IPCC), established by the United Nations Environmental Programme and the World Meteorological Organization, declares that there is a ninety-five percent probability that most of the warming in the past sixty years is due to human activities.[7] The AR5 is the most comprehensive synthesis of climate change science to date. Experts from more than 130 countries contributed to this assessment, which represents six years of work. More than 450 lead authors received input from more than 800 contributing authors, and an additional 2,500 experts reviewed the draft documents.

Increasingly, climate change is about verifiable facts on the ground and not just predictions. Almost weekly there are reports of severe droughts, heat waves, storms, flooding, wildfires, and unprecedented melting of polar icecaps and glaciers. Scientists consider all of these to be symptoms of a climate that is becoming more extreme and chaotic due to a warming planet. There are many sources for facts about climate change:[8]

- Every decade since the 1970s has been warmer than the previous decade, and all of the 17 warmest years since temperature records were kept in 1880 have been since 1998. 2015 is the warmest year recorded, breaking the record set by the previous year. All the 11 months from April 2015 to March 2016 set temperature records for that month, some by significant amounts.
- Polar icecaps and glaciers worldwide have been melting rapidly, faster than climate experts projected.
- There has been an increase in the number and severity of droughts,

http://www.ucsusa.org/global_warming/science_and_impacts/science/scientific-c onsensus-on.html#.VUq4Z86268E

7. Dana Nuccitelli, "Global warming: why is IPCC report so certain about the influence of humans?" The Guardian, September 27, 2013.

8. Sources for updated information about climate change include the following websites: http://climate.nasa.gov, http://data.worldbank.org/topic/climate-change, and http://climatechange.ws/facts/.

wildfires, storms, and floods. California has been subjected to so many severe climate events recently that its governor, Jerry Brown, stated that "Humanity is on a collision course with nature."

- What is especially frightening is that all the severe climate events have occurred due to a temperature increase of about one degree Celsius (about 1.8 degrees Fahrenheit). Climate experts hope the total increase can be limited to 2 degrees Celsius (3.6 degrees Fahrenheit), largely because that is the best that can be hoped for in view of present greenhouse gas emissions and a momentum factor. While such an increase would mean far more serious climate events, the world is now on track for an increase of four to five degrees Celsius, which would be catastrophic for the world.

- Many climate experts, including James Hansen, former director of the National Aeronautics and Space Administration (NASA) Goddard Institute for Space Studies, believe that a safe threshold value for carbon dioxide in the atmosphere is 350 parts per million (ppm). This is why the current most active group working to reduce climate change was named 350.org. However, we reached 400 ppm in 2014, and CO_2 levels are growing by 2–3 ppm per year – yet another indication that major changes in human behavior must be made very soon.

What worries Hansen and other climate scientists most is the prospect that climate change could reach a tipping point within just a few years due to positive feedback loops. This would unleash a vicious cycle of rapid climate alterations leading to disastrous consequences – melted ice caps, flooded cities, mass species extinctions and spreading deserts, among other events – unless humanity soon begins to use energy far more effectively.

Here is an example of a positive feedback loop: When incoming sunlight strikes Arctic ice, about 70% is reflected back into space. But once the ice has melted, leaving much darker soil or water, only about 6% is reflected and about 94% is absorbed by the darker soil or water and converted into heat. The more ice that melts, the more heat is absorbed, creating a potential vicious cycle that accelerates the melting of the Arctic Sea ice cover, effectively destroying one of the planet's major "ice boxes." Another example of a positive feedback loop is that as temperatures increase, people use more air conditioning. This means more fossil fuels are burned, resulting in more greenhouse gas emissions, and thus more warming. Which leads back to more air conditioning . . . and the vicious cycle continues.

Military leaders in the US and other countries see climate change as a potential catalyst of multiplier effect for increased violence. A 2014 report by 16 retired U.S. generals and admirals concluded that tens of millions of hungry, thirsty, desperate refugees fleeing the effects of climate change could make instability, violence, terrorism, and war more likely.[9] Military and intelligence strategists in many countries are revising their planning to take climate change effects into account.

CLIMATE CHANGE AND OTHER ENVIRONMENTAL THREATS TO ISRAEL

What makes the inadequate response of the Jewish community, especially the Orthodox, to climate change and other environmental problems even more disturbing is the fact that Israel, like most other countries, is already suffering from the effects of climate change. It has had many years of drought recently and when rain or snow has come, it has often been in severe storms that caused much flooding and other damage. Israel experienced the worst forest fire in her existence in December 2010, a fire made far worse because of the very dry conditions due to the lack of rain. Israeli climatic conditions are likely to get much worse. The Israel Union for Environmental Defense (IUED, or *Adam, Teva v'Din*, in Hebrew) projected in 2014 that global warming will cause Israel to suffer from many additional severe heat waves, with an average temperature increase of up to 6 degrees Fahrenheit, an average decrease of precipitation of up to 33%, an increase of major storms, an inundation of the coastal plain where most Israelis live caused by a rising Mediterranean sea, and increased desertification.[10]

---

9. "National Security and the Accelerating Risks of Climate Change," CNA Military Advisory Board, May 2014.
10. "Report: Global warming disastrous for Israel," Ynet Israel News, July 5, 2007.

WHY IS THERE SO MUCH SKEPTICISM
ABOUT CLIMATE CHANGE?

With all of this powerful scientific evidence confirming anthropogenic (human-caused) climate change, why there is so much public skepticism? A major study of opinions of people in many countries about climate change was carried out in 2014 by ipsos MORI, one of UK's largest market research companies.[11] It found that, despite all the scientific evidence and many wake-up calls in terms of severe weather events, only 54% of Americans agreed with the statement "The climate change we are currently seeing is largely the result of human activity." This put the U.S. last in a list of 20 countries considered in the survey, ten points below the next lowest countries, Australia and Britain. The survey also found that while 93% of people from China agreed with the statement "We are heading for environmental disaster unless we change our habits quickly," only 57% of Americans concurred, again making the U.S. last among the 20 nations surveyed.

According to James Hoggan, author of *Climate Cover-Up: The Crusade to Deny Global Warming,* the oil, coal, and other industries that are profiting from the status quo are willing to go to great lengths to mislead people, so that they can continue to receive huge profits. Hoggan, who was initially a skeptic about climate change himself, writes that it is a "story of betrayal, a story of selfishness, greed, and irresponsibility on an epic scale . . . a story of deceit, of poisoning public judgment . . ."

Another clue comes from the results of a study called "Balance as Bias," which considered a random sample of 636 articles about climate change in the *New York Times, Washington Post, Los Angeles Times,* and *The Wall Street Journal.*[12] More than 50% of the articles gave roughly equal weight to both the scientific view and the scientifically discredited view that humans do not play a major role in climate change. This would be similar to having a debate on the shape of our planet, and giving equal time to the Flat Earth Society. In addition, some conservative politicians and

---

11. Michael Roppolo "Americans more skeptical of climate change than others in global survey," *CBS News,* July 23, 2014.
12. Maxwell T. Boykoff and Jules M. Boykoff, "Balance as bias: global warming and the US prestige, press," http://www.eci.ox.ac.uk/publications/downloads/boykoff04-gec.pdf

commentators downplay the significance of climate change. As indicated previously, U. S. Senator James Inhofe, for example, calls it the "greatest hoax ever perpetrated on the American people." No wonder many folks are so confused. On one side you have vociferously opinionated media pundits, bloggers, and politicians like Senator Inhofe, the climate change denier who received close to a million dollars from the oil and coal industries between 2000 and 2008. On the other side are the real experts, typically more cautious in their assertions.

Meanwhile, the media, leaning over backward to be perceived as balanced and reasonable, often gives equal time to both "sides" of the issue. The vast majority of climate scientists, virtually all peer-reviewed articles in respected scientific journals, and statements from scientific academies worldwide agree that the scientific probability is extremely high that climate change poses an existential threat to life as we know it – and that humans are the cause *and* the potential solution.

Another reason there is so much skepticism about climate change, despite the strong scientific consensus surrounding it, is the bias of Fox News. An internal e-mail written in December 2009 and published by liberal-media-watchdog group Media Matters for America on December 16, 2010, revealed that Bill Sammon, Fox News's Washington bureau chief, told Fox journalists to "refrain from asserting that the planet has warmed (or cooled) in any given period without *immediately* pointing out that such theories are based upon data that critics have called into question. It is not our place as journalists to assert such notions as facts, especially as this debate intensifies."[13]

While it is true that there have been a few examples of scientific error and misbehavior among climate scientists, these have been unfairly seized upon and exaggerated by climate change deniers. Follow-up investigations have demonstrated that the mistakes were honest ones, and there were no efforts by the scientific community to mislead the public.[14]

---

13. Victoria Bekiempis, "How the Media fails to Cover Climate Science," *Newsweek*, June 26, 2014.
14. "Debunking Misinformation About Stolen Climate Emails in the 'Climategate' Manufactured Controversy," Union of Concerned Scientists report, http://www.uc susa.org/global_warming/solutions/fight-misinformation/debunking-misinformati on-stolen-emails-climategate.html#.VUq1xs6268E

Many people dismiss climate change as just "liberal politics." They give more weight to the views of Glenn Beck, Rush Limbaugh, and other reactionary commentators than to the scientific consensus. These climate deniers should be made aware of the previously mentioned little-known conservative group ConservAmerica (www.ConsrvAmerica.com), formerly known as "Republicans for Environmental Protection." There is an abundance of material about climate change and other environmental threats on their website, including responses to many of the questions that climate deniers raise. ConservAmerica has the slogan "Conservation IS Conservative." It deserves much greater recognition and to have its voice heard. Climate change is not a partisan, political issue, but arguably the greatest moral, environmental, economic, and social justice issue of our time.

If we follow the strenuous recommendations of climate scientists, we have the potential for a far better, environmentally sustainable world. However, if we follow the advice of the skeptics and do not try to address climate change soon, we will likely end up with a climatic cataclysm.

THE CALL OF THE HOUR

There is a need for major changes if the world is to avoid increasingly severe threats from climate change and other environmental problems. In 1992 over 1,670 scientists, including 104 Nobel laureates – a majority of the living recipients of the Prizes in the sciences – signed a "World Scientists' Warning to Humanity."[15] The introduction states:

> Human beings and the natural world are on a collision course. Human activities inflict harsh and often irreversible damage on the environment and on critical resources. If not checked, many of our current practices put at serious risk the future that we wish for human society and the plant and animal kingdoms, and may so alter the living world that it will be unable to sustain life in the manner that we know. Fundamental changes are urgent if we are to avoid the collision our present course will bring about.

---

15. Union of Concerned Scientists report, http://www.ucsusa.org/about/1992-world-scientists.html#.VYiysmAqe8E

The scientists' analysis discusses threats to the atmosphere, rivers and streams, oceans, soil, living species, and forests.

> We the undersigned, senior members of the world's scientific community, hereby warn all humanity of what lies ahead. A great change in our stewardship of the earth and the life on it is required, if vast human misery is to be avoided and our global home on this planet is not to be irretrievably mutilated.

It is essential that the Jewish community apply our rich tradition concerning environmental responsibility and stewardship to the world's fragile ecology. Too often the Jewish establishment has been silent while our climate is rapidly changing, our air is bombarded by poisons that threaten life, our rivers and streams are polluted by industrial wastes, our fertile soil is eroded and depleted, and the ecological balance is endangered by the destruction of rain forests and other vital habitats.

The Jewish community must become more actively involved. We must proclaim that it is *chillul Hashem* (a desecration of God's name) to pollute the air and water which God created pure, to slash and burn forests which existed before there were human beings, and to wantonly destroy the abundant resources that God has so generously provided for all of humanity to enjoy and sustain itself from. We have a choice as indicated in the following Torah verse:

> I call heaven and earth to witness concerning you this day, that I have set before you life and death, the blessing and the curse; therefore choose life, that you may live, you and your descendants. (Deuteronomy 30:19)

The following Midrash provides an early warning about the importance of preserving the environment:

> In the hour when the Blessed Holy One [God] created the first human being [Adam], God took him and let him pass before all the trees of the Garden of Eden and said to him: "See my works, how fine and excellent they are! All that I have created, for you have I created them. Think upon this and do not ruin and destroy My world. For if you ruin it, there is no one to set it right after you." (Ecclesiastes *Rabbah* 7:28)

In ancient times, people may have wondered about the significance of this Midrash. How could it be possible to destroy the world that God had made? Did anybody have such power? And what could it mean, that if they did ruin it, nobody could fix it again? Wouldn't God fix everything? Now, however, it has become all too relevant. We do indeed have the power to destroy the world.

Judaism offers very powerful teachings on our environmental obligations, and these teachings are urgently needed today. Applying them would not only help to revitalize Judaism, but could also help avert the many current threats to humanity. (Additional suggestions for improving the environment are in Appendix B.)

In summary, Judaism requires Jews to act to preserve God's creation – to protect our planet and all life forms on it. Failure to do so would be a complete betrayal of Judaism and future generations.

Chapter 12

Judaism and Animal Rights

*T*here are probably no creatures that require more the protective Divine word against the presumption of man than the animals, which like man have sensations and instincts, but whose body and powers are nevertheless subservient to man. In relation to them man so easily forgets that injured animal muscle twitches just like human muscle, that the maltreated nerves of an animal sicken like human nerves, that the animal being is just as sensitive to cuts, blows, and beating as man. Thus man becomes the torturer of the animal soul.

– RABBI SAMSON RAPHAEL HIRSCH[1]

*H*ere you are faced with God's teaching, which obliges you not only to refrain from inflicting unnecessary pain on any animal, but also to help and, when you can, to lessen the pain whenever you see an animal suffering, even through no fault of yours.

– RABBI SAMSON RAPHAEL HIRSCH[2]

THE QUOTATIONS ABOVE ARE just two examples of Judaism's powerful teachings concerning the proper treatment of animals. Unfortunately, the Torah's magnificent teachings on compassion for animals are often overlooked in a world where animals suffer enormously at the hands of humans. It is marvelous to have such beautiful

---

1. Samson Raphael Hirsch, *Horeb*, Chapter 60, Section 415.
2. *Ibid*, section 416.

teachings, but it would be even better if they were applied to reduce the current widespread mistreatment of animals.

THE RELATIONSHIP BETWEEN GOD AND ANIMALS

Judaism provides very powerful teachings about the proper treatment of animals. If Jews took these teachings seriously, we would be among the strongest protesters of many current practices related to animals.

The Torah teaches that animals are part of God's creation and that people bear special responsibilities toward them. The Jewish tradition clearly indicates that we are forbidden to be cruel to animals and that we are to treat them with compassion. These concepts are summarized in the Hebrew phrase *tsa'ar ba'alei chayim*, the Torah mandate not to cause "pain to living creatures." The Talmud states this is *d'oraita*, meaning a law that comes from the Torah (as opposed to one enacted by the rabbis later), and therefore is to be observed more strictly.

Psalms 104 and 148 describe God's close identification with the animals of the field, the creatures of the sea, and the birds of the air. In the book of Genesis, we see the close connection between animals and people at the time of the Creation:

- Sea animals and birds receive the same blessing as people: "Be fruitful and multiply" (Genesis 1:22).
- Animals were initially given a vegetarian diet, similar to that of people (Genesis 1:29, 30).
- The important Hebrew term *nefesh chayah* (a "living being") is applied in Genesis (1:21, 1:24) to animals as well as people.

Although the Torah clearly indicates that humans are to have "dominion over the fish of the sea, and over the fowl of the air, and over every living thing that creeps upon the earth" (Genesis 1:26), a cooperative and mutual relationship is intended (see chapter 11). The rights and privileges of animals are not to be neglected or overlooked. Animals are also God's creatures, possessing sensitivity and the capacity for feeling pain; hence they must be protected and treated with compassion and justice. God even made treaties and covenants with animals just as with humans:

> "As for me," says the Lord, "behold I establish My Covenant with you and with your seed after you, and with every living creature that is with

you, the fowl, the cattle, and every beast of the earth with you; of all
that go out of the Ark, even every beast of the earth."

(Genesis 9:9–10)

And in that day will I make a covenant for them with the beasts of the
field and with the fowls of heaven and with the creeping things of the
ground. And I will break the bow and the sword and the battle out of
the land and I will make them to lie down safely.   (Hosea 2:20)

God includes animals, as well as people, when he admonishes Jonah: "and
should I not have pity on Nineveh, that great city, wherein are more than
120,000 persons . . . and also much cattle" (Jonah 4:11).

The Psalms portray God's concern for animals: "His tender mercies
are over all His works" (Psalms 145:9). They picture God as "satisfying
the desire of every living creature" (Psalms 145:16), "providing food for
the animals and birds" (Psalms 147:9), and "preserving both man and
beast" (Psalms 36:7).

God provides each animal with the attributes necessary for survival in
its environment. For example, the camel has a short tail, so that it won't
become ensnared when it feeds upon thorns; the ox has a long tail, so that
it can protect itself from gnats when it feeds on the plains; the feelers of
locusts are flexible, so that they won't be blinded by their feelers breaking
against trees.

JEWISH TEACHINGS ON COMPASSION FOR ANIMALS

Jews are mandated to imitate God's positive attributes and to be *rachmanim
b'nei rachmanim*, "compassionate children of compassionate ancestors"
(*Beitza* 32b). In Judaism, animals are not considered equal to human
beings, but that does not mean that they can be mistreated. Perhaps the
Jewish attitude toward animals is best summarized by the statement
in Proverbs 12:10, "The righteous person regards the life (*nefesh*) of his
animal." This is the human counterpoint of "The Lord is good to all, and
God's tender mercies are over all His works" (Psalms 145:9). In Judaism,
one who is cruel to animals cannot be regarded as a righteous individual.
The Torah mandates numerous laws requiring compassion to animals,
including:

• An ox is not to be muzzled when threshing the grain [so it does not suffer from being unable to eat food it sees and smells all day] (Deuteronomy 25:4).

- A farmer must not plow with an ox and a donkey together [so that the weaker animal would not suffer pain in trying to keep up with the stronger one] (Deuteronomy 22:10).
- Animals, as well as people, must be allowed to rest on the Sabbath day (Exodus 20:10). The importance of this verse is indicated by its inclusion in the Ten Commandments and its recitation in the Shabbat morning *Kiddush* blessing in many traditions.
- Based on the question of the angel of God to Balaam, "Why have you hit your donkey these three times?" (Numbers 22:32), the Talmud states that animals are to be treated humanely.
- Based on Deuteronomy 11:15, "And I will give grass in the fields for your cattle and you shall eat and be satisfied," the Talmud teaches that a person should not eat before first feeding his or her animals.

Many great Jewish heroes were chosen because they showed compassion to animals. Moses and King David were considered worthy to be leaders because of their kind treatment of the sheep in their care when they were shepherds (Exodus *Rabbah* 2:2). Rebecca was judged suitable to be Isaac's wife because of her kindness in providing water to the ten thirsty camels cared for by Eliezer, Abraham's servant (Genesis 24:14). All of these teachings should lead us to care for the welfare of animals, and to raise our voices in protest when they are mistreated. Unfortunately, many Jews are not protesting, perhaps because they are not aware of the extreme cruelty involved in the modern meat, egg, and dairy industries.

With regard to the treatment of animals, I have long seen my role to be that of a bridge between people with two extreme, opposite viewpoints, each of which expresses only part of the overall picture. One group consists of religious Jews who are admirably meticulous in carrying out *mitzvot* (commandments) but who overlook how grievously the *mitzvot* related to the proper treatment of animals are being violated on factory farms, as well as in laboratories, circuses, rodeos, and other settings. The other group is made up of dedicated animal rights activists who protest diligently against animal abuses, but who misrepresent religious teachings and often see religion as an enemy, rather than a potential ally in efforts to improve conditions for animals. In this chapter, I am attempting to help bring these two sides together in respectful dialogue.

SOME EXAMPLES OF THE MISTREATMENT
OF ANIMALS TODAY ON FACTORY FARMS

As indicated above, the Jewish tradition stresses compassion for animals and commands that we strive to avoid causing them pain (*tsa'ar ba'alei chayim*). Unfortunately, the conditions under which animals are raised for food today are quite different from any that the Torah would endorse. Below are just a few examples of the mistreatment of animals on factory farms.[3]

Chickens are raised for slaughter in long, windowless, crowded sheds, unable to see sunlight, breathe fresh air, or get any exercise. When the tiny chicks arrive, there is plenty of room, but they have progressively less and less room as they grow, and the shed becomes too crowded for the birds to move properly. Just prior to slaughter, the area that each chicken occupies – about half a square foot on average – is barely enough to move. Overcrowding and stress mark the lives of these "broiler" (meat) chickens, and they are generally slaughtered when only about six weeks old. By contrast, a normal chicken's lifespan is eight to ten years.

In his April 14, 2003 article in the *New Yorker*, Michael Specter describes his first visit to a chicken farm:

> I was almost knocked to the ground by the overpowering smell of feces and ammonia. My eyes burned and so did my lungs, and I could neither see nor breathe. . . . There must have been thirty thousand chickens sitting silently on the floor in front of me. They didn't move, didn't cluck. They were almost like statues of chickens, living in nearly total darkness, and they would spend every minute of their six-week lives that way.[4]

---

3. Abuses of farmed animals are described in detail in *Diet For a New America* and *The Food Revolution* by John Robbins; *Old McDonald's Factory Farm* by C. David Coats; *Eating Animals* by Jonathan Safran Foer, and many other powerful books. There are also many videos online of undercover investigations that show the horrors of factory farming.

4. Leah Garcia, "Why We Haven't Seen Inside a Broiler Chicken Factory Farm in a Decade," *Foo Factory News*, January 24, 2013.

There is also much cruelty in the raising of chickens to produce eggs. Layer hens are extremely crowded, with five hens generally squeezed into an 18 by 20 inch cage. Crowding is so bad that a hen cannot fully stretch even one wing. The results of these very unnatural conditions are that the birds are driven to pecking at each other, which harms and sometimes kills their fellow cellmates, thus reducing the producers' profits. To avoid this, the lighting is kept very dim (chickens are diurnal and not as active in low light), and the chickens are de-beaked. De-beaking is a very painful, often debilitating procedure that involves cutting off part of the beak with a hot knife while the hen's head is held by hand or in a vise. This is the industry's cruel strategy for obtaining maximum profit, rather than providing the hens more space and other improvements in their living conditions.

Because male chicks have no value to the egg industry and have not been genetically programmed to produce much flesh, they are discarded shortly after birth and disposed of by "chick-pullers." Each day, U.S. workers stuff over half a million live chicks into plastic bags, where they crush and suffocate them, or grind them up while still alive to use them as fertilizer, or to feed them to other animals.

Today's modern milk factories raise cows for maximum milk production at minimum cost, resulting in much cruelty to the cows. Farmers artificially inseminate each cow annually, and then take her calf away almost immediately, so that the mother cow will constantly produce milk for human consumption. She lives with an unnaturally enlarged and sensitive udder and is milked up to three times a day.

While the dairy industry would like people to believe that its cows are contented, today's factory-bred cows have to be fed tranquilizers to reduce their anxiety. As soon as their milk production decreases, after only a few years, they are slaughtered to produce hamburgers.

The following story by Dr. Michael Klaper, who spent much of his childhood summers working on his uncle's dairy farm and is now a leading advocate for vegan diets, dramatically illustrates the cruelty of the dairy industry.

The very saddest sound in all my memory was burned into my awareness at age five on my uncle's dairy farm in Wisconsin. A cow had given birth to a beautiful male calf. The mother was allowed to nurse her calf but for a single night. On the second day after birth, my uncle took the calf from the mother and placed him in the veal pen in the barn – only ten yards away, in plain view of the mother. The mother cow could see her infant, smell him, hear him, but could not touch him, comfort him, or nurse him. The heartrending bellows that she poured forth – minute after minute, hour after hour, for five long days – were excruciating to listen to. They are the most poignant and painful auditory memories I carry in my brain.

Since that age, whenever I hear anyone postulate that animals cannot feel emotions, I need only to replay that torturous sound in my memory of that mother cow crying her bovine heart out to her infant. Mother's love knows no species barriers, and I believe that all people who are vegans in their hearts and souls know that to be true.[5]

The following two selections summarize the inhumane treatment of animals raised for food:

How far have we the right to take our domination of the animal world? Have we the right to rob them of all pleasures in life simply to make more money more quickly out of their carcasses? Have we the right to treat living creatures solely as food-converting machines? At what point do we acknowledge cruelty?[6]

Every year millions of animals are born and bred for the sole purpose of satisfying those who like the taste of meat. Their lives vary in length from a few weeks to a few years; most live a fraction of the time they would in more natural conditions. They die in slaughterhouses where, if the tranquilizers have their effect, they know only a few moments of the awful fear of death before they are stunned and their throats cut. This is what all meat-eaters actively support, for there would be no batteries, no sweatboxes, no need to castrate male animals or artificially inseminate females, no cattle markets and no slaughterhouses if there was no one insensitive enough to buy their products.[7]

---

5. "Choose life over death, kindness over killing," *Vegan Peace* information compilation, http://www.veganpeace.com/veganism/compassion.htm
6. Ruth Harrison, *Animal Machines*, (London: Vincent Street, 1964), 12.
7. John Harris, "Killing for Food," in *Animals, Men, and Morals*, S. R. Godlovitch and John Harris, eds. (New York: Taplinger Publishing Co., 1972), 98.

British author Ruth Harrison eloquently summarizes how animals are raised on factory farms:

> To some extent . . . man has always exploited farm animals in that he rears them specifically for food. But until recently they were individuals, allowed their birthright of green fields, sunlight, and fresh air; they were allowed to forage, to exercise, to watch the world go by, in fact to live. Even at its worst . . . the animal had some enjoyment in life before it died. Today the exploitation has been taken to a degree that involves not only the elimination of all enjoyment, the frustration of all natural instincts, but its replacement with acute discomfort, boredom, and the actual denial of health. It has been taken to a degree where the animal is not allowed to live before it dies.[8]

The conditions under which animals are raised today are totally contrary to the Jewish ideals of compassion and avoiding tsa'ar ba'alei chayim:

- Instead of animals being free to graze on the Sabbath day to enjoy the beauties of creation, they are confined for all of their lives in darkened, crowded stalls and cages without air, natural light, or room in which to exercise.
- Whereas the Torah mandates that animals should be able to eat the products of the harvest as they work in the fields, today animals are fed chemical fatteners and other additives in their food, based on computer programs.
- Whereas Judaism indicates consideration for animals by prohibiting the yoking of a strong and weak animal together, veal calves spend their entire lives standing on slats, their necks chained to the sides, without sunlight, fresh air, or exercise.

Rabbi Aryeh Carmell, a 20th century Torah scholar in Jerusalem, stated: "It seems doubtful from all that has been said whether the Torah would sanction factory farming, which treats animals as machines, with apparent insensitivity to their natural needs and instincts. This is a matter for decision by *halachic* authorities."[9]

---

8. Harrison, *Animal Machines*, 3.
9. Carmell, Rabbi Aryeh, *Masterplan: Judaism – Its Programs, Meanings, Goals* (New York/Jerusalem: Feldheim, 1991), 69.

Rabbi David Rosen, former chief rabbi of Ireland, uses even stronger language: "The current treatment of animals in the livestock trade definitely renders the consumption of meat as *halachically* unacceptable as the product of illegitimate means."[10] He makes clear that he is not referring only to the production of veal and goose liver, the "most obvious and outrageous" examples of animal mistreatment, but also to common practices in the livestock trade, such as massive drug dosing and hormonal treatment.[11]

The vicious cycle of misery that results from our addiction to meat is powerfully described by C. David Coats in his book, *Old McDonald's Factory Farm*:

Aren't humans amazing? They kill wildlife – birds, deer, all kinds of cats, coyotes, beavers, groundhogs, mice and foxes by the million in order to protect their domestic animals and their feed.

Then they kill domestic animals by the billion and eat them. This in turn kills people by the million, because eating all those animals leads to degenerative – and fatal – health conditions like heart disease, stroke, kidney disease, and cancer. So then humans spend billions of dollars torturing and killing millions more animals to look for cures for these diseases.

Elsewhere, millions of other human beings are being killed by hunger and malnutrition because food they could eat is being used to fatten domestic animals.

Meanwhile, few people recognize the absurdity of humans, who kill so easily and violently, and once a year send out cards praying for "Peace on Earth."

In light of the horrible conditions under which most animals are raised today, Jews who eat meat raised under such conditions seem to be supporting a system contrary to basic Jewish principles and obligations. I believe that Jews should seriously consider becoming vegetarians, and preferably vegans, to be most consistent with basic Jewish teachings.

---

10. Rosen, Rabbi David, "Vegetarianism: An Orthodox Jewish Perspective," in *Rabbis and Vegetarianism: An Evolving Tradition*, Roberta Kalechofsky, ed. (Marblehead, MA: Micah Publications, 1995), 53.
11. *Ibid*, 54.

RESPONSES TO JUSTIFICATIONS FOR EATING MEAT

Many apologists for the exploitation of animals seek justification in Jewish scripture, but their analysis is largely based on a misunderstanding of two important Torah verses in Genesis that, when better understood, actually endorse the struggle to improve conditions for animals. The first misunderstanding is the common claim that the Torah teaching granting humans dominion over animals (Genesis 1:26, 28) gives us a warrant to treat them in whatever way we may wish. This interpretation is incorrect, as is demonstrated by the fact that immediately after God gave humankind dominion over animals (Genesis 1:26), He prescribed vegan foods as the diet best suited to humans (Genesis 1:29). This mandate is almost immediately followed by God's declaration that all of Creation was "very good" (Genesis 1:31).

Adam and Eve's original vegan diet was consistent with the kind and gentle stewardship that God entrusted to them and to all humankind. Another indication of the true message of "dominion" is the Torah verse that indicates God put Adam, the first human being, into the Garden of Eden "to work it and to guard it" (Genesis 2:15). To guard something implies that one must protect it, not exploit it. Based on these statements in Genesis, the Jewish sages saw human dominion as based on responsible and caring stewardship.

In support of this analysis, Rabbi Abraham Isaac Kook, Chief Rabbi of pre-state Israel and one of the outstanding Jewish thinkers of the twentieth century, stated in his booklet (edited by Rabbi David Cohen) "A Vision of Vegetarianism and Peace":

> There can be no doubt in the mind of any intelligent person that [the Divine empowerment of humanity to derive benefit from nature] does not mean the domination of a harsh ruler, who afflicts his people and servants merely to satisfy his whim and desire, according to the crookedness of his heart. It is unthinkable that the Divine Law would impose such a decree of servitude, sealed for all eternity, upon the world of God, Who is "good to all, and Whose compassion is upon all His works" (Psalms 145:9).

The second error the apologists for animal exploitation make is the presumption that the necessary implication of the Biblical teaching that only human beings are created "in the Divine Image" is that God places little or no value on animals. While the Torah does state that only human beings are created "in God's Image" (Genesis 1:27, 5:1), animals are also God's creatures, possessing sensitivity and the capacity for feeling pain. So the fact that humans are in a different spiritual category than animals does not give us the right to treat animals as mere objects or machines for our pleasure. God is concerned that they are protected and treated with compassion and justice. In fact, the Jewish sages state that to be "created in the Divine Image" means that people have the capacity to emulate the Divine compassion for all creatures. In his book, *The Vision of Eden: Animal Welfare and Vegetarianism in Jewish Law and Mysticism*, referring to the Talmudic teaching that we are to emulate God's ways, Rabbi David Sears states that "compassion for all creatures, including animals, is not only God's business; it is a virtue that we too must emulate. Moreover, compassion must not be viewed as an isolated phenomenon, one of a number of religious duties in the Judaic conception of the Divine service. It is central to our entire approach to life."

In his classic work *Ahavat Chesed* ("The Love of Kindness"), the revered Chofetz Chaim (Rabbi Yisrael Meir Kagan of Radin) discusses this teaching at length. He writes that whoever emulates the Divine love and compassion to all creatures "will bear the stamp of God on his person."

Some meat-eaters point to the biblical animal sacrifices as a justification for their eating meat today. But, according to Maimonides, the sacrifices were a concession to the primitive conditions in biblical times. Since sacrifices were the universal expression of religion in that period, if Moses had tried to eliminate them, his mission might have failed and Judaism might have disappeared. Instead, limitations were placed on sacrifices in Judaism: They were confined to one central location (instead of each family having a home altar), and the human sacrifices and other idolatrous practices of the neighboring pagan peoples were forbidden.

The prophets speak of sacrifices as an abomination to God if not carried out along with deeds of loving-kindness and justice. After the destruction of the Temple, the rabbis stated that prayer and good deeds should replace sacrifices in the absence of the designated site for burnt offerings, based on the statement from the prophet Hosea: "Take words and return to the Lord; instead of calves we will offer the words of our lips" (Hosea

14:2).[12] In the early 20th century, Rav Kook wrote that there will be only non-animal sacrifices, such as fruits and grains, in the Messianic period when the Temple is rebuilt (may it come speedily in our day!).

In addition, we should note that sacrificial animals had to be perfect specimens without any blemishes (Deuteronomy 17:1). This means they must have been treated very gently and kindly, to avoid causing any injuries that would have disqualified them for use in the Temple service. Given the horrendous conditions under which most meat animals are raised today, it is doubtful that any of them would qualify as sacrifices.

IS TODAY'S MEAT REALLY 'KOSHER'?

The kosher industry tends to focus only on the actual moment of slaughter, and the packing and preparation of the meat afterward. Very little, if any, attention is paid to how the animals are treated *before* slaughter. One has to wonder if this can be reconciled with *kashrut*, because *kashrut* is designed to be humane. But how can it be humane if most kosher meat, dairy, and eggs come from the same abominable factory farm conditions as does non-kosher food? Shouldn't we be concerned – indeed alarmed – about the ways that food is being produced?

In the past, farm animals ran free in pastures or open country, grazed on grass, and were slaughtered only for special occasions, such as when Abraham slaughtered a calf for his angelic guests. Chickens were hatched naturally under mother hens and usually eaten by Jews only on Shabbat and holidays – and then only after the birds had a life of freedom to scratch, peck, and live as a chicken was created to do. There was nothing remotely resembling the year-round factory farm conditions under which food animals are raised today. Therefore, although the Torah does permit eating meat, the conditions under which animals are raised today are a far cry from those for the flocks of our ancestors.

Given that Jews should be *rachmanim b'nei rachmanim* (compassionate

---

12. In Hebrew, the word *dvarim* means both "words" and "things." Hosea is therefore using a play on words that gets lost in translation: Instead of physical objects *(dvarim)*, one can bring verbal words *(dvarim)*. After the destruction of the Temple, reciting the passages about the sacrifices replaced the actual sacrifices themselves. To this day, the appropriate sacrificial passages are read as part of the Orthodox Jewish liturgy.

children of compassionate ancestors), can kosher consumers justify the cruelty of factory farms to mass-produce meat that we do not really need for nourishment? Can we justify the force-feeding of ducks and geese to create *pate de foie gras*? Can we justify taking day-old calves from their mothers so that they can be raised in very cramped conditions to be eaten as "tender" veal? Can we justify the killing of over 250 million male chicks in the U.S. alone immediately after birth at egg-laying hatcheries – a total waste of sentient animal life – because they cannot lay eggs and have not been genetically programmed to grow as much flesh as the meat-producing breeds? Can we justify artificially impregnating cows every year on what the industry calls "rape racks," so that they will be able to produce more milk? Or artificially inseminating turkeys to get fertile hatching eggs, because the birds have been bred to get so fat they can no longer mate naturally? Can we justify the many other ways that animals are unnecessarily exploited and mistreated in our society to meet consumer's claimed needs?

Another practice that raises questions about the modern treatment of animals is *Kapparos* (or *Kapparot*), a ritual performed annually by some Orthodox and Hasidic Jews between Rosh Hashanah and Yom Kippur. *Kapparos* involves waving a live chicken over the head of the participant and reciting a special prayer, after which the chicken is slaughtered and the meat donated to poor people. Unfortunately, the donations to the poor do not always occur today. As with kosher meat in general, the chickens for this ceremony now come from factory farms, often trucked in from miles away without any food or water – raising some serious questions about cruelty to animals. In his new book, *Kapporos Then and Now: Toward a More Compassionate Tradition*, Rabbi Yonassan Gershom discusses the origins of this ritual and the Kabbalistic meanings behind it. He comes to the conclusion that, while our ancestors were able to do it with the proper mystical focus (*kavannah*) and "raise the holy sparks" within the chickens, the cruelty involved in raising and transporting chickens under modern conditions cancels out the spiritual value of the ceremony. He therefore concludes that nowadays it is best to do *Kapparos* with the *halachically*-acceptable substitution of money instead of using a chicken.

ADDITIONAL ISSUES CONCERNING OUR
OBLIGATION OF COMPASSION TO ANIMALS

Is Wearing Fur Consistent with Jewish Teachings on Compassion for Animals?

Jewish worshipers chant every Sabbath morning "The soul of every living being shall praise God's name" (*Nishmat kol chai t'varech et shim'chah*). Yet, some people come to synagogue during winter months wearing coats that required the cruel treatment of some of those living beings whose souls, we declare, are praising God.

Should Jews wear fur? Several factors should be considered:

- What does the Jewish tradition teach about the treatment of animals? As discussed above, Judaism expresses very strong laws and attitudes on the proper treatment of animals.
- How much suffering do animals who are raised or trapped for their fur actually experience?
- Does the wearing of fur coats have any redeeming factors that would override Jewish teachings about the proper treatment of animals?

The Pain of Fur-Bearing Animals

Fur is obtained from animals who are either trapped or raised on ranches. Both methods involve violent and abusive treatment of animals, which are far from Jewish teachings on the dignity and sensibility of animals.[13]

Animals caught in steel-jaw leg traps suffer slow, agonizing deaths. Some are attacked by predators, while others often freeze to death or chew off their own legs to escape. It has been said that one can get a "feel for fur" by slamming your fingers with a car door.

Over 100 million wild animals are killed for their pelts every year. Many species of animals killed for their furs have become endangered or have disappeared completely in some localities. Millions of animals not wanted by trappers, including dogs, cats, and birds, die in traps annually

---

13. Many facts about the cruelty involved in producing fur garments can be found in "Truth About Fur," http://truthaboutfur.com/en/home?gclid=CjoKEQjwmqyq BRC7zKnO_f6iodcBEiQA9T996ENFD-m_W4968WsU5boxGhOKo-_WUujtOm 3_nb1Mad4aAj488P8HAQ

and are discarded as trash animals. Many trapped animals leave behind dependent offspring who are doomed to starvation.

Treatment of animals raised on "fur ranches" is also extremely cruel. Sentenced to lifelong confinement, millions of foxes, beavers, minks, ocelots, rabbits, chinchillas, and other animals await extinction with no stimulation, little room to move, and all their natural instincts thwarted. The animals are simply a means to the maximization of production and profit, without regard for their physical, mental, or emotional well-being. Unnatural confinement and lack of privacy cause wild animals to exhibit neurotic behaviors, such as compulsive movements and self-mutilation. In the end, they suffer hideous deaths by electrocution rods thrust up their anuses, by suffocation, by poisoning (which causes painful convulsions), or by having their necks broken.

According to the International Society for Animal Rights, Inc., to make one fur garment requires up to 400 squirrels, 240 ermine, 200 chinchillas, 120 muskrats, 80 sables, 50 martens, 30 raccoons, 22 bobcats, 12 lynx, or five wolves.

Is Wearing Fur Really Necessary?

Judaism puts human beings, uniquely created in the image of God, on a higher level than animals and specifies that animals may be harmed and even killed to meet an essential human need. However, is the wearing of fur truly necessary for people to stay warm during wintry weather? There are now many non-fur coats and hats, available in a variety of styles, that provide plenty of warmth and are much lighter and easier to care for than fur. As for style, imitation fur is produced at such a high level of quality that even among Hasidim there is a small but growing trend to wear synthetic *shtreimlach* (fur-trimmed hats).

Based on the prohibition of *tsa'ar ba'alei chayim*, Rabbi Chaim David Halevy, former Sephardic Chief Rabbi of Tel Aviv, issued a *p'sak* (rabbinic ruling) in March 1992 mandating that Jews should not wear fur.[14] Rabbi Halevy asked: "Why should people be allowed to kill animals if it is not necessary, simply because they desire the pleasure of having the beauty

---

14. Shmuly Yanklowitz, "The Religious Case Against Wearing Fur or Leather," *Jewish Journal*, January 26, 2015.

and warmth of fur coats? Is it not possible to achieve the same degree of warmth without fur?"

Inspired by Rabbi Halevy's prohibition and by Israel's strict laws against mistreating animals, there have been several attempts to pass a law in the Knesset banning the manufacturing of fur in Israel, with an exception for Hasidic *streimels* for religious reasons. Had this law passed, it would have made Israel the only country in the world with such a ban. However, the bill has been blocked so far, despite widespread support, possibly by Knesset members who felt that attempts to ban the production of meat would follow.[15]

Do we really need the Knesset to pass a law to tell us what is right? In his book, *The Jewish Encyclopedia of Moral and Ethical Issues*, Israeli author and educator Rabbi Nachum Amsel states: "If the only reason a person wears the fur coat is to 'show off' one's wealth or to be a mere fashion statement, that would be considered to be a frivolous and not a legitimate need." Rabbi Amsel also points out that hunting for sport is prohibited because it is not considered a legitimate need (based on *Avodah Zarah* 18b).

Rabbi Yona Metzger, former Ashkenazic chief rabbi of Israel, recently ruled against fur imports from China, where animals are often skinned alive.[16] There is a growing awareness of the many cruelties involved in producing fur. One has to wonder what kind of lesson young people are learning when they see worshippers arriving at the synagogue in fur coats on the Sabbath day. Instead of reinforcing the many beautiful Jewish teachings about compassion to animals, we are teaching them that expensive status symbols and conspicuous consumption are more important than respect for God's creatures.

If there was a reduction in the wearing of fur, not only would tens of thousands of animals benefit from our compassion and concern – we, too, would benefit by becoming more sensitive and more humane Jews and civilized human beings. We would be setting an example for the rest of the world that says there is no beauty in cruelty.

---

15. Marilyn Kretzer, "Are Dirty Politics Holding Up Ban On Fur in Israel?" PETA, May 5, 2015.

16. "Rabbi Yona Metzger says no to fur," *Orthomom*, February 20, 2007.

Animal Experimentation

Because Judaism puts a higher priority on human life than on animal life, it is not, in principle, opposed to all uses of animals if there are significant benefits for humans that could not be obtained in any other way. But results from animal experiments should generally be viewed with some skepticism for the following reasons:[17]

- It is difficult to gain insight into a human disease by studying an artificially-induced pathology in animals, no matter how superficially similar the two may seem.

- Because of differences between species, studies conducted on animals cannot always reliably be extrapolated to humans. Many times, animals react to medicines differently than people. Aspirin, for example, is poisonous to cats. There is an ever-growing list of drugs deemed safe after very extensive animal testing, which later are proven to be carcinogenic, mutagenic (causing birth defects), or toxic to humans. Guinea pigs generally die when given penicillin; aspirin causes birth defects in rats and mice, but not in people; thalidomide was helpful when tested on laboratory animal, but causes birth defects in people; and insulin causes deformities in laboratory animals, but not with people.

- Contrary to the beliefs of most people, including supporters of animal experimentation, key discoveries in such areas as heart disease and cancer were achieved through clinical research, observations of patients, and human autopsy, *not* through animal testing. The greatest medical advancements were the result of improved hygienic approaches. Animal tests gave results that, at best, paralleled previous findings in humans.

- Misleading animal test results can sometimes be devastating for human health. In a number of cases, effective therapies were delayed because of misleading animal models. For example, the animal model for polio resulted in a misunderstanding of the mechanism of infection, delaying the discovery of a vaccine.

- Reliance on animal experiments and transplants from animals keeps people from considering their basic responsibility for their own health. If the billions of dollars spent on animal experimentation were instead spent on educating people about better nutrition and other positive

---

17. Many facts about animal experimentation can be found at "11 Facts About Animal Testing," https://www.dosomething.org/facts/11-facts-about-animal-testing

lifestyle changes, there would be far greater benefits for human health. Of course there are other factors that affect humans' health – including genetics – that are beyond people's control, but lifestyle changes can make major differences in many cases.

Perhaps because of the above factors, animal experimentation has produced relatively little progress in many areas of medicine. Despite (or perhaps because of) relying heavily on extensive animal experimentation for medical advancement, health costs in the U.S. have been soaring in recent years, which has led to major budgetary problems in many cities and states and nationally, with the result that spending for many other human needs has had to be reduced. Health expenditures have been increasing more rapidly than any other element of the federal budget; total health costs grew from 6% of total GDP in 1960 to 17% in 2013, and are still rising.[18]

THE QUESTION OF NECESSITY – AGAIN

Many laboratory experiments on animals are completely unnecessary. Must we force dogs to smoke to reconfirm the health hazards of cigarettes? Do we have to starve dogs and monkeys to understand human starvation? Do we need to cut, blind, burn, and chemically destroy animals to produce another type of lipstick, mascara, or shampoo?

A reduction in animal experiments would not mean that experiments have to be done on people. Healthier lifestyles would avoid the need for many experiments. Many alternative approaches to advancing medical knowledge have been developed that are often more accurate and cost effective. These include epidemiological studies, computer and mathematical models, genetic research, cell and tissue cultures, stem cell research, clinical pharmacology, diagnostic imaging (MRI, CAT, and PET scans), and autopsies.

Human health can best be advanced by improvements in hygiene, better diets and other lifestyle changes, and through clinical studies. As the poet Alexander Pope put it, "The proper study of mankind is man."

---

18. "Health expenditures, Total (% of GDP), World Bank, http://data.worldbank.or g/indicator/SH.XPD.TOTL.ZS

HUNTING AND OTHER BLOOD SPORTS

Throughout the ages, rabbis have strongly disapproved of hunting as a sport. A Jew is permitted to capture animals only for purposes of human food, or for what is considered an essential human need. But to destroy an animal for "sport" constitutes wanton destruction and is to be condemned. Based on the statement "not to stand in the way of sinners" (Psalms 1:1), the Talmud prohibits association with recreational hunters (*Avodah Zarah* 18b). A query was addressed to Rabbi Yechezkel Landau (1713–1793) by a man wishing to know if he could hunt in his large estate, which included forests and fields. Rabbi Landau's response in his classic collection of *responsa Nodah b'Yehudahis* follows:

> In the Torah the sport of hunting is imputed only to fierce characters like Nimrod and Esau, never to any of the patriarchs and their descendants . . . I cannot comprehend how a Jew could even dream of killing animals merely for the pleasure of hunting . . . When sport prompts killing, it is downright cruelty.   (*Yore Deah*, Second Series, 10)

It should be noted that meat from animals killed by hunting with a gun or bow would not be considered kosher, and would therefore be a violation of *bal tashchit*, the prohibition against unnecessary destruction or waste. Because Judaism opposes any cruel treatment of animals, it also looks unfavorably on rodeos, animal fighting events, fishing contests, dog racing, and the use of animals in circuses, because the animals are often mistreated while being trained for their acts.

HORSE RACING

Like many other industries involving animals, the racing industry is built on the exploitation of animals, with cruelty and abuse common. While horse racing currently exists in Israel only in a very small way, there are plans to expand the races to involve as many as 2,000 horses and to initiate gambling on the races. The group Concern for Helping Animals in Israel (CHAI) is working to educate lawmakers, and also the public, about current horse abuse in Israel and how it will be multiplied manifold if gambling on racing is legalized. CHAI stresses that in England and the

United States, when gambling is involved, the welfare of the horses is sacrificed.

Nina Natelson, founder and director of CHAI, summarized the cruelty involved in horse racing in a personal email to me:

> Thousands of horses are bred annually, but only the few fastest are chosen to race, with most of the rest sent to the slaughterhouse. Trained and raced by age two, before their bones have hardened, they often incur catastrophic injuries. Pushed beyond their limits, they suffer bleeding in the lungs, which can be fatal, and chronic ulcers. They are drugged to improve performance and so they can race even while injured, which worsens the injury. Corruption is inherent in this industry based on greed, so, for example, the legs of horses not fast enough to win have been broken to collect on insurance policies. When they are too old to possibly win, at around six (though their natural lifespan is around 25), even champions are often sent to the slaughterhouse or sold into a downward spiral of abuse. The U.S. Congress held hearings on the industry due to the high level of breakdowns and deaths in training and on the track. At the hearings, industry leaders admitted that the industry could not police itself and asked the government to start policing for illegal drug use and other corrupt practices.

On July 30, 2006, Rabbi Shlomo Amar, the Sephardic Chief Rabbi of Israel, issued a *p'sak halachah* (rabbinical ruling) against horse racing. The ruling concludes: "It seems self-evident that one ought . . . not to participate in horse-races – neither in establishing them, nor by watching them: because of the pain to animals caused thereby, because it is 'a dwelling place of scoffers,' and because it is 'playing with dice' (the Talmudic term for gambling)."[19] Among the reasons the Chief Rabbi cited for his conclusion:

- Racing involves the premature death of many horses, and this violates the Jewish law against wanton destruction.
- Horse slaughter would create a risk that horsemeat would be sold in Israel, violating Jewish law.

---

19. "Ruling of Chief Rabbi of Israel Against Racing," report from 'Concern for Helping Animals in Israel,' http://www.chai.org.il/en/campaigns/racing/campaigns_racin g_psak.htm

- Whoever shows compassion is shown compassion by God.
- Using horses for racing is unnecessary; it involves cruelty, and is conducted only for the purpose of making some rich people richer; therefore it is prohibited.
- Judaism discourages gambling because it enriches one person at the expense of another.

RESTORING AND TRANSFORMING THE ANCIENT NEW YEAR FOR ANIMALS

As discussed above, Judaism mandates that animals be treated kindly. It is essential that this message be spread and put into practice in order to help create a society more consistent with Jewish values, and to help end the horrendous conditions under which so many animals currently suffer. Because of the wide disparities between Judaism's powerful teachings on compassion to animals and the horrible ways that animals are mistreated on factory farms and other settings, Jewish Veg (formerly known as Jewish Vegetarians of North America), of which I am president emeritus, has worked with a coalition of Jewish groups and individuals to restore and transform the ancient and largely forgotten Jewish holiday of *Rosh Hashana LaBeheimot* (New Year's Day for Tithing Animals for sacrifices when the Jerusalem Temple stood) into a day devoted to increasing awareness of Judaism's beautiful teachings on compassion to animals and how far current realities for animals is from these teachings.

Many religious Jews are properly diligent in "building fences" around some *mitzvot*. For example, there is great care on the part of religious Jews to fulfill the laws related to removing *chametz* before Passover. But other *mitzvot*, including *tsa'ar ba'alei chaim*, are often downplayed or ignored. Perhaps this is not surprising when one considers that with regard to animals the primary focus of Jewish religious services, Torah readings, and education is on the biblical sacrifices, animals that are kosher for eating, and laws about animal slaughter, with relatively little time devoted to Judaism's more compassionate teachings. It is essential that this emphasis on the killing and sacrifice of animals be balanced with a greater consideration of Judaism's more compassionate teachings about animals. Hence the need to restore and transform the ancient, long forgotten holiday.

There is a precedent for the restoration and transformation of a holiday in Jewish History. *Rosh Hashanah Lailanot,* a day initially intended for tithing fruit trees for Temple offerings, was reclaimed in the 17th Century by mystics in Sefat, Israel, as a day for celebrating nature's bounty and healing the natural world. Many Jews now regard this increasingly popular holiday, Tu B'Shvat, as an unofficial "Jewish Earth Day."

It is hoped that the transformed New Year for Animals will also serve as a *tikkun* (healing or repair) for the current widespread mistreatment of animals previously discussed in this chapter. Awareness about *tsa'ar ba'alei chaim* is even more important because animal-based diets and agriculture are significantly contributing to many diseases that are afflicting Jewish and other communities, as well as climate change and other environmental problems that threaten all life on the planet. A major shift to plant-based diets is essential to help shift our precious, but imperiled, planet to a sustainable path. In addition, as discussed in more detail in the next chapter, the production and consumption of meat and other animal products arguably violate Jewish mandates to preserve human health, treat animals with compassion, protect the environment, conserve natural resources, and help hungry people.

Restoring the New Year for Animals would have many additional benefits, including (1) showing the relevance of Judaism's eternal teachings to today's critical issues, (2) improving the image of Judaism for many people by showing its compassionate side, and (3) attracting disaffected Jews through reestablishing a holiday that they find relevant and meaningful. *Rosh Hashanah LaBeheimot* occurs on Rosh Chodesh Elul, the first day of the Hebrew month of Elul, one Hebrew month before Rosh Hashanah. Since Rosh Chodesh Elul ushers in a month-long period of introspection, during which Jews are to examine their deeds and consider how to improve their words and actions before the holidays of Rosh Hashanah and Yom Kippur, this is an ideal time for Jews to consider how to apply Judaism's splendid teachings on compassion to animals to reduce the current massive mistreatment of animals on factory farms and in other settings.[20]

---

20. I have four articles on this initiative at a special section at www.JewishVeg.com/schwartz.

Chapter 13

Should Jews Be Vegetarians – or Even Vegans?

And God said, "Behold, I have given you every herb bearing seed, which is upon the face of the earth, and every fruit tree yielding seed; to you it shall be for food . . ."

– GENESIS 1:29

*T*he dietary laws are designed to teach us compassion and to lead us gently to vegetarianism.

– RABBI SHLOMO RISKIN, CHIEF RABBI OF EFRAT, ISRAEL

*W*hat was the necessity for the entire procedure of ritual slaughter? For the sake of self-discipline. It is far more appropriate for man not to eat meat; only if he has a strong desire for meat does the Torah permit it, and even this only after the trouble and inconvenience necessary to satisfy his desire. Perhaps because of the bother and annoyance of the whole procedure, he will be restrained from such a strong and uncontrollable desire for meat.

– RABBI SOLOMON EFRAIM LUNCHITZ
IN HIS WORK KLI YAKAR

AS A VEGETARIAN AND later a vegan activist in the Jewish community for about 35 years, I believe it is essential that Jews consider how plant-based diets are most consistent with basic Jewish teachings. Plant-based diets can improve the health of Jews and others, can help stabilize the world's climate, and can help reduce human hunger and environmental dangers. I hope this chapter starts a respectful dialogue about if Jews should be vegetarians, or even vegans. I think such a dialogue would be a *kiddush Hashem* (a sanctification of God's name), since it would help make Jews (and others) aware of the many benefits of non-meat diets, and how they can assist in creating healthier people and a healthier planet. Widespread discussions of the many moral issues related to our diets can also help revitalize Judaism by showing the relevance of eternal Jewish teachings to our most critical problems.

SIX WAYS THAT ANIMAL-BASED DIETS VIOLATE BASIC JEWISH TEACHINGS

As I have been arguing for many years, animal-based diets conflict with basic Jewish values in at least six important areas:

- While Judaism mandates that people should be very careful about preserving their health and their lives, *"v'nish-martem me'od l'nafsho-te-ichem"* (Deuteronomy 4:9), numerous scientific studies have linked animal-based diets directly to heart disease, stroke, cancer, and other chronic, degenerative diseases.
- Even though Judaism forbids *tsa'ar ba'alei chayim*, inflicting unnecessary pain on animals, animals are raised on "factory farms" where they live in cramped, confined spaces. They are often drugged, mutilated, and denied fresh air, sunlight, exercise, and any enjoyment of life before they are consumed.
- While Judaism teaches that "the earth is the Lord's" (Psalm 24:1) and that we are to be God's partners and co-workers in preserving the world, modern livestock agriculture contributes to climate change, soil erosion and depletion, air and water pollution, overuse of chemical fertilizers and pesticides, destruction of tropical rainforests and other habitats, and other forms of environmental destruction far more than plant-based agriculture.
- While Judaism mandates *bal tashchit*, that we are not to waste or unnecessarily destroy anything of value nor use more than is needed to accomplish a purpose, the production of animal-source protein is built on an extremely wasteful pyramid of resources (compared to plant protein production): overuse and waste of feed, land, fresh water, energy (most of it "dirty"), and other resources. For example, it takes up to thirteen times more water to produce food for a person on an animal-based diet than for a person on a plant-based diet, largely because of the huge amounts of water needed to irrigate feed crops.

- While Judaism stresses that we are to provide for the poor and share our bread with the hungry, over 70% of the grain grown in the United States is inefficiently funneled through animals to produce meat, milk, and eggs, while millions of people worldwide die each year from hunger and its effects. If we produced fewer animals and ate more "bread" ourselves (grains and beans, fruits and vegetables), we could share so much more of the loaf with the world's nearly one billion chronically hungry people.

- While Judaism teaches that we must seek and pursue peace – and that violence can result from unjust conditions – diets high in animal protein monopolize resources, creating a shortage of affordable land, food, water, and energy for the poor, especially in the underdeveloped world. This exacerbates the tension between haves and have-nots and often produces social unrest, violence, and war.

One could say *dayenu* (it would be enough) after any one of these arguments. Each one by itself constitutes a serious conflict between Jewish values and current practices that should encourage every conscientious Jew to seriously consider adopting a plant-based diet. Combined, they make an even more compelling ethical case.

Animal-centered diets violate and contradict each of these important Jewish mandates: to preserve human health, to attend to the welfare of animals, to protect the environment, to conserve resources, to help feed the hungry, and to pursue peace. Therefore, it would seem to be an important mitzvah for committed Jews (and others) to replace as much of the animal food in their diets as they can with nutritionally superior plant alternatives: tofu, stir fried vegetables, veggie burgers, beans, chick pea curries, lush salads, and a variety of fruit, nuts, and seeds. These arguments are presented in more detail in my book *Judaism and Vegetarianism* and my over 200 articles and 25 podcasts of my talks and interviews, all of which are online at www.JewishVeg.com/Schwartz.

THE POWERFUL VEGETARIAN TEACHINGS
OF RABBI DAVID ROSEN

The powerful, challenging words about vegetarianism of Rabbi David Rosen, former chief rabbi of Ireland, can make a major difference. (They can all be found in the book, *Rabbis and Vegetarianism*, edited by Roberta Kalechofsky.)

As it is halachically prohibited to harm oneself and as healthy, nutritious vegetarian alternatives are easily available, meat consumption has become halachically unjustifiable [contrary to Jewish law]. . . . the current treatment of animals in the livestock trade definitely renders the consumption of meat as halachically unacceptable as the product of illegitimate means.

Indeed a central precept regarding the relationship between humans and animals in halacha [Jewish law] is the prohibition against causing cruelty to animals, *tsa'ar ba'alei chayim*. As mentioned, practices in the livestock trade today constitute a flagrant violation of this prohibition. I refer not only to the most obvious and outrageous of these, such as the production of veal and goose liver, but also to common practices in the livestock trade, such as hormonal treatment and massive drug dosing.

Aside from the fact that both the original Garden of Eden and the Messianic vision of the future reflect the vegetarian ideal in Judaism, it is of course such a dietary lifestyle that is most consonant with the goal and purpose of Torah to maximize our awareness, appreciation, and sensitivity to the Divine Presence in the world. It is therefore only natural for us to affirm – as did Rav Kook (Kuk), the first Ashkenazi Chief Rabbi in [pre-state] Israel – that a redeemed world must perforce be a vegetarian world.

Today not only are we able to enjoy a healthy balanced vegetarian diet as perhaps never before, and not only are there in fact the above mentioned compelling halachic reasons for not eating meat, but above all, if we strive for that which Judaism aspires to – namely the ennoblement of the spirit – then a vegetarian diet becomes a moral imperative . . . [an] authentic Jewish ethical dietary way of life for our time and for all times.

. . . [E]vidently the more sensitive and respectful we are toward' God's Creation, in particular God's creatures, the more respectful and reverential we actually are towards God.

Indeed, Judaism, as a way of life, seeks to inculcate in us a consciousness of the Divine Presence in the World, and respect for life accordingly. The more we care for life, the closer we are in fact to God.

Accordingly, an ethical vegetarian way of life expresses the most sublime and noble values and aspirations of Judaism itself, bringing us to an ideal vision for society as a whole. Is it anything less than a *chillul Hashem* (desecration of God's Name) to declare veal for example, which is produced through wanton human cruelty to a calf to be kosher, simply because at points "Y" and "Z" the animal was slaughtered and prepared in accordance with halachic dictates, after the commandments affecting human responsibility towards animal life have been desecrated from points "A" to "X". . . . Today's concept of kashrut is more permeated with crass indulgence and economic exploitation than the ennoblement of the human spirit that our sages declare to be its purpose. Today as never before, the cruelty in the livestock trade renders meat eating and true kashrut incompatible . . .

Having such a distinguished Israeli Orthodox rabbi strongly arguing that eating meat today is halachically unjustifiable provides a very valuable message that should no longer be generally ignored.

IMAGINING A VEGAN WORLD

The late Senator Robert Kennedy often said, "Some see things as they are and ask why. I dream of things that never were and ask why not." So yes, why not? Why not a vegetarian world? Or even better, since we are dreaming after all, why not a vegan world? When one considers all the harm that comes from the current widespread production and consumption of animal products, it is hard to believe that many more people have not recognized the importance of moving toward such a world. So let us imagine what a vegan world would be like.

It would be a world with far healthier people.[1] Numerous studies show that plant-based diets can sharply reduce the risk factors for heart disease, various types of cancer, strokes, and other chronic degenerative diseases.

---

1. An excellent book on the health benefits of plant based diets is *The China Study* by Colin Campbell, Ph.D. Professor Campbell was the lead investigator for the Cornell, Oxford, China Study, the 'grand prix of epidemiology,' according to the New Your Times, the world's largest epidemiological study, which showed the many benefits of plant-based diets.

Dr. Dean Ornish, Dr. Caldwell Esselstyn, and others have shown that a well-planned vegan diet, along with other positive lifestyle changes, can reverse severe heart-related problems. Currently about 1.3 million Americans die annually from diseases linked to the consumption of animal products. This number would be sharply reduced when people eat a wide variety of foods from what the Physicians Committee for Responsible Medicine (PCRM) calls the "New Four Food Groups": fruits, vegetables, whole grains, and legumes.

It would be a far more humane world.[2] We could eliminate the current abuse of the nine billion animals in the United States and 70 billion animals worldwide raised annually for slaughter. Animals would no longer be bred and genetically programmed to produce far more flesh, milk, and eggs than is natural. The many horrors of factory farming, including the force-feeding of geese, de-beaking of hens, and branding, dehorning, and castrating of cattle would be eliminated. We would no longer need to feel shame when considering Gandhi's statement: "The greatness of a nation and its moral progress can be judged by how its animals are treated."

It would be an environmentally sustainable world. If we were no longer raising 70 billion farmed animals worldwide annually for slaughter, most under very cruel conditions, there would be a sharp reduction in the current significant contributions that modern intensive livestock agriculture makes toward a wide variety of environmental crises: global climate change; rapid species extinction; soil erosion and depletion; massive pollution of land, water, and air; destruction of tropical rain forests, coral reefs, and other valuable habitats; desertification; and other ecological disasters.

Without the need to feed so many animals, we could let land lie fallow on a rotating basis, and thus restore its fertility. There would be far less need for pesticides and chemical fertilizers to produce feed crops for animals. Of course, changes would also have to be made in our production, transportation, and other systems to improve the environment as much as possible, but the shift to veganism would be a major step.

---

2. The horrible ways animals are treated on factory farms was discussed in the previous chapter.

It would be a world where hunger and thirst would be sharply reduced, if not eliminated. When we no longer feed 70% of the grain grown in the U.S. and 40% of the grain grown worldwide to animals destined for slaughter, using vast amounts of agricultural resources to do so, we will have the potential to reduce hunger for the almost one billion of the world's people who are severely malnourished. We will also have the potential to save the lives of many of the millions of people who currently die annually of hunger and its effects. When we shift away from current animal-centered diets that require up to 13 times more water to produce the food per person than vegan diets do, we can help reverse current trends that have been leading to an increasingly thirsty world. Also, since current typical diets require large amounts of energy, a shift to vegan diets and other positive choices would reduce energy drain, and give us more time to develop sustainable forms of energy.

It would be a far more peaceful world. Some may question this point, but please consider that the slogans of the vegetarian and peace movements could be the same: "All we are saying is give PEAS a chance." More seriously, the Jewish sages, noting that the Hebrew words for bread (*lechem*) and war (*milchamah*) come from the same root, deduced that when there are shortages of grain and other resources, people are more likely to go to war. History has verified this many times. Therefore, a vegan world, in which far less water, land, energy, and other resources are required for our diets, would reduce the potential for war and other conflicts.

Creating a vegan world may sound utopian today when so much meat is consumed in the developed world and as newly affluent people in several countries and areas, including China, India, South America, and South Asia shift toward animal-centered diets. However, our current dietary and other practices threaten major catastrophes for humanity because of climate change, loss of biodiversity, water and food shortages, and other threats that are worsened by producing animal based foods. Therefore, it is essential that we alert people to the necessity of moving toward a vegan diet. Fortunately, there has been about a 10% decrease in meat consumption in the last decade in the U.S.

As the song from the musical *South Pacific* says, "You gotta have a dream. If you don't have a dream, how you gonna have a dream come true?" So it is essential that we keep the dream of a vegan world alive. And as the Zionist leader Theodore Herzl famously said, "If you will it, it is no dream." So, we must do more than just dream; we must work diligently to make that dream come true.

WHY IT IS FAR EASIER TO BE A VEGETARIAN OR VEGAN TODAY

Being a vegetarian or vegan is far more acceptable today. While in the past, people wondered why someone would adopt such a diet, there is more recognition of the mistreatment of animals and of the health and other benefits of plant-based diets. Upon learning that a person has such a diet, people today often defensively respond "I now eat less meat," or "I only eat meat from animals raised humanely," or "I do not eat red meat."

There are far more resources today for vegetarians and vegans, including a wide variety of books, recipes, videos and other informative sources on the Internet. As indicated in Appendix C, there are now very active Jewish vegetarian/vegan groups in the U.S., the U.K., Israel, and other countries.

Under the leadership of its new executive director Jeffrey Cohan, Jewish Vegetarians of North America (JVNA) – renamed Jewish Veg in 2015 to reflect that promoting veganism is part of the organization's mission – has become very active recently, with a new board of directors, rabbinic council, advisory council, a website (www.JewishVeg.org), and the creative use of a Facebook page and other social media. Similar increased vegetarian activism has recently occurred in the U.K., under the direction of Lara Smallman, and in Israel, under coordinator Yossi Wolfson. In addition, I have over 200 veg-related articles, 25 podcasts of my talks and interviews, and the complete text of the third edition of my book, *Judaism and Vegetarianism*, at www.JewishVeg.com/schwartz. Hopefully, all these resources will continue the momentum of Jews toward vegetarian and vegan diets.

HOW A SWITCH TO VEGANISM CAN HELP STABILIZE THE CLIMATE

Much has been written about the many health benefits of a vegetarian diet and how shifts away from animal-based diets would reduce animal suffering. One area, however, has been largely neglected in the public debate: the impact of animal-based diets on the environment and their contribution to climate change.

As discussed in Chapter 11, climate change is a major threat to the kind of world we just envisioned above. Because of the attention focused by Al Gore and others, climate change is now on people's minds, but the many connections between typical American (and other Western) diets and climate change have generally been overlooked. Even Al Gore himself missed this important point when he produced his award-winning film, *An Inconvenient Truth*. (Since then he has seen the light and become a vegan.) So let's examine how a major switch to plant-based diets can play a significant role in stabilizing climate.

Current modern intensive livestock agriculture, even on small farms, and the consumption of meat and other animal products greatly contribute to the four major gases associated with the greenhouse effect: carbon dioxide, methane, nitrous oxides, and chlorofluorocarbons. The burning of tropical forests to create grazing land or land to grow feed crops releases tons of carbon dioxide into the atmosphere and destroys the trees that can absorb much carbon dioxide and release oxygen. In effect, trees are the lungs of our planet. Yet these forests are being cut down or burned on every continent to help the livestock industry.

The highly mechanized agricultural sector, much of which is devoted to producing feed for food animals, uses enormous amounts of fossil fuel to produce pesticides, chemical fertilizer, and other agricultural resources, as well as to transport the animals and their products. Operating the tractors, trucks, and other equipment used to produce feed also contributes to carbon dioxide emissions. The large amounts of petrochemical fertilizers used to produce feed crops create significant quantities of nitrous oxides, a very potent greenhouse gas. In addition, the increased refrigeration necessary to prevent animal products from spoiling adds more chlorofluorocarbons to the atmosphere, which contributes to the destruction of the Earth's ozone layer.

"LIVESTOCK'S LONG SHADOW" – THE POWER OF OUR FOOD CHOICES TO REDUCE CLIMATE CHANGE

Most global warming discussions over the past 20 years have focused on implementing changes in energy use, but have given little attention to the impact of our diets. This trend began to change upon publication of a landmark 2006 report by the United Nations Food and Agricultural

Organization (FAO), "Livestock's Long Shadow."[3] The report estimated that, globally, livestock production is responsible for more greenhouse gas emissions (GHGs) in CO_2 equivalents than is emitted by all the world's cars, planes, ships, and all other means of transportation combined. The FAO report projected that the world's current annual consumption of about 70 billion farmed animals will double by mid-century, if human population growth and dietary trends continue. The resulting increase in GHGs would largely negate reduced GHG emissions from all conservation and improved efficiencies in transportation, electricity, and other sectors. This could make it extremely difficult, if not impossible, to reach the GHG reductions that climate experts believe essential to avoid a climate disaster. In view of the above, it is troubling that in the face of livestock's major role in warming the planet, many countries continue to encourage expanded consumption of animal products.

More recently, an in-depth analysis called "Livestock and Climate Change" by World Bank Group environmental specialists Robert Goodland and Jeff Anhang appeared in the November/December 2009 issue of *World Watch* magazine.[4] The authors found sources of GHGs from the livestock sector that were overlooked, underrepresented, or placed in the wrong sectors in the FAO report, and concluded that the livestock sector is responsible for *at least 51%* of all human-induced GHGs.

A major reason that animal-based agriculture is such a major contributor to climate change is that methane emitted by cows and other animals is far more potent per molecule than CO_2 in warming the atmosphere – 23 times as potent in the standard 100 year reference periods. But since methane is only in the atmosphere for about twenty years, it is actually from 72 to 105 times as potent during that period. Leading climate experts have focused increasingly on the role of food production in causing global warming, pointing out that there is no more powerful environmental action that any individual can take than adopting a plant-based diet.

In the fall of 2008, Dr. Rajendra Pachauri, chair of the Inter-governmental Panel on Climate Change, which shared the Nobel Peace Prize with Al

---

3. Livestock's Long Shadow," UN Food and Agriculture Organization (FAO), Rome, 2006. http://www.fao.org/docrep/010/a0701e/a0701e00.HTM

4. Robert Goodland and Jeff Anhang, "Livestock and Climate Change," Worldwatch Institute, June 21, 2015.

Gore in 2007, called on people in the developed world to "give up meat for one day [a week] initially, and decrease [meat consumption] from there."[5] NASA's James Hansen, perhaps the most prominent scientific advocate of aggressive action to combat global warming, told an interviewer, "If you eat further down on the food chain rather than eating animals, which have produced many greenhouse gases and used much energy in the process of growing that meat, you can actually make a bigger contribution in that way than just about anything. So, that, in terms of individual action, is perhaps the best thing you can do."[6]

More recently, economist Lord Nicholas Stern, author of the British government-commissioned *Stern Review on the Economics of Climate Change*, declared that people need to shift toward plant-based diets if the world is to conquer climate change. "Meat is a wasteful use of water and creates a lot of greenhouse gases," the economist told *The Times of London*. "It puts enormous pressure on the world's resources. A vegetarian diet is better."[7]

CONCLUSION

The aims of vegans and environmentalists are very similar: to simplify our lifestyles, show regard for the earth and all forms of life, and apply the awareness that "the earth is the Lord's." In view of the many negative effects of animal-based agriculture on the earth's environment, resources, and climate, it is becoming increasingly clear that a shift toward vegan diets is imperative to move our precious but imperiled planet away from its present catastrophic path.

Jews constitute only a small percentage of the world's population, but we have powerful environmental teachings that can make a major difference if properly applied. It is imperative that Jews strive to be "a light unto the nations" and to work for *tikkun olam* – the healing and repair of our unjust and endangered world. This mission must include lightening

---

5. Juliette Jowit, "UN says eat less meat to curb global warming," *The Observer*, September 6, 2008.

6. Amanda Radke, "Why Ranchers Should Care About the Documentary 'Cowspiracy,'" BEEF Daily, July 21, 2014.

7. David Batty and David Adam, "Vegetarianism is better for the planet, says Lord Stern," *The Guardian*, October 26, 2009.

the immense burden of human diets on animals, the environment, and the world's poor and hungry. To do so is to demonstrate the relevance of Judaism's eternal teachings to the problems of the world today. It is urgent that Jews lead efforts to respectfully convince people to begin making the necessary changes before it is too late.

Chapter 14

How Can Prayer Inspire Activism?

$\mathcal{P}$rayer is meaningless unless it is subversive, unless it seeks to overthrow and to ruin the pyramids of callousness, hatred, opportunism, and falsehoods. The liturgical movement must become a revolutionary movement, seeking to overthrow the forces that continue to destroy the promise, the hope, the vision.

– RABBI ABRAHAM JOSHUA HESCHEL[1]

BASED ON RABBI HESCHEL'S challenging statement above, prayers should help transform people and inspire them to actively strive to create a more humane, compassionate, just, peaceful, and environmentally sustainable world. But unfortunately the opposite is often the case.

A study published in 2005 by the Pew Forum on Religion and Public Life found that while Jews generally are more liberal than any other American religious group, there are significant differences between Jews who regularly attend religious services and those who do not. The study found that Jews who attend synagogue services at least once a week were twice as likely to support the war in Iraq and define themselves as politically conservative than were Jews who seldom or never go to synagogue.[2]

I have been a member of my Orthodox synagogue since 1968. My experiences there have been the most important in shaping my views

---

1. Rabbi Abraham Joshua Heschel. Quoted in "On Prayer," in *Moral Grandeur and Spiritual Audacity,* Susannah Heschel, ed. (New York: Farrar Straus Giroux, 1996), 257.
2. Ori Nir, "U.S. poll: Synagogue-goers more likely to be politically conservative." *Haaretz,* February 7, 2005.

about the failure of synagogue services to inspire people to become more actively involved in relating Jewish values to society's ills. I appreciate the many prayer leaders for their great skill and dedication to keep the *minyanim* (prayer groups) moving along without a hitch. Day by day, week by week, the services are carried out very well. But as for the long-range goals of preserving our planet, feeding its people, and ending its wars, there is little awareness or efforts to connect the powerful messages in the prayers to current issues.

As I attend Shabbat services in my modern Orthodox synagogue, I often think about the tremendous collective wisdom, skills, and generosity among the hundreds of *daveners* (worshippers), and what an important impact their abilities and positive traits could achieve if addressed toward climate change – the most urgent, immediate problem facing the world today – as well as other critical societal threats. I believe that God would welcome that kind of involvement along with, and inspired by, our prayers. But the *davening* does not seem to impel worshippers to apply the challenging words of the prayers toward improving the precious world that God has given us.

Of course I am not recommending that Jews (or others) attend religious services less often. Rather, I would like to see them try to apply the lessons contained in the *siddur* (prayer book) about God's compassion and other ideals into their practical and communal lives.

SOME SHABBAT MORNING PRAYERS THAT ADDRESS THE ENVIRONMENT AND ANIMALS

The Shabbat morning prayers remind us of Judaism's tremendous concern for the environment and for animals, both of which have many implications for activism. If we would only heed the messages of the prayers we recite, they would be a spur to action that would help revitalize Judaism and ultimately help shift our world from its current dangerous path.

For example, in the *Baruch Sheh'amar* prayer the *siddur* says: "Blessed is the One (God) Who has compassion on the earth; blessed is the One Who has compassion on the creatures [animals and people]." What a far better world it would be if, consistent with the key Talmudic principle that we are to imitate God's qualities, more Jews understood that these statements in the *siddur* obligate us to help feed the hungry, protect the environment, and work to end the current widespread mistreatment of people and animals.

In the Shabbat services, God is called *Rachum* (the Merciful One) and *Av Ha-Rachamim* (Father of Mercies). Since we are to imitate God, we too should be merciful. The Talmud states that Jews are to be *rachmanim b'nai rachmanim* (compassionate children of compassionate ancestors), and that one who is not compassionate cannot truly be of the seed of Abraham, our father (*Bezah* 32b). It also states that Heaven grants compassion to those who are compassionate to others, and withholds it from those who are not (*Shabbat* 151b).

In the important *Ashrei* (Psalm 145), recited twice during every morning service, the Psalmist states (verse 9) that "God is good to all, and God's mercies are over all of God's works [including both people and animals]." According to Rabbi Dovid Sears in his book *The Vision of Eden: Animal Welfare and Vegetarianism in Jewish Law and Mysticism*, this verse is "the touchstone of the rabbinic attitude toward animal welfare, appearing in a number of contexts in Torah literature." Referring to the Talmudic teaching that we are to emulate God's ways, he states, "Therefore, compassion for all creatures, including animals, is not only God's business; it is a virtue that we too must emulate. Moreover, compassion must not be viewed as an isolated phenomenon, one of a number of religious duties in the Judaic conception of the Divine service. It is central to our entire approach to life."

ALL OF CREATION IS TO PRAISE GOD

Ashrei is followed by a number of psalms extolling God that begin and end with *halleluyah* – literally "praise God!" The final psalm in that grouping ends with, "Let all souls praise God. Halleluyah!" The Hebrew word for "soul" used here is *neshamah*, a word that is etymologically related to the word for breath. Based on this, some translations render it as "Let *everything that has breath* praise God," which would certainly include animals as well as people.

Perek Shira, "A Chapter of Song," is a mystical hymn dating from the 5th to 7th centuries found in many traditional *siddurs*, although not generally part of services today. It portrays all living creatures singing their individual songs in praise of the Creator. The universe is filled with hymns as cows, camels, horses, mules, roosters, chickens, doves, eagles, butterflies, locusts, spiders, flies, sea creatures, fish, frogs, and many more creatures offer songs of praise to God. Several Shabbat morning prayers also reinforce this concept:

- The beautiful *Nishmat* prayer begins with, "The soul [or breath] of every living being shall bless Your Name, Lord, our God; the spirit of all flesh shall always glorify and exalt Your remembrance, our Ruler."
- Shortly after the *Barchu* call to prayer, the *Hakol Yoducha* prayer indicates that "All will thank You and all will praise You . . . all will exalt you . . ." The Artscroll *siddur* commentator states, "Thus every facet of the universe will join in thanking and lauding God."
- The *Keil Adon* prayer that is generally sung by the *chazzan* (prayer leader) and congregation together indicates that God "is blessed by the mouth of every soul."

Ideally, all of nature should be singing praises of God in a celestial chorus. It is hard to see this happening today though, when so many animals are so cruelly treated on factory farms and other settings, and so much of nature is being rapidly destroyed in the name of progress. One cannot help but wonder how many animal voices are now missing from that chorus.

An appreciation of nature can make our prayers more meaningful. Unfortunately, most Jews today, including me, do not get out to see nature during hikes and other activities as much as we used to, now that we have become urbanized and spend so much time using technical gadgets for communication and recreation. Not only Jews, but our whole society in general, is suffering from what has recently been called "nature deficit disorder." As Rabbi Heschel states, we should be looking on the world with a sense of awe, wonder, and radical amazement. He also points out that the greatest threat to religion is taking things for granted. The special *brachot* (blessings) to be recited when, for example, we see a rainbow or a fruit tree blossoming for the first time each year, as well as on more common occasions such as eating particular foods, are designed to slow us down and make us appreciate those experiences. They should remind us that, as a song in the Rogers and Hammerstein musical *Flower Drum Song* puts it, "A hundred million miracles are happening every day. And those who say they don't agree are those who cannot hear or see."

IMPORTANT ENVIRONMENTAL MESSAGES

There is a very powerful environmental lesson in the book of Deuteronomy that is recited twice daily during services as the second paragraph of the *Shema*, one of Judaism's most important prayers:

> And it will come to pass that if you continually hearken to My commandments that I command you this day, to love the Lord your God, and to serve God with all your heart and with all your soul – then I will provide rain for your land in its proper time, the early rains and the later rains, that you may gather in your grain, your wine and your oil. I will provide grass in your fields for your cattle and you will eat and be satisfied. Beware lest your heart be seduced and you turn astray and serve other gods and bow to them. Then the wrath of God will blaze against you. God will restrain the heaven so that there will be no rain and the ground will not yield its produce. And you will swiftly be banished from the goodly land that God gives to you.

The message seems clear. If we put God's teachings into practice and take care of the earth as we are commanded, then we will have blessings of prosperity and peace. However, if we turn to false modern gods, such as materialism, egoism, hedonism, and chauvinism, and put these traits before our wise *mitzvot*, then we will be cursed with many environmental and other societal problems. If Jews would take this message to heart – a message that is recited morning and evening by religious Jews as well as at bedtime by many – and apply it toward working for a better world, what a wonderful difference that could make!

Another important prayer, *Aleinu*, which is recited near the end of every synagogue service, tells us what our role should be: *L'takein olam b'malchut Shaddai* – "to perfect the world under the reign of the Almighty." This is the basis of the Jewish mandate for *tikkun olam*, to heal, repair, and transform the world. If this challenging message were taken seriously and applied on a daily basis, what a far better world it would be. As indicated in Appendix C, there are Jewish groups already applying this message, but far more needs to be done.

A PERSONAL SYNAGOGUE EXPERIENCE
THAT AFFECTED MY LIFE

I had a personal experience that illustrates how an inspiring moment at a synagogue service can make a difference. In the early 1970s, I was asked to be Third Vice President of my synagogue, with the responsibility of seeing that the youth programs ran smoothly. At the time, I was busy with family and professional responsibilities, and I felt alienated by the lack of social consciousness of many people in the synagogue. After some soul searching, I decided to not accept the position.

Then came Yom Kippur, during which we recite the *al chet,* a long list of communal sins. Suddenly I was faced with the *al chet* (for the sin) of casting off responsibility. I thought back to my reasons for refusing the youth program position. Was I casting off my responsibility? Yes, I was. So I decided to accept the position and make sure that Jewish values such as *gemilut chesed* (doing acts of kindness) were an essential part of the synagogue's youth activities. Every year since then, I try to pay special attention to that specific *al chet* and to ask myself, "Are there any responsibilities I am casting off by taking the easy way out?"

TEACHINGS THAT CAN ENHANCE
PRAYER EXPERIENCES

The following are some anonymous statements about prayer and activism from a handout I received many years ago as part of a High Holidays (Rosh Hashanah and Yom Kippur) package of inspirational material. To this day, I still find them helpful, and review them annually during these important holidays:

- Pray as if everything depends on God and act as if everything depends on you.
- Prayer does not change God, but it changes him (or her) who prays.
- Our prayers are answered not when we are given what we ask for, but when we are challenged to be what we can be.
- True worship is not a petition to God; it is a sermon to ourselves.
- Prayer is answered when it enables us to act as God desires.

"RELIGIOUS BEHAVIORISM" OR
ACTIVE INVOLVEMENT?

Unfortunately, as indicated before, worship services do not always inspire people to greater activism in working for a better world. Many people (often including me) settle for what Rabbi Heschel called "religious behaviorism." We recite the prayers mechanically, without really considering how the holy words can inspire us to change our communities and ourselves and face up to local and global problems. For some Jews, attendance at prayer services is often a social event, based more on tradition and habit than on a desire for genuine communion with God or a desire to be inspired to greater awareness and activism.

It is my hope that more rabbis, educators, and other Jewish leaders will use sermons, classes, articles and other strategies to help *daveners* better absorb and apply the many powerful messages in the eternal Jewish prayers. Involvement in trying to improve the environment and conditions for the world's people can also make the *davening* experience more meaningful. As Rabbi Heschel states, "Prayer and prejudice cannot dwell in the same heart. Worship without compassion is worse than self-deception; it is an abomination."[3] Prayers and social justice activities can ideally complement each other.

This is consistent with an approach that Rabbi Arthur Waskow, director of the Shalom Center, stresses: to apply the challenging teaching of Rabbi Abraham Joshua Heschel that one should carry on politics as if it were prayer and carry out prayer as if it were politics. After marching with the Reverend Martin Luther King in the second civil rights march from Selma to Montgomery, Alabama, Rabbi Heschel said, "I felt as if my legs were praying."

If more Jews took this approach and strove to put the messages in the prayers into practice, this could release a great potential to help revitalize Judaism. It could also move our imperiled planet toward a more just, humane, and environmentally sustainable path, toward a time when "no one shall hurt nor destroy in all of God's holy mountain" (Isaiah 11:9).

---

3. Rabbi Abraham Joshua Heschel, *The Insecurity of Freedom* (New York: Farrar, Straus and Giroux, 1959), 87.

Chapter 15

How Can We Revitalize Judaism?

*L*ittle does contemporary religion ask of man. It is ready to offer comfort; it has no courage to challenge. It is ready to offer edification; it has no courage to break the idols, to shatter callousness. The trouble is that religion has become "religion" – institution, dogma, ritual. It is no longer an event. Its acceptance involves neither risk nor strain. — ABRAHAM JOSHUA HESCHEL[1]

*W*e must cultivate a sense for injustice, impatience with vulgarity, a capacity for moral indignation, a will to readjust society itself when it becomes complacent and corrupt. — ABRAHAM JOSHUA HESCHEL[2]

*W*hat young people need is not religious tranquilizers, religion as a diversion, but spiritual audacity, intellectual guts, power of defiance. Our task is not to satisfy complacency but to shatter it. Our duty is confrontation rather than evasion. — ABRAHAM JOSHUA HESCHEL[3]

ORKING TO MEET THE challenge expressed in the three quotations above can help revitalize Judaism. Rabbi Heschel expressed the central role that Judaism must play in helping

---

1. Abraham Joshua Heschel, *The Insecurity of Freedom* (New York: Ferrar, Strauss, and Giroux, 1967), 218.
2. *Ibid,* 49.
3. *Ibid,* 1–2.

to solve contemporary problems. Much of my own Jewish philosophy comes from Rabbi Heschel, whom I often quote in this book. I regard him as the ideal Jew, because he not only took Jewish prayer and ritual seriously and wrote beautifully on such a wide variety of issues, but also put Jewish teachings into practice in active involvement in many social issues, including supporting freedom for Soviet Jews, working for civil rights, helping improve relations between Catholics and Jews, and opposing what he regarded as an unjust, immoral war in Vietnam.

Unfortunately, relatively few Jews are familiar with his writings nowadays. I strongly believe that if many more Jews read Rabbi Heschel's books and essays and tried to live by them, we would have a far more sensitive and dedicated Jewish community. This, in turn, would lead to a revitalized Judaism and a far better world. Heschel writes:

> Our civilization is in need of redemption. The evil, the falsehood, the vulgarity of our way of living cry to high heaven. There is a war to be waged against the vulgar, against the glorification of power, a war that is incessant, universal. There is much purification that needs to be done, ought to be done, and could be done through bringing to bear the radical wisdom, the sacrificial devotion, the uncompromising loyalty of our forefathers upon the issues of our daily living.[4]

SUGGESTIONS FOR REVITALIZING JUDAISM

Building On Jewish Progressive Teachings

As indicated in Chapter 3, Judaism is in many ways a radical religion, in the best sense of the word "radical." However, our Jewish schools and synagogues seem to be grooming mostly contented and complacent individuals, people unwilling to apply Jewish values to help change an unjust status quo. I believe that in this time of violence, oppression, bigotry, selfishness, and materialism, there should be greater stress on Judaism's powerful, radical teachings. These include:
- "Justice, justice shall you pursue" (Deuteronomy 16:20).
- "Seek peace and pursue it" (Psalms 34:14).

---

4. *Ibid*, 218

- "Be kind to the stranger, for you were strangers in the land of Egypt" (This appears in various forms 36 times in the Hebrew scriptures).
- "Love your neighbor as yourself" (Leviticus 19:18).
- "*Bal tashchit*" You shall not waste or destroy (Deuteronomy 20:19–20).
- Be a "light unto the nations" (Isaiah 42:6).
- "If I am not for myself, who will be for me? If I am only for myself, what am I? And if not now, when?" (Hillel, *Pirkei Avot* 1:14).

These and other challenging teachings in the Jewish tradition should become watchwords in synagogues, and Jewish schools, institutions, and homes. This would help return Judaism to its radical roots and help Jews apply its teachings to societal problems.

USING THE JEWISH FESTIVALS AS A SPUR TO ACTIVISM

Many important Jewish teachings are reflected in Jewish holidays. Rabbi Irving Greenberg, author of *The Jewish Way: Living the Holidays* and other books, has written, "The Holy Days are the unbroken master code of Judaism. Decipher them and you will discover the inner sanctum of your religion. Grasp them and you hold the heart of the faith in your hand."[5] Judaism's rich and beautiful holidays can help raise awareness of how our tradition speaks to modern social issues:

Shabbat: We can highlight the important environmental benefits of Shabbat as a day of rest, putting aside computers, TV sets, cars, and other items that are so prevalent during the workdays, and refraining from striving to increase one's wealth. As Rabbi Heschel states in his classic book *The Sabbath*:

> To set aside one day a week for freedom, a day on which we would not use the instruments which have so easily been turned into weapons of destruction, a day for being with ourselves, a day of detachment from the vulgar, of independence of external obligations, a day on which we stop worshipping the idols of technical civilization, a day on which we use no money, a day of armistice in the economic struggle with our

---

fellow men and the forces of nature – is there any institution that holds out a greater hope for man's progress than the Sabbath?

Rabbi Samuel Dresner, a devoted student of Rabbi Heschel, suggests that the Sabbath should represent an armistice in battles between people and society, between people and nature, and between people with themselves. We are not to even pick a flower on Shabbat, not only because we should not harvest things on that day, but also because we are to be at peace with everything, as in the Garden of Eden, for which reason we do not make or destroy anything on the Sabbath day.

I always welcome Shabbat with joy as a chance to recharge my batteries, to renew family relationships and conversations, to catch up on my reading and, of course, to commune with God and God's creations. I sometimes wonder how I would manage without Shabbat. I get some of my best work done on Saturday evenings after a restful Shabbat, perhaps partly because by turning away from the endless barrage of messages, tasks, and data, I return refreshed and able to see things anew. Of course we must maintain the sanctity of Shabbat and other Jewish holy days, but we can also direct the great peace and strength we gain from observing these days toward greater involvement on the other days of the week. I agree with Rabbi Arthur Waskow that the entire world needs a Shabbat, or perhaps an entire Sabbatical Year, to pause from efforts to constantly produce and amass more and more goods, to reassess where we are heading, and stop or reform the practices that are harmful to the environment.

Rosh Hashanah: On this day that commemorates the creation of the world, we should consider how the wonderful world that God has created is now imperiled by climate change and many other environmental threats, and vow to work with others to turn things around in the coming New Year. In praying for a healthy year for our loved ones, and ourselves, we should recognize that having a healthful, meat-free diet is the best way to reduce risks of disease and increase chances for a longer life.

Yom Kippur: On this Day of Atonement and repentance, we should consider how we can repent and atone for all the ways we, as individuals, communities, and societies, have exploited and savaged our environment and vow to work to restore and improve it.

Sukkot: On this harvest festival, as Jews in their holy booths (*sukkahs*), exposed to the elements and smelling plants and tree branches, we might focus on Jewish teachings about food and preventing hunger. The poetic references to the cycles of sun, wind, and water in the book of Ecclesiastes, which we read on the Shabbat during Sukkot, could inspire discussions of renewable energy. Our prayers for rain on Shemini Atzeret can remind us of the importance of conserving water, especially in this time when many areas face severe droughts.

Chanukah: The importance of non-conformity and fighting for one's beliefs should be stressed, with the victory of the holy few (the Maccabees) against the far stronger, pagan Syrian-Greeks as an example. It is also a good opportunity to consider how we can make our oil last longer through conservation and improved efficiencies, just as it occurred miraculously in the holy Temple.

Tu B'Shvat: An event on the Jewish calendar that is ideally suited to raising environmental awareness and activism is Tu B'Shvat, the "birthday of the trees," which has become a kind of "Jewish Earth Day" in some Jewish circles.[6] The traditional foods served at a Tu B'Shvat seder are all grains and fruits, which make it a good opportunity to consider Jewish teachings on the environment, vegetarianism, and veganism, like the ones in lessons from trees discussed in the next section. When the holiday falls on Shabbat, it can be turned into an environmentally-themed Shabbat, including a Tu B'Shvat seder overflowing with plant-based foods, especially fruits and nuts from trees that grow in Israel, plus environmentally-oriented sermons, talks, panel discussions, and debates, nature walks, and other appropriate activities. If Tu B'Shvat falls during the week, besides having a seder, it provides a good opportunity for school children to get close to nature by taking hikes, planting trees, studying relevant texts, reading and writing appropriate material, singing songs, and in other ways learning

---

6. Connections between this holiday and the environment were made long before the invention of the secular Earth Day. In Israel, Tu B'Shvat comes at tree-planting time, and it is a time-honored tradition to plant trees in someone's honor or memory on this day. Much of the early reforestation of Israel was done with donations for planting trees on Tu B'Shvat.

to appreciate our deep connection to nature. The holiday also provides an opportunity to discuss threats to Israel (and the U.S. and the entire world) from climate change and other environmental problems and from resource scarcities.

Passover: The themes of liberation and freedom from oppression can lead to seder table discussions about democracy and civil liberties. It is also a good time to consider the implications of the oft-quoted Jewish mandate that we should be kind to the stranger since "we were slaves in Egypt."

Shavuot: On this holiday that commemorates the giving of the Torah to the Jewish people, we might study, during the traditional all-night gatherings to learn Torah, some of the Torah's teachings about justice, compassion, peace, environmental preservation, community, kindness, and helping our neighbors. The book of Ruth that is read on Shavuot is an especially valuable source for discussions on kindness.

Tisha B'Av: On this sad day that commemorates the destruction of both our ancient holy Temples, we should recognize that today it is not only holy temples and the residents of the holy city of Jerusalem that are threatened with destruction, but the whole world as well. We should actively work to avert an impending, climate catastrophe and other threats to the planet. Every Jewish holiday provides an excellent occasion to increase awareness and sensitivity about Jewish teachings that speak to current crises. I suggest connections between Shabbat and all of the Jewish festivals and other sacred days to vegetarianism in my articles in the holidays section at www.JewishVeg.com/Schwartz. We can similarly tie all the Jewish holy days to other environmental and social justice issues.

Rabbi Arthur Waskow has written an excellent book called *Seasons of our Joy,* which follows the holiday cycle and explains how each of the holy days not only commemorates a historical event, but is also connected to the natural cycles of the earth. Each sacred day has its own theme and its own special energy. When a Jew is conscious of and tuned into this cycle, it can become the story of one's own life as well. There is plenty of room for authentic creativity and innovation within Jewish tradition.

I am writing these words shortly after Tu B'Shvat, the birthday of the trees, in 2015. Below is the *dvar Torah* (Torah teaching) that I presented at the Tu B'Shvat *Seder* at my synagogue:

Some of my most important lessons in life I learned from Jewish verses about trees. From the following I learned that I should be an environmental activist, working to help preserve the world:

> In the hour when the Holy one, blessed be He created the first person, He showed him the trees in the Garden of Eden, and said to him: "See My works, how fine they are; Now all that I have created, I created for your benefit. Think upon this and do not corrupt and destroy My world, For if you destroy it, there is no one to restore it after you."
>
> (Ecclesiastes Rabbah 7:28)

From the following and the rabbinic commentaries on it I learned that I should avoid destruction and should conserve resources:

> When you shall besiege a city a long time, in making war against it to take it, you shall not destroy (*lo tashchit*) the trees thereof by wielding an ax against them; for you may eat of them, but you must not cut the down; for is the tree of the field a man, that it should be besieged by you? Only the trees of which you know that they are not trees for food, them you may destroy and cut down, that you may build bulwarks against the city that makes war with you, until it fall.
>
> (Deuteronomy 20:19, 20)

The following verse helped convince me that I should be a vegan:

> And God said: "Behold, I have given you every herb yielding seed which is upon the face of all the earth, and every tree that has seed-yielding fruit – to you it shall be for food." (Genesis 1:29)

From the following I learned that as a Jew I should strive to serve as a positive example:

And they came to Elim, where were 12 springs of water and 70 palm trees; and they encamped here by the waters (Deuteronomy 15:27). Rabbi Bachya saw a very deep message in this apparently simple verse. He stated that the 12 springs represent the 12 tribes of Israel, and the 70 palm trees represent the 70 then nations of the world. He stated that just as the 12 springs nourished the 70 palm trees, the 12 tribes (the Jewish people) should serve to "nourish" the world by serving as a good example.

From the following I learned to consider the consequences of my actions on future generations:

While the sage Choni was walking along a road, he saw an old man planting a carob tree. Choni asked him: "How long will it take for this tree to bear fruit?" "70 years," replied the man. Choni then asked: "Are you so healthy a man that you expect to live that length of time and eat its fruit?" The man answered: "I found a fruitful world because my ancestors planted it for me. Likewise, I am planting for my children."

(Ta'anis 23b)

From the following I learned how important it is to be involved in the natural world:

In order to serve God, one needs access to the enjoyment of the beauties of nature – meadows full of flowers, majestic mountains, flowing rivers. For all these are essential to the spiritual development of even the holiest of people. (Rabbi Abraham ben Maimonides, cited by Rabbi David E. Stein in *A Garden of Choice Fruits*, Shomrei Adamah, 1991).

From the following I learned the importance of acting on my knowledge and beliefs:

Whoever has more wisdom than deeds is like a tree with many branches but few roots, and the wind shall tear him from the ground. . . . Whoever has more deeds than wisdom is like a tree with more roots than branches, and no hurricane will uproot him from the spot.

(Pirke Avot 3:17)

From the following I learned the importance of working for a more peaceful world:

> And He shall judge between many peoples, and shall decide concerning mighty nations afar off; and they shall beat their swords into plowshares, and their spears into pruning hooks; nation shall not lift up sword against nation, neither shall they learn war any more. But they shall sit every man under his vine and under his fig tree; and none shall make them afraid; for the mouth of the Lord of hosts hath spoken.
>
> (Micah 4:3–5)

Last but far from least, from the following I learned how the Torah is a guide to a happy, productive, and fulfilling life:

> [The Torah is] a tree of life to those who hold fast to it and all who cling to it find happiness. Its ways are ways of pleasantness, and all its paths are peace.　　　　　　　　(Proverbs 3: 17–18)

BUILDING PROGRESSIVE JEWISH VALUES INTO BAR AND BAT MITZVAH CEREMONIES AND OTHER JEWISH EVENTS

Bar and Bat Mitzvah ceremonies are a big part of the lives of 12 year-old Jewish girls and 13-year old Jewish boys. Such occasions often end up focusing on materialism and lavish parties and indulgence, especially as the boys and girls attend and compare many parties of friends and classmates in a short period of time, not to mention competition among the parents to "keep up with the Cohens." However, with a change of focus, these events could also provide an opportunity for young Jews to reflect on and apply important Jewish values.

One group that helps infuse such occasions and other events with Jewish values is Areyvut, which means responsibility. This organization emphasizes that Jews should feel responsible for other Jews and should play an active role in creating a better community and a better world. Founded and led by Daniel Rothner, Areyvut's mission is to infuse the lives of Jewish youth and teenagers with the core Jewish values of *chesed* (kindness), *tzedakah* (charity), and *tikkun olam* (social action). Areyvut offers Jewish day schools, congregational schools, synagogues, community centers, and families a variety of opportunities to empower and enrich their youth by creating innovative programs that make these core Jewish values real and meaningful to them.

Areyvut's fundamental belief is that sparking a passion for service in the young can inspire a lifelong commitment to charity, kindness, and social justice. Therefore, Areyvut creates programs that reach out to Jewish youth, building on their individual interests and putting their experiences into a meaningful Jewish and communal context. They encourage young people to engage in both hands-on service and philanthropy, in the belief that all of God's gifts should be used to improve our world. Areyvut also believes that community service can benefit – and change – both the recipient and the provider of the service. Their target audience is middle school and high school students from all denominations of Judaism, in all types of Jewish educational settings, and of every kind of Jewish communal affiliation.

Among Areyvut's many programs are mitzvah clowning, Jewish teen philanthropy, and mitzvah and *chesed* fairs. Areyvut organizes hands-on, community service fairs for schools, synagogues, and community centers to educate students about the many different ways they can make a difference in their community. More information about Areyvut and its programs can be found at www.areyvut.org.

GETTING STUDENTS MORE INVOLVED

Much of the apathy and very conservative values in the Orthodox Jewish community seem to be continuing among our youth. Schools are doing a fine job teaching students how to learn Jewish texts, how to *daven*, and how to carry out *mitzvot* and lead a religious Jewish life. But they generally are not inspiring students to apply the Jewish teachings they are learning about in efforts to make the world more consistent with the highest of Jewish values. Changing this will not be easy, but here are some suggestions for ways to involve students in order to help imbue them with Jewish teachings and values, and encourage them to relate Jewish teachings in response to current challenges:

- High school students could be asked to submit papers – perhaps as part of an essay contest – and make class presentations that use Jewish teachings to address current issues such as climate change, energy conservation, hunger, poverty, peace, health, animal rights, vegetarianism, and many more.

- Debate teams could be set up, and students could learn the value of researching positions they don't personally agree with. The chapters in this book and many other books can be used as starting points for debating many topics pro and con. Many Jews today are afraid to expose their children to opposing views, but they shouldn't be. The Talmudic rabbis were not afraid of intense debate, and even preserved the ideas that were voted down, so we could learn from the process. Judaism is a strong religion that has stood the test of time; it can certainly withstand the questioning of today's teenagers. Students should learn that there is not necessarily one correct answer to an issue, and that they should respect others' opinions even while disagreeing with them.
- Having guest speakers with a wide variety of opinions, consistent with Jewish law and values, would create much interest in a wide variety of current topics.
- Students could be encouraged to come up with their own questions and issues that they would like to investigate. Use of the Internet gives students wonderful opportunities to explore issues.
- When students learn to lead the *davening* in preparation for adulthood, there should be an effort to relate the prayers to the issues that they are addressing in their research, discussions, and debates. For example, what are the implications of the verse, "Blessed is the One (God) who has compassion on all the creatures," or "God is good to all, and God's compassion is over all of God's works?" How would these verses apply to the way we treat animals and the environment? The same could be done with many other statements in *davening*. We should be making a conscious effort to connect the words with our actions in the world.

There are many other creative ways through which we can help revitalize Judaism. It is my hope that wiser people than me will build on the few ideas in this chapter and suggest additional ideas, so that Judaism may become more of what it was always intended to be: a light unto the nations, a kingdom of priests and a holy people, and God's witnesses on earth.

Chapter 16

Summary and Conclusions

In this hour we, the living [post-Holocaust Jews], are "the people of Israel." The tasks begun by the patriarchs and prophets and continued by their descendants are now entrusted to us. We are either the last Jews or those who will hand over the entire past to generations to come. We will either forfeit or enrich the legacy of ages.

— ABRAHAM JOSHUA HESCHEL
(THE EARTH IS THE LORD'S), 107

WHAT A WONDERFUL PATH JUDAISM IS!

- Judaism proclaims a God who is the Creator of all life, whose attributes of kindness, compassion, and justice are to serve as examples for all our actions.
- Judaism stresses that every person is created in God's image and therefore is of supreme value.
- Judaism teaches that people are to be co-workers with God in preserving and improving the world. We are mandated to serve as stewards of the world's resources to see that God's bounties are used for the benefit of all.
- Judaism asserts that nothing that has value may be wasted or unnecessarily destroyed (*bal tashchit*).
- Judaism stresses that we are to love other people as ourselves, to be kind to strangers, "for we were strangers in the land of Egypt," and to act with compassion toward the homeless, the poor, the orphan, the widow, and all of God's creatures.

- Judaism urges efforts to reduce hunger. A Jew who helps to feed a hungry person is considered, in effect, to have "fed" God.
- Judaism mandates that we must seek and pursue peace. Great is peace, for it is one of God's names, all God's blessings are contained in it, it must be sought even in times of war, and it will be the Messiah's first blessing.
- Judaism exhorts us to pursue justice, to work for a society in which each person has the ability to obtain, through creative labor, the means to lead a dignified life.
- Judaism teaches that God's compassion is over all of God's works, that the righteous individual considers the well-being of animals, and that Jews should avoid *tsa'ar ba'alei chayim*, causing pain to animals.
- Judaism stresses involvement, nonconformity, resistance to oppression and injustice, and a constant struggle against idolatry.

PRODUCING A BETTER WORLD BY APPLYING JEWISH VALUES

This ancient, marvelous Jewish outlook, applied to the planet's gravest problems, can help shift the planet away from its present perilous course to produce a far better world. Strategies to obtain a better world include:

- There should be a central focus in Jewish life on the preservation of our natural environment and the improvement of economic and social conditions. Synagogues, yeshivas, Jewish centers, and other Jewish institutions should increase the awareness of Judaism's powerful messages about justice, peace, environmental sustainability and other values, and how these teachings can be applied to the problems of today. Hopefully other religions will apply their own teachings and join in these efforts.
- We should seek a fairer tax system, with a reduction of major tax breaks for the wealthiest Americans and highly profitable corporations. The increased tax revenues should be used to finance a major effort to rebuild our decaying infrastructure, produce more renewable energy, improve our educational systems and research capacities, and make other necessary investments that will create jobs, increase tax revenue, and help improve the economy, while providing dignity and confidence to workers.

- We should promote major changes in response to the overwhelming consensus among climate scientists that climate change is happening, that it poses a grave threat to life on earth and human civilization, and that we – humanity – are both a major cause of current climate change and are the only potential solution. Preventing the climate catastrophe that many climate scientists are predicting should be a major focus in all aspects of Jewish life today.

- A Global Marshall Plan should be established, led by the United States and other developed nations, including European Union nations and Israel, to sharply reduce world poverty, hunger, illiteracy, pollution, disease, and other societal problems. This would improve the image of the U.S. and Israel, potentially reducing future acts of terrorism.

- There should be a major effort to resolve the Israeli/Palestinian conflict and other Middle Eastern conflicts, as well as conflicts throughout the world, for the great benefit of all the people involved, and so that more money, time, and attention can be applied to addressing today's many global challenges. Israel cannot avert renewed conflict and increased diplomatic isolation, effectively respond to her serious economic, environmental, and other domestic problems, and remain both a Jewish and a democratic state, without an enduring Middle East peace. While recognizing the many obstacles related to Palestinian statements and actions, we should encourage increased efforts to reach a resolution of the conflicts. The U.S. and other nations should support Israel in every attempt to achieve a comprehensive, just, and sustainable peace.

- There should be a widespread effort to increase awareness that a large-scale shift toward plant-based (vegan) diets would provide numerous benefits, including significantly improving human health and reducing climate change, deforestation, desertification, rapid species losses, soil erosion, and many other environmental threats. There is no way that the world will be able to avoid an unprecedented climate catastrophe and meet increasing needs for food, energy, water, and other resources, without a major societal switch toward vegetarian, and preferably vegan, diets, along with other positive changes.

- We should stress that plant-based (vegan) diets are the diets most consistent with basic Jewish teachings on preserving health, treating animals with compassion, protecting the environment, conserving natural resources, helping hungry people, and seeking and pursuing peace.

- A commission of highly respected religious leaders, environmentalists, educators, politicians, and other experts should be formed to investigate and report on the best approaches to reduce current threats and greatly improve conditions worldwide.

Of course, it will not be easy to carry out the strategies listed above. However, we must recognize the seriousness of the threats we face today, and that business as usual is no longer an option. Unprecedented changes in thinking and action must be made very soon and Jews, along with others, must play a major role in increasing awareness in the urgency of these changes in order to avoid a catastrophic future. This should be a priority in all aspects of Jewish life. Failure to apply Jewish values to address current threats will result in a very dismal future, with increased poverty, hunger, terrorism, war, pollution, and severe climate events.

Many Jews today justify their lack of involvement with the world's problems by stating that Jews have enough troubles of their own, and that we can leave it to others to involve themselves in "non-Jewish" issues. Certainly, Jews must be actively involved in battling anti-Semitism, working for a secure and just Israel, and engaging with numerous other Jewish needs and obligations. But can we divorce ourselves from active involvement with wider problems? Are efforts to obtain justice, peace, environmental sustainability, etc., really "non-Jewish" issues? Don't Jews also suffer from polluted air and water, resource shortages, the effects of climate change, and other societal threats? Can we ignore issues critical to the future of our community, nation, and world? When people are poor, hungry, oppressed, disease-ridden, and victimized by violence, does our tradition not mandate that we respond, and is it not also very much in the self-interest of our own safety and advancement? Perhaps the situation is, in mathematical terms, one of conditional probability. If conditions in the world are good, it is still possible that Jews will suffer. But if these conditions are bad, it is almost certain that Jews will be hurt along with everyone else. Jews must be involved in working for a just and harmonious world for the sake of our ethical values as well as our own self-interest.

It is essential that Jews, along with others, actively apply Jewish values to current critical problems. We must be "God's loyal opposition" to injustice, greed, and immorality, rousing the conscience of humanity. We must shout "no" when others are whispering "yes" to injustice. We must involve Judaism in the universal task of "comforting the afflicted and afflicting the comfortable." We must act as befits "descendants of the prophets," reminding the world that there exists a God of justice, compassion, and kindness. Nothing less than global survival is at stake.

As indicated by the list of activist Jewish groups in Appendix C, there are many dedicated Jews who recognize that Judaism has splendid values that can play major roles if applied to today's critical issues. It would be very helpful if many more Jews educated themselves on the issues, got more involved in Jewish life, and spoke out.

There is a battle worldwide between the forces seeking harmony, tolerance, common ground, and solutions and the forces of fear, obstruction, hatred, bigotry, and demonization of people who are different in views, nationality, or religion. This book is a calling to join with the many, although yet too few, activist Jews serving our Covenant with God, with actions that respond to God's call for our partnering in building a more caring humanity and a better existence for all God's creatures.

The afternoon service for Yom Kippur includes the prophetic reading of the book of Jonah, who was sent by God to the city of Nineveh to urge the people to repent and change their evil ways in order to avoid their destruction. The people of Nineveh listened and changed their actions – but will we? Today the whole world is like Nineveh, in danger of annihilation and in need of repentance and redemption. Each one of us must be a Jonah, with a mission to warn the world that it must turn from greed, injustice, and materialism, in order that we may avoid global catastrophe.

SOME QUESTIONS TO PONDER

I would like to conclude this chapter with some questions that I have been trying to raise for many years about current Jewish life. I ask these questions (addressed to me as well as everyone else) with great love and respect, because I hope they will lead to positive changes that will be a *kiddush Hashem* (a sanctification of God's Name):

- Are we defining Judaism too narrowly? Shouldn't a definition of a religious Jew include a passion for social justice, a moral sensitivity, a strong feeling for ethics and morals?
- Is coming to the synagogue more important than what happens there? Are we transformed by our services to become better people, to do something about the injustices and indignities suffered by our fellow humans?

- Have we forgotten who we are and what we stand for and Whom we represent? Have we forgotten our roles: to be a chosen people, chosen to be God's servants and witnesses, a light unto the nations, a holy people, descendants of the prophets, the original champions of social justice?
- Are we too complacent, too ready to believe that we need not change? The patriarch Abraham began the history of Judaism by a radical break with the past, by smashing the idols of his society. Are we ready, too easily, to accept modern idols of conformity, materialism, secularism, and permissiveness?
- Do we realize that the task of religion is to be a challenge to the status quo, to prejudices, and to a herd mentality, and that complacency and taking things for granted are not consistent with Judaism?
- Are we taking our ethical ideals and prophetic teachings seriously enough? If Judaism teaches "justice, justice, shall you pursue" and "let justice well up as waters and righteousness as a mighty stream," why is there so much complacency about poverty, exploitation, corruption at every level of government, and corporate actions that negatively affect our health and safety?
- Why are there so few dreams of a better world through Jewish ideals?
- Are we segregating God in our synagogues? If God is sanctified by justice and righteousness, why are we so complacent in the face of an unredeemed, immoral, and unjust world?
- What would the prophets say about our society today? About Judaism in our time? About activities in our synagogues and other Jewish institutions?
- Moses said, "would that all God's people were prophets" (Numbers 11:29), but where is the voice of prophecy in our synagogues and other aspects of Judaism today?
- Have we forgotten, amidst our many study groups, that it is not study that is the chief thing, but action?
- If "to save one life is to save an entire world," why such silence in the face of conditions that lead to the deaths of millions of people annually due to hunger?
- If every person is created in God's image and we all have one Creator, why aren't there greater efforts to combat racism, anti-Semitism, sexism, homophobia, and other forms of discrimination?
- Consistent with our prayers to a God of compassion, shouldn't we feel more compassion toward all of God's creatures?

- Considering the many threats to our (and God's) world, from climate change, destruction of tropical rain forests, depletion of the ozone layer, acid rain, rapid loss of bio-diversity, soil erosion and depletion, and widespread air and water pollution, and in light of Judaism's strong environmental messages, shouldn't the preservation of the global environment be given greater priority on the Jewish agenda?
- If all Jews put our splendid teachings into practice in efforts to improve the world, can you imagine the effects? Would there be so much crime, violence, distrust, prejudice, and discord, and air, water and land pollution? Would we have so much "private affluence along with public squalor?" Would we have the misguided priorities that lead to spending so many billions of dollars for the military and not enough for human needs and a better environment?
- When considering what Judaism can and must become, shouldn't we consider the statement that Robert Kennedy often made: "There are those who look at things the way they are, and ask, 'Why?' I dream of things that never were, and ask, 'Why not?'"
- In summary, since Judaism is such a wonderful, challenging, dynamic religion, why isn't this translated more into Jews' lives today?

*

This has indeed been a very difficult book to write, but as I did the research and writing, I saw Israel increasingly isolated, facing what former Israeli Defense Minister Ehud Barak called a looming "diplomatic tsunami." I saw the United States and many other countries facing difficult economic conditions, and signs of climate change occurring more frequently. And I saw many Jews and others in denial about such issues and/or backing very conservative policies and politicians. As I saw these things, the importance of this book became increasingly clear. I hope that people will respond with an open mind and a desire to apply the arguments I have presented in pursuit of a more sustainable future. I very much hope that many respectful dialogues result, and that they lead to solutions to current problems.

My intent was not to offend, and I apologize to anyone who was offended. I certainly mean everything in a positive way, "for the sake of Heaven," with the hope that the book will help revitalize Judaism (and perhaps other religions, from our example), improve Israel's security and well-being, reduce anti-Semitism, reduce climate change and other environmental threats and, in general, lead to a far better future.

I hope this book will help revitalize Judaism and enable Jewish groups and individuals to truly apply Jewish values in their lives and communities, in efforts to create a more compassionate, just, healthy, peaceful, and environmentally sustainable world.

—Richard Schwartz

The Making of a Jewish Activist:
An Author's Bio

I AM A BA'AL T'SHUVAH – meaning "one who has returned" – a Jew who started practicing Judaism late in life. I did not grow up in a religious family, and I did not receive a yeshiva education as observant Jewish children generally do today. Most of my current Jewish learning comes not from formal education, but from extensive reading and conversations with Jews from many different backgrounds, plus Torah classes and lectures over the past few decades.

Like most Jewish boys growing up in New York during the 1940s, I went to a Talmud Torah school a couple of afternoons a week after public school in order to prepare for my bar mitzvah. But I was not particularly interested in Jewish teachings or societal issues. Rather, like most of my friends and classmates who did not go to Hebrew school, I was primarily interested in swimming in the nearby Atlantic Ocean, playing handball, baseball, basketball, and other sports with friends, and rooting for the New York Yankees. I would devour every sports section when the Yankees won, but a Yankee defeat would make me very sad. Nowadays I've lost most of my interest in spectator sports. I still support most New York teams, but very seldom spend any time watching them.

One aspect of Judaism that did interest me in my early years was the wisdom teachings contained in a section of the *Mishnah* called *Pirkei Avot*, the "Ethics of the Fathers." This tractate, which contains short, pithy sayings from the early Talmudic rabbis and scholars, is a basic manual on how to be a good Jew. *Pirkei Avot* is still my favorite section of the *Mishnah*, and its teachings have helped guide me through life, especially the following:

• You are not required to complete the task, but neither are you free to desist from [doing all that you can] (2:21).

- Be of the disciples of Aaron [the brother of Moses]: love peace and pursue peace, love all people, and bring them closer to the Torah (1:12).
- Who is rich? The person who rejoices in his or her portion (4:1).
- Who is wise? The person who learns from every other person (4:1).

After graduating from high school in 1952, I was not sure what career to pursue. I finally decided to study civil engineering, mainly because that was the field that my older brother had chosen. Because I didn't want to go to an out-of-town college, and tuition was free at the city university, I attended the City College of New York. Since the campus was far from my home in Far Rockaway, I decided to take advantage of the option of taking my pre-engineering courses for two years at Queens College, which was closer to home. This decision was a major turning point in my life. Had I started at City College, I would have interacted primarily with engineering students, people interested mostly in mathematical, scientific, and technical courses and concepts. At Queens College, I took liberal arts courses along with students who had a broader range of views and outlooks.

Because I didn't drive a car at the time, I rode in various car pools to and from the campus. This put me in contact with a wide variety of people and views, ranging from very conservative to extremely radical. I started investigating current issues in order to refute some of the radical ideas that I was hearing for the first time. I soon began to recognize the injustices in the world and became imbued with the idea that I should be involved in struggling against these injustices. I began reading books like *The Grapes of Wrath* and viewing films like *Mr. Smith Goes to Washington*, which inspired me to try to learn more and to strive to improve society.

During this time, my involvement with Judaism diminished to practically nothing. I viewed the synagogues and Jewish groups as being primarily concerned with ritual for the sake of ritual, and with maintaining their membership rolls and social status. The Jewish institutions did not seem to be involved with the societal causes of the day, and they were totally irrelevant to me.

I was now so committed to working to end society's injustices that I seriously considered becoming an English major, in order to write and make others aware of what I was learning. I loved reading novels and non-fiction books about historical events and social issues. I yearned to learn more and to apply my knowledge in the struggle toward a more just, peaceful world.

However, family members, fellow students, and college advisors all pointed out how well I was doing in my pre-engineering classes (I had the top grade point average of all the students in the department) and stressed that I would have a much easier time making a living as an engineer than as a writer. I took their advice and remained in civil engineering, but my feelings about social issues were so strong that I seriously considered not being involved in the world of commerce and business. Instead, I thought about moving to Israel after graduation to work on a kibbutz. I saw that system of communal living, cooperative efforts, and desire to serve one's community as a model of an ideal community most consistent with my views at that time. I even planned a trip to Israel immediately after graduating from City College, in order to further explore that possibility.

Then, in my final semester, something occurred that represented another major turning point in my life. Because I had the top grade point average in my Civil Engineering class, I was offered a position as an instructor in the Department of Civil Engineering at City College, starting in the spring semester of 1957. I saw this as a great opportunity and quickly accepted the position. This would enable me to help people, and I would stay out of the business world, which I then regarded as a "rat race" that involved advancing one's career at the expense of others. As a college instructor, I would be able to apply and teach the many concepts I had learned in my studies. I would also be working with material that I had mastered and enjoyed.

I did go to Israel in the summer of 1957, and I did spend some time working on a kibbutz. But my great excitement at teaching, and the honor I felt at being chosen to be a member of City College's Civil Engineering Department working side-by-side with teachers whom I greatly admired, reduced my interest in living on a kibbutz. I recall spending my last day in Israel excitedly preparing lecture notes for the course on "Strength of Materials" that I would be teaching shortly after my return. At the same time, I had a deep love for Israel, which I regarded as a modern day miracle. Shortly after I returned to the United States, I gave a talk at a "cousin's club" meeting at which I extolled many aspects of life in Israel.

*

The next major change in my life came when I married Loretta Susskind in 1960 (yes, we have been married now for over 55 years). When I began dating Loretta, she was a social worker at a center in Harlem. We shared an interest in addressing social ills and helping less fortunate people. Loretta came from a more religious family and background than I did. She had continued her Jewish studies beyond the pre-teen Talmud Torah classes and had graduated from Marshalia Hebrew High School. Loretta wanted to introduce Jewish rituals into our family life once we were married. So she presented me with some books on the Sabbath, the *mikveh* (Jewish ritual bath), and other Jewish practices.

I read these books somewhat reluctantly at first, and then with increasing interest. I began to see that my ideas about working for a better world were included in the Jewish worldview. I now understood the "task" from which *Pirkei Avot* says we are not free to desist is the ongoing process of improving the world. There was plenty of opportunity for a fulfilling spiritual, socially-activist life within my own tradition! In fact, the whole saga of Jewish history involved a struggle to maintain the Jewish people and its ethical teachings in the face of oppression, widespread anti-Semitism, hatred, antagonism, and violence.

The more I read, the more I became interested in learning about all aspects of Judaism. In the process, I began to incorporate some Jewish practices into my own life. At first I didn't attend synagogue services on Shabbat mornings, but would find a nice quiet place outdoors and read Jewish books on a wide variety of topics. Around this time, Loretta and I purchased a set of five wonderful anthologies: *A Treasury of Jewish Quotations, A Treasury of Jewish Poetry, A Treasury of Jewish Folklore, A Treasury of American Jewish Stories,* and *A Modern Treasury of Jewish Thought.*

As I read *A Modern Treasury of Jewish Thought,* I became increasingly thrilled to discover that there were brilliant Jewish thinkers who wrote eloquently about applying Jewish values to the world. I was especially excited by the writings of Rabbi Abraham Joshua Heschel. I relished his radical analysis of Judaism and his challenging criticism of "religious behaviorism," which he defined as performing the *mitzvot* without any real devotion or any attempt to relate them to the realities of our society. And I loved the powerful but poetic ways that he expressed his challenging ideas.

It was also very important to me that Heschel was both a religious Jew and an activist. He marched with Martin Luther King, advocated early on for the liberation of Soviet Jews, and spoke out courageously against what

I regarded as an illegal, unjust, and immoral war in Vietnam – despite the disapproval from many Jewish leaders of his views and activities. Through Heschel I recognized that my earlier rejection of Judaism was not because of any problems inherent in the religion itself; rather, it was because of what the practice of Judaism in the mid-twentieth century had become. As Heschel put it, in a challenging statement that I previously quoted:

> Religion declined not because it was refuted, but because it became irrelevant, dull, oppressive, insipid. When faith is completely replaced by creed, worship by discipline, love by habit; when the crisis of today is ignored because of the splendor of the past; when faith becomes an heirloom rather than a living fountain; when religion speaks only in the name of authority rather than with the voice of compassion, its message becomes meaningless.[1]

I increasingly found that all my social ideals were included within Judaism, and that Judaism provides a structure for leading a meaningful and involved spiritual life – if only people would really practice it! I was amazed to learn how the Jews had maintained their beliefs and practices in spite of persecutions and harassment in many lands and historical periods. The more I learned, the more I was able to relate Jewish theology to current social issues.

Discovering the writings of Martin Buber further reinforced my emerging belief that it was actually the distortion of religion that I was so much against. I concluded that, to some extent, my religion had been "stolen." Back then in the 1960s, many observant Jews around me seemed to be locked into ritual for its own sake, without seeing or applying the deeper values that could challenge an unjust status quo. People were reading about Moses confronting Pharaoh in the Torah, but few were confronting the oppressors of our own time.

While teaching at City College, I studied for my master's degree in civil engineering. I was enjoying my teaching and interactions with students so much that I decided to make college teaching my career. However, I didn't want to seek a PhD, because it would involve doing research in a relatively narrow area. Back then, many engineering colleges were

---

1. Abraham Joshua Heschel, *The Insecurity of Freedom*, (New York: Ferrar, Strauss, and Giroux, 1967), 1–2.

accepting professional engineering licenses in lieu of a PhD, so I decided to pursue that path instead. This involved getting some experience working in industry and passing several tests. My teaching experience and strong academic background made passing the tests a relatively easy matter, but I had to leave teaching for a while in order to get the required experience.

Before entering the engineering field, I decided to take care of my military obligations. At that time, the United States was in a major technological race against the then Soviet Union. In 1958 the Soviets surprised the world by launching Sputnik I, the world's first artificial satellite. This was a wake-up call to the U.S. government, a warning that we were falling behind in technology. As a result, engineers were classified by the military into a special category called "Critical Skills." The government's philosophy at the time was that everyone should get some basic training in order to be ready if the United States was attacked, but that people with special skills should not be taken away for long periods from the important work of improving the nation's technological abilities.

Therefore, I only had to be in the U.S. Army for three months. Those few months in the army were the only substantial time in my adult life when I was not focused on studying for tests, preparing class lectures and other talks, researching and writing articles and books, and dealing with other professional concerns. It was a valuable time for organizing my thoughts about social issues. After leaving the army, I worked at Ammon & Whitney, the engineering company in lower Manhattan that designed the Verrazano-Narrows Bridge connecting Staten Island and Brooklyn. I did not work on that project, but I did work on many other civil engineering design projects. Although I enjoyed working with other engineers and applying what I had learned, my desire to return to college teaching remained strong. As soon as I had sufficient practical experience, I arranged to take the necessary tests for my professional engineering license. Fortunately, because of my academic and teaching background, I easily passed.

My next step was to seek a position teaching civil engineering at a college. I thought that my academic achievements, my teaching experience, my professional experience, and my professional engineer's license would make this easy, but that was not the case. The only Civil Engineering Department willing to hire me was at Rutgers University, and then only if I also enrolled as a PhD candidate there. Seeing no other possibility that would enable me to resume teaching, I agreed. So I moved to New Brunswick, New Jersey, with my wife and first child, Susan Esther.

I enjoyed my new teaching activities, and once again did well in my engineering studies. However, I had difficulty choosing a topic for my PhD thesis. This was a source of great frustration to me. I loved teaching and wanted very much to continue it, but I absolutely hated the idea of spending endless hours researching a relatively minor topic that few people outside a specialized field would ever be interested in. I would much prefer to spend the time teaching and promoting positive causes. I became so frustrated over this that I even thought of dropping out of the PhD program altogether. When people warned me that this would end my chances of maintaining a college teaching position, I replied that I would just teach at a two-year college.

Had I dropped out of the PhD program it would have greatly hindered my teaching career, because even community colleges began to require PhD degrees for full-time teachers. Fortunately, I finally found a workable topic, "Analysis of Circular Plates on Elastic Foundations Under Radially Symmetrical Loadings," that enabled me to use my mathematical skills as well as others. I also received National Science Foundation grants for two consecutive summers, which provided me with some income, enabling me to work full-time on the project. In 1967 I received my PhD in Applied Mechanics. This enabled me to continue my teaching career until my retirement from the College of Staten Island as a full professor in 1999.

As I was completing my PhD requirements, I was informed that Rutgers had a "no inbreeding" policy. This meant that they did not continue employing people who had taught at Rutgers while getting their PhD degrees there. The Rutgers philosophy was that, by hiring people from a wide variety of other schools, they would get the greatest possible cross-fertilization of ideas. An academically laudable position, but one that left me without a job.

So once again I sent out resumes, and this time I received an invitation to teach at Pratt Institute in Brooklyn. They offered me a position as an assistant professor with the possibility of a rapid promotion to associate professor, and I accepted. Pratt did not have a civil engineering department, so I served in the mechanical engineering department; many of the courses that I had taught were equally applicable to both civil and mechanical engineering.

In 1968, my wife and I moved to Staten Island to be closer to Pratt Institute. By then we had three children: Susan Esther, David Elliot, and

Deborah Ann. In 1970 I learned that there was an opening at Staten Island Community College (SICC). The college was only about five minutes by car from my house, which would make it easier to help out with the kids. The position had a better salary and benefits as well, so I decided to apply. I was accepted, but only as a substitute in the civil technology department for a professor who had left for a year to help set up Hostos Community College in the Bronx. I was told that the professor for whom I was substituting probably wouldn't return. However, he did decide to return, and that put me in a very difficult position. I had given up a tenured position at Pratt Institute to be a substitute at SICC. Now it looked like I would have to leave. My efforts at finding another position were not panning out, and I was becoming increasingly desperate.

Fortunately, the City University started its "Open Admissions" policy at that time, providing remediation to students who did not meet entrance requirements in Mathematics and English. Because of that program, I was able to join the SICC mathematics department, teaching remedial math. It wasn't the ideal job, but it provided a salary which helped feed my family. Needless to say, this was a very difficult time in my life. But, as the Chinese philosopher Lin Yutang said in his book *The Importance of Living*, one does not know what is "good luck" or "bad luck" until the end of a sequence of events, because what appears to be a negative event often leads to a positive result and vice versa. In the Jewish tradition, there is a similar teaching. Joseph, who is sold into slavery by his brothers, ends up becoming an important official in Egypt and saves many people from famine, including those very same brothers who had betrayed him in the first place.

And so it turned out for me, that my "bad luck" became my good fortune. During the difficult period when I was trying to find a new teaching position, I went to the director of an experimental department at SICC known as The Place, which offered a number of interdisciplinary courses. I asked about the possibility of teaching in their department. They had no opening at the time, but later, after I was teaching in the mathematics department, they asked me to teach a course on "The Impact of Science on Human Values and Problems."

At first I hesitated; this topic was completely different from anything I had previously taught or even considered before. At the same time, it offered the possibility of applying my interest in social issues. I decided to accept the offer. That was a major turning point in my life, because teaching that course started me on the path of environmental activism that I still pursue today.

Through the study of essays, short stories, and plays, the students and I explored the implications of the rapid explosion of scientific and technological advances on society and its problems. This was right after the first Earth Day in April 1970, when there was widespread interest in environmental threats, so we devoted a lot of discussion time to ecological issues. As I became increasingly concerned about the environment, the original course was replaced by a new one called "Environmental Issues on Staten Island."

I was a relatively new resident of Staten Island, so I had to rely on local resources to help me teach the course. I pored over old newspapers and reports, interviewed Staten Island environmentalists, invited guest speakers, and showed films and videos. We also went on field trips to places like Fresh Kills landfill (then the world's largest garbage dump). We also visited different types of housing developments, sewage treatment plants, and natural areas. Instead of a final examination, the students were required to write a report and give an oral presentation about some current environmental issue impacting Staten Island.

Because this course was so different from anything I had previously taught, I devoted a great deal of my time, energy, and thinking to developing it. In the process, I became increasingly active in responding to environmental issues, often writing letters to the editor for publication in the *Staten Island Advance* about local and national environmental and other societal concerns. I also spoke on these topics to various groups at the college and in the community.

After a number of years teaching "Environmental Issues on Staten Island," budgetary considerations led to an end of The Place. As a result, I was no longer able to offer the course. At first, this was a big disappointment. But I soon recognized that this "disaster" had, in fact, freed up a lot of time and energy that I could now devote to other activities. I was determined to continue educating people about environmental issues, and it dawned on me that perhaps I could teach a course that related mathematics to environmental and other global concerns.

At the time, I was teaching a basic math course for liberal arts majors. This was a course that students had to take in order to fulfill the requirements for their degrees. Most of the students were poorly prepared and even less motivated. So instead of the usual course that included a smorgasbord of unconnected topics, I decided to offer a course called "Mathematics and the Environment," in which basic mathematical concepts and problems would be used to explore current critical problems. Using basic calculations, ratios and proportions, circle diagrams, bar charts, line graphs, scatter plots, sequences, and elementary statistics and probability, we considered such issues as pollution, resource scarcities, hunger, energy, population growth, nutrition, and health. In short, my course covered similar mathematical concepts to those in the old course, but all the examples and exercises connected with environmental concerns. The course was well received. I found plenty of valuable material in the daily newspapers and weekly magazines, which I used to create mathematical problems. The annual *World Population Data Sheet* of the Population Reference Bureau and that group's many demographic reports were also very valuable. The class considered issues like percentages of the world's population in the United States versus China, projected increases in world population, effects of infant mortality, etc.

Analyzing the computer-generated graphs in a book entitled *The Limits to Growth,* we saw that the world would face severe future problems if global population and industrial production continued to increase exponentially. Once again, instead of a final exam, I required written and oral reports on environmentally related topics, using the mathematics that students had learned in the course.

Designing this course resulted in my reading, thinking, and teaching about a wide variety of environmental crises. As I worked with the statistics related to these issues, I became increasingly aware of environmental threats and the urgent need to respond to them. During my first sabbatical, in the 1978–79 academic year, I wrote a course text called *Mathematics and Global Survival.* This book was updated and revised every few years to reflect changing conditions, and became the foundation for my later book, *Judaism and Global Survival,* which is still in print today.

*

Throughout my academic career, my involvement in Judaism was also growing. After moving to Staten Island in 1968, my family immediately joined the local modern Orthodox synagogue. I have met wonderful, generous, sincere, deeply committed people in this congregation. I have found many members to be extremely charitable, kind, and deeply involved in learning and *davening.* Given these involvements and my personal friendships, as well as an awareness of own limitations and weaknesses, it is not easy to be critical of my own community. But I think some constructive criticism might be valuable. Through the application of Jewish teachings on social activism, we can join in the process of moving our endangered planet to a more just, peaceful, and environmentally sustainable path. It is no longer enough to ask "Is it good for the Jews?" We must now also ask "Is it good for the planet?"

I am deeply disturbed by the seeming lack of concern for universal issues among many of my religious Jewish brethren (as well as most other people). Within their own communities they are very caring and generous, but they often seem oblivious to issues that affect the rest of humanity. It sometimes seems that one can be more readily accepted in the Orthodox Jewish community today if one has intolerant, reactionary ideas than if one has a commitment to Jewish universal values.

For this reason, I often need to go outside my immediate synagogue group in order to find support for my Jewish activism. Through my articles, talks, books, and letters to editors, I am able to express my societal concerns, but I often feel alienated from my local community in the process. How grateful I am to be living in the age of email and the Internet! The electronic age has enabled me to be in regular contact with many like-minded people around the world, express my ideas to a wider audience, and to reach beyond the limitations of my own community.

In the early 1970s, partly in an attempt to increase my synagogue's involvement in social justice issues, I became co-editor of the synagogue's newsletter and frequently contributed articles. I was (and still am) searching for ways to demonstrate Judaism's meaning and relevance to the world. I sensed a great gap between the glorious Jewish teachings that I was learning about and the realities that I was seeing in my synagogue and Jewish community. Jews have been chosen to be God's servants, a light unto the nations and a holy people, descendants of the prophets, the original champions of social justice. Why, then, was there so much complacency in the face of so many critical problems? Why so few dreams of a better world through the application of Jewish teachings?

I saw great potential for applying the values I was reading about in Jewish texts to the real world around us. I wanted to help revitalize Judaism, to harness it to help save our imperiled planet. My reaction to the Judaism of the time is summed up in the following paragraph from one of my articles for the synagogue newsletter:

It is generally not religious values that dominate in churches and synagogues today, but rather materialistic, middle-class values. The problem is that far too few people (sometimes including myself) take God and religious teachings seriously enough. If we did, would we fail to protest against the destruction of the precious planet that God has given us as our home? Would we be so apathetic while millions of people die of hunger and its effects annually (when God has provided sufficient food for every person on earth), and additional millions suffer from poverty and a lack of shelter, clean water, and other necessities, while hundreds of billions of dollars are spent creating newer and better ways to wage war? If a person took God and religious values seriously, he or she would be among the greatest critics of society, where religious values are generally given lip service, at best. She or he would be among the greatest champions of peace and justice.

Unfortunately, these editorials were like crying into the wilderness. Nobody appeared to be listening. I felt as if I were tilting at windmills, engaging in a quixotic quest for "The Impossible Dream." This book is my latest attempt to turn these dreams into practical realities.

The "Mathematics and the Environment" course had another profound effect on my life: it set me on the road toward vegetarianism. Up until 1978, I was a typical American meat and potatoes eater. My mother would be sure to prepare my favorite dish – pot roast – whenever I came to visit with my wife and children. It was a family tradition that I would be served a turkey drumstick every Thanksgiving. And yet, I not only became a vegetarian (and later a vegan), but also now devote a major part of my time to writing, speaking, and teaching about the benefits of vegetarianism. What caused this major change?

While reviewing material on world hunger for my "Mathematics and the Environment" course in the 1970s, I became increasingly aware of the tremendous waste of grain that results from the production of beef. Over 70% of the grain produced in the United States and about 40% of the grain produced worldwide is fed to animals destined for slaughter, while millions of people – many of them children – die of hunger and its effects annually. In spite of my own eating habits, I often led class discussions on the possibility of reducing meat consumption as a way of helping hungry people. After several semesters of this, I listened to my own advice and gave up eating red meat, while continuing to eat chicken and fish.

I then began to read about the many health benefits of vegetarianism and about the horrible living conditions of animals raised on factory farms. As a result, I was increasingly attracted to the vegetarian way of life. I was very fortunate to take a course on "Judaism and Vegetarianism" at Lincoln Square Synagogue (LSS) in Manhattan taught by Jonathan Wolf, founder and first president of Jewish Vegetarians of North America. I learned many things and gained much insight from him.

On January 1, 1978, I decided to join the International Jewish Vegetarian Society. The membership form offered two choices: (1) practicing vegetarian (one who refrains from eating any flesh), or (2) non-vegetarian (one who is in sympathy with the movement, but not yet a vegetarian). I decided to become a practicing vegetarian. I checked that box on the form, and ever since that moment I have avoided eating any meat, fowl, or fish. In 2000, I became a vegan, abstaining from knowingly using any animal products, except those employed for religious purposes to make such ritual objects as Torah scrolls, *mezzuzot*, and *tefillin*.

After becoming a vegetarian in 1978, I learned a great deal more about vegetarianism's connections to health, nutrition, ecology, and animal welfare. Plus, I began wondering about the deeper connections between my vegetarianism and Judaism. I learned that the first biblical dietary regimen (Genesis 1:29) was strictly vegan, and that the future age of world peace and harmony, the Messianic period, will also be a vegan time. I soon became convinced that there are important Jewish mandates to preserve our health, be kind to animals, protect the environment, conserve natural resources, share with hungry people, and seek and pursue peace – all of which point to vegetarianism as the ideal diet for Jews. To get this message out to a wider audience, I wrote *Judaism and Vegetarianism*, which was first published in 1982, with revised and expanded editions published in 1988 and 2001.

The more I have learned about the wastefulness of meat production, the negative health effects of animal-based diets, and the cruelties of factory farms – and their inconsistencies with Jewish values – the more I have come to see a switch toward vegetarianism as not only a personal choice but as societal and Jewish imperatives. Reducing meat consumption is an essential component in the solution of many national and global problems, as well as an important symbolic religious move toward the peaceable kingdom envisioned by the prophets.

In recent years, I have been devoting considerable time and energy toward making others aware of the importance of switching toward vegetarian diets, both for themselves and for the world. I have appeared on many radio and cable television programs, contributed many letters and several op-ed articles in a variety of publications, spoken frequently at conferences and meetings, given dozens of talks, and met with four Chief Rabbis and other religious and political leaders in Israel, while visiting my two daughters and their families. In addition:

- I am now president emeritus of Jewish Veg (formerly known as Jewish Vegetarians of North America), and while I was president I produced and sent out almost weekly e-mail newsletters to keep Jewish vegetarians informed.
- I have over 200 articles, 25 podcasts of my talks and articles, and the complete texts of my other Judaica books at JewishVeg.com/schwartz.
- In 1987, I was selected as "Jewish Vegetarian of the Year" by the JVNA.
- In 2005, I was inducted into the "Hall of Fame" of the North American Vegetarian Society.
- I am also president of the Society of Ethical and Religious Vegetarians (SERV), an interreligious group dedicated to spreading vegetarian messages in many religious communities.
- I served for several years as director of Veg Climate Alliance, a group dedicated to spreading awareness that a major shift to plant-based diets is essential to avert an impending climate catastrophe.
- I also helped produce and appear in the documentary *A Sacred Duty: Applying Jewish Values to Help Heal the World*, which premiered in Jerusalem in November 2007. Because the issues are so important and the threats are so great, we have given out over 40,000 complimentary copies of the DVD and made it freely available on You Tube. It was produced as a labor of love and dedication, with no professional fee being received, by multi-award winning producer, director, writer, and cinematographer Lionel Friedberg, along with his wife Diana, a professional film editor. The documentary has been acclaimed by Jews, Christians, and others and has had a significant impact.
- In 2015, I spent two months in Israel increasing awareness of the importance of switches to plant-based diets to efforts to avert a climate catastrophe and other potential environmental disasters. I gave eight talks and two radio interviews, and interviewed key Israeli environmen-

talists, animal rights activists, rabbis, and other influential Israelis. The interviews and five of my talks were filmed and uploaded to YouTube. The links can be found at my *Times of Israel* blog.

As I reflect on all of the above, I am so thankful that I have been blessed by God to have been able to make at least a small difference in trying to help produce a better world. Of course there is much more that needs to be done, and I hope to be able to devote much of the time that I will be granted by God to continuing the struggle. I hope that this book will help inspire many others, especially young people, to work in the struggle to shift our very imperiled planet to a healthier, more just, peaceful, more humane, environmentally sustainable path.

Appendix B

Action Ideas:
Putting Jewish Values into Practice

T HE WORLD FACES A very dangerous situation today. As Woody Allen cynically put it, "More than any other time in history, mankind faces a crossroads. One path leads to despair and utter hopelessness. The other, to total extinction. Let us pray we have the wisdom to choose correctly." While that may often seem true, we also have a chance to show that there is another path – a path to a far better world – by truly applying Jewish values to present crises. To help do this, some action suggestions are below. They are consistent with the Talmudic teaching that "it is not study that is the chief thing, but action" (*Kiddushin* 40b).

In attempting to change the world, sometimes we have to start by changing ourselves. Rabbi Israel Salanter, the founder of the Mussar (ethics) movement in Lithuania, taught: "First a person should put his house together, then his town, then his world." If you feel that global crises are so overwhelming that your efforts will have little effect, then consider the following. Judaism teaches: "You are not obligated to complete the task, but neither are you free to desist from it" (*Pirkei Avot* 2:21). Each of us must make a start and do whatever he or she can to help improve the world. Judaism also teaches that a person is obligated to protest when there is evil and, if necessary, to proceed from protest to action. Each person is to imagine that the world is evenly balanced between good and evil, and that each good deed tips the whole world toward the side of good. Therefore, her or his actions can determine the destiny of the entire world. Even if little is accomplished right away, the act of trying to make improvements will prevent the hardening of one's heart and will affirm acceptance of an obligation to try to improve conditions. Even the act of consciousness-raising itself is important, because it may lead to future action for change.

In considering how much to become involved, please consider that the world is approaching climate, food, energy, water, and other environmental catastrophes, as well as other threats. Consider how essential it is that major changes soon be made so that future generations will have a decent world in which to live. Here are some things each person can do:

- Become well informed. Learn the facts about current environmental and other societal problems and the applicable Jewish teachings from this and other books (see Bibliography).

- Check rumors you receive by email against the facts before passing them on to others. Snopes.com is an excellent resource for verifying whether or not a particular Internet rumor is a hoax. Remember: spreading *lashon hara* (evil gossip) is contrary to Jewish teachings, and this includes material you send by email.

- Try to influence public policy on the issues discussed in this book. Organize letter-writing campaigns and group visits to politicians to lobby for a safer, saner, more stable world. Run for office if you feel inclined to do so. Members of city councils, school boards, and other local institutions can have a big impact. Think globally, act locally.

- Help inform others. Write timely letters to editors of publications. Set up programs and discussions. Become registered with community, library, or school speakers' bureaus. Wear a button. Put bumper stickers where many people will see them. Make and display posters.

- Simplify your life-style. Conserve energy. Recycle materials. Buy and wear used clothing. Bike or walk whenever possible, rather than drive, and learn to combine errands on your trips. Share rides. Use mass transit when appropriate.

- Become a vegetarian, and preferably a vegan, or at least sharply reduce your consumption of animal products. As discussed in Chapter 13, veganism is the diet most consistent with such Jewish values as showing compassion to animals, taking care of one's health, preserving the environment, sharing with hungry people, conserving natural resources, and pursuing peace. Even if you don't feel you can give up meat and other animal products right now, try having a meatless day each week, when you try new vegan recipes at home, or eat out in a vegetarian or vegan restaurant.

- Work with organizations and groups on some of the significant issues discussed in this book. If your time is limited, then choose one issue and devote yourself to that. For contact information for Jewish groups working on such issues see Appendix C. If there are no local groups, or if you differ with such groups on some important issues, set up a group in your synagogue, Jewish Center, or JCC.

- Encourage your public and congregational libraries to order, stock, and circulate books on global issues and Jewish teachings related to them. Donate any duplicate copies. Request that libraries regularly acquire such books. Subscribe to relevant magazines, and, if you can afford it, buy some to donate.

- Speak or organize events with guest speakers and/or audio-visual presentations on how Jewish values address current critical issues. Consider requesting a complimentary DVD of the documentary film *A Sacred Duty: Applying Jewish Values to Help Heal the World* at aSacredDuty.com. Schedule a showing of the film at your synagogue or other local organization. Offer it to your local film festival or other arts event.

- Ask rabbis and other religious leaders to give sermons and/or classes discussing Judaism's teachings on social justice, sustainability, reducing hunger, peace, conservation, and other Jewish values and how they can be applied to current issues. Ask principals of yeshivas and day schools to see that their curricula reflect traditional Jewish environmental, peace, and justice teachings. Volunteer to speak to classes and to help plan curricula.

- Contact editors of local newspapers and ask that more space be devoted to current threats and on religious teachings related to them. Write articles and letters using information from this book and other books and magazines.

- Consult with rabbis and religious educators and leaders on how to apply to today's critical issues such Jewish mandates as "seek peace and pursue it," *bal tashchit* (you shall not waste), "justice, justice shall you pursue," and "love your neighbor as yourself."

- As an outgrowth of Jewish teachings on helping feed hungry people and conserving resources, work to end the tremendous amount of waste associated with many Jewish organizational functions and celebrations: Encourage friends and institutions to simplify, reduce wastefulness, and serve less food at celebratory events. Put this into practice at your own celebrations. Reclaim left over edible food from *simchas* (Jewish celebrations) to donate to shelters and food kitchens. Recommend to people hosting a celebration that they donate a portion of the cost of the event to Mazon (an organization discussed in Appendix C) or another group working to reduce hunger.

- Request that meat not be served at Jewish events, since the production of meat wastes grain, land, water, and other resources and contributes substantially to pollution, deforestation, desertification, loss of biodiversity, and climate change. Refraining from eating meat also expresses identification with the millions of people who lack an adequate diet, as well as the billions of farmed animals slaughtered each year.
- Start a community garden, or participate in one already established. Buy your food from local farmers' markets as much as possible.
- Help set up a committee to analyze and reduce energy consumption in your synagogue. Apply steps taken to reduce synagogue energy use as a model for similar action on other buildings and homes in the community.
- Set up a social action committee at your synagogue, temple, Jewish Center, day or afternoon school, or campus, to help people get more involved in educational and action-centered activities. Build coalitions with other social justice groups in your community.
- Raise the consciousness of your synagogue members and other local Jewish organizations and individuals about how Jewish teachings can be applied to respond to current societal problems. Ask respectful but challenging questions, such as those presented in Chapter 16.

Appendix C

Guide to Jewish Activist Organizations

L ISTED BELOW ARE SOME of the Jewish organizations working in
a wide variety of areas to improve the world and to involve Jews in
changing society. Many of the descriptions below are taken from
the groups' web sites, as sometimes indicated by quotation marks. Most
of these web sites have links to numerous other groups.

Inclusion of an organization in this list does not necessarily mean agreement with every position, action, and statement issued by the group or
its representatives. Rather, it means that they are doing some positive
things toward a more humane, compassionate, just, peaceful, and environmentally sustainable planet. Conversely, omission from this list does
not necessarily imply disapproval, only limited space. Readers are strongly
encouraged to investigate these and other organizations for themselves,
and make their own decisions about which ones to support and/or join.

AMERICAN JEWISH ENVIRONMENTAL ORGANIZATIONS

Aytzim: Ecological Judaism hosts Jewcology, the largest Jewish-environmental website; the Green Zionist Alliance, a green group able to
help write and implement Israeli environmental laws; and GreenFaith,
Shomrei Breishit: Rabbis and Cantors for the Earth. Their work in Israel
has led to more than two-million trees planted in Israel; the building of
hundreds of miles of bike paths; the declaration of nature preserves, saving
endangered species from extinction; the generation of more than 1,000
Jewish-environmental educational resources; and the commitment of over
100 Jewish clergy to become carbon neutral. www.aytzim.org

Canfei Nesharim (Wings of Eagles) connects traditional Jewish texts with contemporary scientific findings. It educates and empowers Jewish individuals, organizations, and communities to take active roles in protecting the environment, in order to build a more sustainable world inspired by Torah teachings. The long-term goal is to build a multi-denominational, multi-generational, regionally diverse community of Jewish environmental activists who are learning from one another and from an expanding set of Jewish-environmental resources how to educate their communities about the Jewish responsibility to protect the environment. www.canfeinesharim.org

The Coalition on the Environment and Jewish Life (COEJL) uses a network of Jewish institutions, leaders, and other individuals to increase the Jewish community's involvement in environmental stewardship. It strives to educate the Jewish community on environmental issues, promotes conservation and renewable energy sources, and provides a Jewish voice in the environmental community and the broader interfaith community and an environmental voice in the Jewish community. www.coejl.org

Hazon works to create healthy and sustainable communities in the Jewish world and beyond through supporting the Jewish environmental movement in the U.S. and Israel. They organize Jewish environmental bike rides to raise money for environmental groups in Israel, promote partnerships between synagogues and local farmers, hold annual conferences to consider Jewish teachings on agriculture and diets, and have a website which features discussions of Jewish teachings on food-related issues. www.hazon.org

Jewish National Fund (JNF) has worked for over 100 years to improve Israel's environment by planting 240 million trees, building over 210 reservoirs and dams, developing over 250,000 acres of land, creating more than 1,000 parks, providing the infrastructure for over 1,000 communities, and bringing life to the Negev Desert. They have educated students around the world about Israel and its environment. In the midst of Israel's recent droughts, they are working to increase the efficiency of Israel's water use. www.jnf.org

The Shalom Center is committed to inspiring the Jewish community to greater awareness and involvement on issues of peace, justice, and environmental sustainability for the planet and all its inhabitants. Working with peace and justice advocates of all faiths, it promotes activities related to Jewish holidays and other occasions to increase awareness of threats from "global scorching" and the importance of a sane energy policy. www.theshalomcenter.org

Teva Learning Center partners with Jewish day schools, congregational schools, synagogues, camps, and youth groups to educate Jews about nature and Jewish environmental teachings. Teva's programs, most of which occur at Surprise Lake Camp in the picturesque mountains at Cold Spring, New York, stress experiential learning to advance the skills of environmental educators and increase the awareness of Jewish youth. They touch the lives of 6,000 participants annually. www.TevaLearning Center.org

ENVIRONMENTAL ORGANIZATIONS IN ISRAEL

Most Israeli websites have both a Hebrew and English version. If a listed website first appears on your screen in Hebrew, find and click on the English icon or link for the translation.

Arava Institute for Environmental Studies is a teaching and research center that stresses regional cooperation in solving environmental problems, with the hope that this will lead to peace and harmony in the region. Located at Kibbutz Ketura, in the Negev, it educates Jewish, Palestinian, Jordanian, and international students with the hope that they will become future environmental leaders in their countries. www.araEcoPeace/va.org

EcoPeace Middle East, formerly Friends of the Earth Middle East (FoEME) brings together Jordanian, Palestinian, and Israeli environmentalists. Their primary objective is the promotion of cooperative efforts to protect our shared environmental heritage, with an emphasis on the Jordan River and the Dead Sea. In so doing, they seek to advance both sustainable regional development and the creation of necessary conditions for lasting peace in the Middle East. They have offices in Tel Aviv, Amman, and Bethlehem. www.foeme.org

Green Course (Megamah Yeruka) is Israel's largest volunteer environmental organization, with over 6,000 student volunteers in 26 chapters on campuses across Israel. Through Green Course, students are active in projects to raise public awareness to environmental issues. The group plans to expand beyond the campuses that have been its central focus. www.israelnonprofitnews.com/directory/environment/green-course/

Heschel Center for Environmental Learning and Leadership, named after Rabbi Abraham Joshua Heschel, trains leaders, produces publications on Israel's environmental problems, holds educational seminars, and cooperates with foundations in order to try to create a healthier, more environmentally sustainable Israel. http://www.israelgives.org/amuta/580237097

Israel Union for Environmental Defense (I.U.E.D.), known in Hebrew as *Adam Teva V'Din*, employs about thirty environmentalists, attorneys, and scientists to work toward a more environmentally sustainable Israel through education, litigation, and cooperation with local groups and efforts to pass stronger environmental legislation. www.iued.org.il

Keren Kayemet L'Yisrael (KKL), Israel's Jewish National Fund, is leading the quest for a more environmental Israel by educating people to appreciate Israel's natural and cultural heritage. KKL's work in Israel is concentrated in six action areas: water, forestry and environment, education, community development and security, tourism and recreation, and research and development. www.kkl.org.il

Life and the Environment (Chaim V'Sviva) serves as the umbrella organization of 130 Israeli organizations that deal with public health, sustainable development, and public participation in planning. Life and the Environment focuses on empowering its member organizations in order to better influence decision-making processes, and it has assumed a leadership role in furthering the integration of issues of sustainable development and environmental justice into the discourse of both civil society and government agencies. www.sviva.net

Society for the Protection of Nature in Israel (SPNI) conducts numerous hikes and educational tours that many Israelis and tourists participate in, and it helps educate the public on environmental issues. It also lobbies to promote a cleaner and greener Israel. It played a major role in preventing a major housing development that would have seriously harmed the Jerusalem Forest. www.natureisrael.org

JEWISH ORGANIZATIONS COMBATING
HUNGER AND POVERTY

Many Jewish groups are working to reduce poverty and to help poor people in the United States and worldwide achieve self-sufficiency. Below are just a few of them.

American Jewish World Service (AJWS) strives to reduce poverty, hunger, and disease for all of the world's people, based on the Jewish imperative to pursue justice. They use education, advocacy, volunteer service, and grants to local grassroots organizations to promote sustainable development and human rights for all people, and also work to educate Jews about Jewish teachings on the responsibilities of global citizenship. www.ajws.org

Bend The Arc: A Jewish Partnership for Justice is building the power and passion of the progressive Jewish movement in American by bringing together Jews from across the country to advocate and organize for a more just and equal society. www.bendthearc.us

Jews For Racial and Economic Justice pursues racial and economic justice in New York City by promoting systemic changes that can improve people's daily lives. They engage individual Jews and key Jewish leaders and institutions in the struggle for economic and racial justice in partnership with minority groups and low-income and immigrant communities. www.jfrej.org

Mazon provides a "Jewish Response to Hunger." The group seeks to reduce hunger worldwide by encouraging Jews to donate three percent of the cost of their festive occasions to Mazon, which allocates these donations to hunger relief organizations in the US, Israel, and around the world to help feed hungry people. www.mazon.org

Ve'ahavta is a Canadian humanitarian and relief organization that is motivated by the Jewish value of *tzedakah* – the obligation to act justly – to
help needy people locally and abroad through volunteerism, education,
and acts of kindness, while building bridges between Jews and others
worldwide. www.veahavta.org/

JEWISH PEACE AND JUSTICE-
RELATED ORGANIZATIONS

Israel/Palestine Center for Research and Information is a joint Pales-
tinian-Israeli public policy organization that is committed to developing
practical solutions for the Israeli-Palestinian conflict. They publish articles
and hold educational meetings to increase awareness and actions that they
hope will lead to greater tolerance, harmony, and peace. http://ipcri.org
/httpdocs/IPCRI/About_Us.html

Jewish Peace Fellowship (JPF) is "A Jewish voice in the peace community and a peace voice in the Jewish community." They are a pacifist group
committed to active nonviolence as a means of resolving conflicts, drawing
on Jewish traditional sources within the Torah, the Talmud, and recent
peacemaking activists like Martin Buber, Judah Magnes and Abraham
Joshua Heschel. They also counsel conscientious objectors. www.Jewis
hPeaceFellowship.org

Jewish Peace Lobby promotes a just, comprehensive resolution of the
Israeli-Palestinian conflict, which they believe will lead to a secure and
humane Israel, within which human rights and democratic values are
protected. They try to be a counterpoint to other pro-Israel lobbying
groups that generally give uncritical support to Israeli government actions.
www.peacelobby.org

J Street is the "pro-Israel, pro-peace" organization that strives to give
political voice to mainstream American Jews and other supporters of
Israel, especially those who, "informed by their progressive and Jewish
values, believe that a two-state solution to the Israeli-Palestinian conflict
is essential to Israel's survival as the national home of the Jewish people
and as a vibrant democracy." www.JStreet.org

Oz v'Shalom/Netivot Shalom is a group of Orthodox Israelis dedicated to seeking a two-state solution of the Israeli/Palestinian conflict and educating Israelis and others about Jewish teachings on peace and justice. The group's approach is discussed in detail in chapter 7. www.netivot-sh alom.org.il

Partners for Progressive Israel is a progressive Zionist organization that promotes a just and durable two-state solution between Israel and the Palestinians, peace between Israel and her Arab neighbors, and equality, social justice, and human and civil rights for all residents of Israel. It is affiliated with the World Union of Meretz. www.Progressiveisrael.org

Peace Now (Shalom Achshav) aims to sway public and governmental opinion toward achieving a just peace and a historic conciliation with the Palestinian people and neighboring Arab countries, in exchange for a territorial settlement based on the formula of "land for peace." They monitor construction on the West Bank and report on their findings, with the hope that increased awareness of the facts will slow settlement expansion. They have a U.S. support group, "Americans for Peace Now." www.PeaceNow.org

Tevel B'Tzedek (The Earth in Justice) is an Israel based non-profit organization promoting social and environmental justice. Its mission is to create a community of Israeli and Diaspora Jews engaging in the urgent issues of global poverty, marginalization and environmental devastation based on a deep commitment to the Jewish people and its ethical and spiritual traditions. www.tevelbtzedek.org

Tru'ah, formerly known as Rabbis for Human Rights (RHR), promotes the Jewish and Zionist tradition of concern for human rights. RHR promotes human rights in Israel and in the territories for which Israel has taken responsibility. www.rhr.org.il

The group has a North American support group called Rabbis for Human Rights North America. www.rhr-na.org

Uri L'Tzedek is an Orthodox social justice organization guided by Torah values and dedicated to combating suffering and oppression. Through community based education, leadership development, and action, Uri

L'Tzedek creates discourse, inspires leaders, and empowers the Jewish community towards creating a more just world. The group organizes many events to educate people about Judaism's powerful message on social justice issues. www.utzedek.org

Alliance to End Chickens as Kapporos is an association of groups and individuals who seek to replace the use of chickens in *kapporot* ceremonies with money or other non-animal symbols of atonement. The alliance does not oppose *kapparot* per se, only the cruel and unnecessary use of chickens in the ceremony. www.endchickensaskaporos.com

Anonymous for Animal Rights, one of Israel's leading animal rights organizations, chose the name "Anonymous" out of their deep solidarity with the suffering of animals who have no name, identity, or voice, and "who are subjected to systematic abuse . . . imprisoned in laboratories, circuses, municipal pounds – but above all on factory farms." They produce literature and conduct demonstrations in efforts to reduce animal suffering. www.anonymous.org.il/cat78.html

Concern for Helping Animals in Israel (CHAI) participated in drafting the Israeli Animal Protection Law, provided help to shelters, imported the first animal ambulance and mobile spay/neuter clinic, and rescued and re-homed hundreds of animals. CHAI co-sponsored educational conferences and projects with government ministries to, for example, introduce humane education into Israeli schools – both Jewish and Arab. CHAI campaigned against cruelties, resulting in the humane oral rabies vaccine replacing mass strychnine poisoning, and in banning cruel horse and donkey-drawn carts on city streets and highways. CHAI wrote extensive humane education materials for all grades. www.chai-online.org

The International Jewish Vegetarian Society has, since 1965, been the center for international Jewish vegetarian activism. Centered in London, they distribute a quarterly publication *The Jewish Vegetarian* that includes articles, news of vegetarian events, recipes, and other vegetarian-related material. www.jvs.org.uk

Israeli Jewish Vegetarian Society (Ginger), centered in Jerusalem, helps educate Israelis about Jewish teachings on vegetarianism, and brings Israeli vegetarians together through lectures, cooking demonstrations, pot-luck meals, and other vegetarian-related events, as well as Tu B'Shvat and Passover seders. www.ginger.org.il

Jews for Animal Rights (JAR) is a resource to educate people about and to answer questions on Jewish teachings on vegetarianism and animal rights. The group is associated with Micah Publications, so many vegetarian and animal rights books are shown on their website. www.micahbooks.com

Jewish Veg, formerly known as Jewish Vegetarians of North America (JVNA), argues that Judaism mandates to preserve human health, treat animals with compassion, protect the environment, conserve natural resources, help hungry people, pursue peace, and make vegetarianism (and preferably veganism) the ideal diet for Jews. To help increase awareness of Jewish teachings on vegetarianism, the group has given away over 40,000 complimentary DVDs with its acclaimed documentary, *A Sacred Duty: Applying Jewish Values to Help Heal the World.* www.JewishVeg.org

Shamayim V'Aretz, a center for Jewish spirituality and leadership, was founded by Rabbi Shmuly Yanklowitz, also a founder of Uri L'Tzedek. Their core mission is to educate about the value of kosher veganism, to empower others to show leadership on animal welfare issues, and to build Jewish spiritual community around these issues. www.shamayimvaretz.org

OTHER ACTIVIST JEWISH ORGANIZATIONS

CLAL, "The National Jewish Center for Learning and Leadership," is a think tank, resource center, and leadership training institute that encourages pluralism and openness, and strives to link innovative scholarship with Jewish wisdom to deepen Jewish involvement in American spiritual and civic life. www.clal.org

Jewish Prisoner Services International (JPSI) serves Jewish inmates and their families worldwide. They provide volunteers (both rabbis and laypersons) to visit inmates, conduct classes, collect Jewish books and ritual items, and correspond as pen pals. In addition, they advocate for Jewish prisoners' religious rights within the prison system. www.jpsi.org

New Israel Fund (NIF) is "a philanthropic partnership of North Americans and Israelis dedicated to strengthening democracy and advancing social justice and religious pluralism in Israel." The group supports hundreds of Israeli NGOs committed to social justice, equality, peace, and tolerance in Israel. www.nif.org

Religious Action Center of Reform Judaism (RAC) for over 50 years has been a center of legislative activity in Washington, DC, based on Jewish social justice teachings. The organization strives to educate and mobilize Reform Jews on involvement in over seventy societal issues, including civil rights, economic justice, civil liberties, religious liberty, and Israel. www.rac.org

ORGANIZATIONS CO-SPONSORED
BY JEWS WITH OTHERS

Neve Shalom/What al-Salam ("Oasis of Peace") is a village jointly established in 1985 by Jewish and Palestinian Arab citizens of Israel. They engage in educational work for peace, equality, and understanding between the two peoples. In addition to sponsoring local programs and a Palestinian children's summer camp, NS-WAS has accommodations for individual visitors and groups, including a 39 room hotel, conference halls, restaurants, and a café. www.wasns.org

The Abraham Fund Initiatives has been working since 1989 to promote coexistence and equality among Israel's Jewish and Arab citizens. Named for the common ancestor of both Jews and Arabs, The Abraham Fund advances a cohesive, secure, and just Israeli society by promoting policies based on innovative social models, and by conducting large-scale social change initiatives, advocacy, and public education. www.abraham.org

Interfaith Encounter Association strives to promote Middle East peace through interfaith dialogue and cross-cultural study. They believe that religious teachings can and should help resolve conflicts that exist in the region and beyond. www.interfaith-encounter.org

Network of Spiritual Progressives (NSP) initiated and actively promotes campaigns for a modern "Global Marshall Plan" (discussed in chapter 10), and a campaign for a constitutional amendment to preserve democracy and require corporate environmental responsibility. www.spiritualprogressives.org

EDUCATIONAL GROUPS

Areyvut aims to infuse the lives of Jewish youth and teenagers with the core Jewish values of *chesed* (kindness), *tzedakah* (charity), and *tikkun olam* (social action). Areyvut offers Jewish day schools, congregational schools, synagogues, community centers, and families a variety of opportunities to empower and enrich their youth by creating innovative programs that make these core Jewish values real and meaningful to them. The group's activities are also discussed in chapter 14. www.areyvut.org

Institute for Jewish Ideas and Ideals fosters an appreciation of legitimate diversity within Orthodoxy. "It wishes to create an Orthodox Jewish life that is intellectually alive, creative, inclusive, open to responsible discussion and diverse opinions, active in the general Jewish community, and in society as a whole, engaged in serious and sophisticated Jewish education for children and adults, committed to addressing the *halakhic* and philosophic problems of our times, [and] drawing on the wisdom and experience of diverse Jewish communities throughout history." www.jewishideas.org

ORTHODOX GROUPS HELPING THE POOR AND NEEDY

The following, in alphabetical order, is a sampling of Orthodox Jewish groups that are involved with helping sick and needy people and performing other charitable acts. As with the other activist lists above, not everything of importance about each group is included, and some very worthy groups are not listed below because of space considerations. Much of the information on the groups is from their websites.

Aleph Institute is the Chabad (Lubavitch) outreach organization for helping Jewish prisoners and their families. Aleph has created and implemented a host of highly acclaimed programs for Jews who are isolated due to incarceration. They provide books, calendars, and ritual items, such as *tallit* and *tefillin*. Chabad rabbis also visit and correspond with inmates, and work with prison chaplains to advocate for prisoner's religious rights. www.aleph-institute.org

Bema'aglei Tzedek (Circles of Justice) works to empower young Israelis to apply Jewish values in becoming powerful agents of social change. They use creative educational tools and social action campaigns to "create a more just Israeli society, informed and inspired by Jewish values." Among the issues they address are reducing poverty, increasing access for handicapped people, and improving conditions for women. They believe in the importance of addressing root causes of Israel's socioeconomic problems and in the power of average Israelis to join together to create a better society, based on Jewish sources. www.mtzedek.org.il/english/AboutUs.asp

Bikur Cholim, "visiting the sick," involves many individuals and groups in Jewish communities providing support and comfort to people who are ill, homebound, isolated, and/or otherwise in distress. Bikur Cholim includes such activities as visiting patients in a hospital, rehabilitation center, or nursing home; visiting people who are restricted to their home because of physical or psychological impairment or social isolation; taking people who are ill or impaired to doctor's appointments, on errands, or field trips; providing telephone contact and reassurance to those who are ill or homebound. www.bikurcholimcc.org/whatisbc.html and www.jbfcs.org/BikurCholim

Chai Lifeline strives to "bring joy to the lives of its young patients and their families through creative, innovative, and effective family-centered programs, activities, and services . . . providing unparalleled support throughout the child's illness, recovery, and beyond . . . offering all services free of charge . . . embodying the ideals of compassion, kindness, and caring for others inherent in Jewish culture and life." www.chailifeline.org

The Chofetz Chaim Heritage Foundation uses innovative methods to promote the Torah's wisdom on human relations and personal development. It uses a vast array of effective communication tools including books, tapes, video seminars, telephone classes, and a newsletter, designed to heighten awareness of such essential values as judging others favorably, speaking with restraint and integrity, and acting with respect and sensitivity. Their programs use Torah values in seeking to build a world of harmony and compassion. www.chofetzchaimusa.org

Friendship Circle builds friendships between children with special needs and teen volunteers. Their shared experiences empower the children, teach the teens the priceless value of giving, and enrich the lives of all involved. Sponsored by local Lubavitch Centers, it has about 80 locations worldwide. www.friendshipcircle.org

Gemachs, an abbreviation for *gemilut chasadim*, "acts of kindness," operate in many Jewish communities to loan gowns and other wedding items for future brides and others, using donations that they receive. Many people have expanded the concept of *gemachs* to include free loans of household items, clothing, books, equipment, services, and advice. Some *gemachs* groups loan costumes for Purim. Still others provide interest-free loans, with easy repayment terms. Contact your local Orthodox synagogue for information on a *gemach* group near you.

Hatzolah is the largest volunteer Emergency Medical Services and ambulance provider in the United States, with numerous branches serving communities throughout the United States and the world. It aims to save lives, as well as prevent, reduce, and treat injuries and illness. Hatzolah uses the latest equipment and has well-trained volunteers who respond to emergencies at a moment's notice. Their efforts have saved many lives. Hatzolah is available 24 hours a day, seven days a week, and they provide care equally to all who are in need, regardless of religion, race, or any other factors. www.hatzolahems.org

Maot Chitim provides matzah, wine, and other Passover needs to poor people before the holiday. Their actions are to help fulfill the opening paragraph of the *Haggadah* recited at the seder: "All who are hungry, let them come and eat." www.maotchitim.org/

Meir Panim relief centers in Israel help address the poverty crisis in Israel that affects over one and a half million people across the country. Meir

Panim is "committed to provide both immediate and long-term relief to the impoverished of Israel – young and old alike – via its dynamic range of food and social service programs in distressed cities throughout Israel, all aimed at helping the needy with dignity and respect." In addition to providing immediate assistance, they provide solutions to help poor Israelis break out of the cycle of poverty and become self-sufficient members of Israeli society. www.meirpanim.org

Ohel provides a wide variety of social services to Jews with a variety of needs. Among their many programs are children and family services, foster care for children who suffer from abuse and neglect, adolescent residential programs, counseling to teenagers and their families on drug, alcohol, gambling, eating disorders, and other addictions, counseling to victims of sexual abuse, providing school-based mental health workshops and other services, and many more. www.ohelfamily.org/

Tomchai Shabbat (Supporters of the Sabbath) involves several Jewish charities in different communities that provide food and other supplies to poor Jews to help them celebrate the Sabbath and the Jewish holidays. Their programs also help those without work find jobs, start businesses, and earn livelihoods. They provide clothing and furniture, assist with utilities and rent in emergency situations, help children obtain Jewish educations, and direct those in need to the proper social service organizations. https://en.wikipedia.org/wiki/Tomchei_Shabbos

Yachad, a group affiliated with the National Council of Synagogue Youth (NCSY), the youth group of the Orthodox Union (OU), is dedicated to addressing the needs of all individuals with disabilities and including them in the Jewish community. Yachad chapters are located throughout the United States and Canada and they have several inclusive activities per month. www.njcd.org

Annotated Bibliography

BOOKS RELATING JUDAISM TO CURRENT ISSUES

AMSEL, NACHUM. *The Jewish Encyclopedia of Moral and Ethical Issues.* Jason Aronson, Northvale, New Jersey, 1996. Short essays summarizing Jewish teachings on many ethical issues.

BEN-AMI, JEREMY. *A New Voice for Israel: Fighting for the Survival of the Jewish Nation.* Macmillan, New York, 2011. The director of J Street argues for respectful dialogues in the Jewish community and for the two-state solution.

BENSTEIN, JEREMY. *The Way Into Judaism and the Environment.* Jewish Lights Publishing, Woodstock, Vermont, 2006. A founder and associate director of Israel's Heschel Center for Environmental Learning and Leadership relates the Torah and other traditional sources to Israeli and world environmental crises, the proper treatment of animals, and dietary concerns.

BERNSTEIN, ELLEN, EDITOR. *Ecology and the Jewish Spirit: Where Nature and the Spirit Meet.* Jewish Lights Publishing, Woodstock, Vermont, 1998. A wide variety of Jewish perspectives on environmental issues.

BERNSTEIN, ELLEN AND DAN FINK. *Let the Earth Teach You Torah: A Guide to Teaching Ecological Wisdom.* Shomrei Adamah, Wyncote, Pennsylvania, 1992. Guidebook for teaching Jewish perspectives on the human relationship with nature.

BROYDE, MICHAEL AND JOHN WITTE (EDS.). *Human Rights in Judaism: Cultural, Religious, and Political Perspectives.* Jason Aronson, Northvale, New Jersey, 1998. A broad range of Jewish approaches on human rights issues.

BUSH, LAWRENCE AND JEFFREY DEKRO. *Jews, Money, and Social Responsibility: Developing a "Torah of Money" for Contemporary Life.* The Shefa Fund, Philadelphia, 1993. Insights on Torah teachings related to obtaining ad donating money.

DORFF, ELLIOT. N. *The Way Into Tikkun Olam.* Jewish Lights Publishing, Woodstock, Vermont, 2005. Addresses current societal challenges and how Jewish teachings can be used to address them.

ELKINS, DOV PERETZ. *Simple Ways for Jews to Help Green the Planet: Jews, Judaism and the Environment, Growth Associates*: Princeton, NJ, 2011. Provides many specific behaviors and actions that Jews (and people of all backgrounds and faiths) can perform to help green the planet.

GERSHOM, YONASSAN. *Eight Candles of Consciousness: Essays on Jewish Nonviolence.* Lulu Press, Raleigh, North Carolina, 2009. Anthology of articles on peace, justice, and ecology. Includes the story of how he became a vegetarian.

————. *Kapporos Then and Now: Toward a More Compassionate Tradition.* Lulu Press, Raleigh, North Carolina, 2015. After presenting a critique of both the practitioners and opponents of this thousand-year-old ceremony, as well as the history and mystical meanings behind it, the author comes to the conclusion that in modern times it is best to substitute money for a chicken in the ritual.

GREENBERG, IRVING. *The Jewish Way: Living the Holidays.* Summit Books, New York, 1988. Insights and background material on all the Jewish holy days.

HESCHEL, ABRAHAM J. *The Insecurity of Freedom: Essays on Human Freedom.* Farrar, Straus and Giroux, New York, 1967. Wide ranging collection of essays addressing Judaism to such issues as Jewish education, civil rights, Soviet Jewry, and Judaism in the Diaspora.

————. *The Prophets.* Jewish Publication Society, Philadelphia, 1962 (two volumes). Excellent analysis of history's greatest protesters against injustice and their messages.

HIRSCH, RICHARD G. *The Way of the Upright: A Jewish View of Economic Justice.* Union of American Hebrew Congregations, New York, 1973. Summary of Jewish ethical teachings related to economic behavior.

————. *Thy Most Precious Gift, Peace in Jewish Tradition.* Union of American Hebrew Congregations, New York, 1974. Provides many sources for traditional Jewish views on war/peace issues.

HIRSCH, SAMSON RAPHAEL. *Horeb*, translated by Dayan I. Grunfeld. Soncino Press, New York/London/Jerusalem, 1962. Analyzes a wide variety of *mitzvot*, including those that teach us how to relate to the earth and its creatures.

————. *The Nineteen Letters.* Feldheim, Jerusalem/New York, 1969. Passionate defense of traditional Judaism through eloquent letters to a skeptic.

JACOBS, JILL. *There Shall Be No Needy: Pursuing Social Justice Through Jewish Law & Tradition.* Jewish Lights, Woodstock, Vermont, 2010. Ancient Jewish texts used to inform our approaches to current issues.

──────. *Where Justice Dwells: A Hands-On Guide to Doing Social Justice in Your Jewish Community.* Jewish Lights, Woodstock, Vermont, 2011.

JEWISH PEACE FELLOWSHIP. *Roots of Jewish Non-Violence.* 2010. Several essays, including one by this book's author, on Jewish teachings on peace, non-violence, conscientious objection, and *tikkun olam.*

KALECHOFSKY, ROBERTA, ED. *Judaism and Animals Rights: Classical and Contemporary Responses.* Micah Publications, Marblehead, Massachusetts, 1992. A wide variety of articles on animal rights, vegetarianism, and animal experimentation, from the perspective of Judaism.

──────. *Vegetarianism and Judaism: A Guide for Everyone.* Micah Publications, Marblehead, Massachusetts, 1992. Nice discussion of all the reasons Jews should consider being vegetarians. Includes an excellent presentation of how the philosophy of René Descartes changed the Western perspective of animals from sentient living beings to mere "machines," thereby opening the way for today's abusive factory farms.

KRANTZ, DAVID, EDITOR. *Jewish Energy Guide.* Jewish Council for Public Affairs and Green Zionist Alliance, New York, 2011. Fifty articles by a wide variety of experts designed to help Jews reduce their energy use.

KUSHNER, TONY AND ALISA SOLOMON, EDITORS. *Wrestling With Zionism: Progressive Jewish-American Responses to the Israeli-Palestinian Conflict.* Grove Press, New York, 2003. A wide variety of essays from progressive perspectives on many aspects of the Mideast conflict.

LANDAU, YECHEZKEL. *Violence and the Value of Life in Jewish Tradition.* Oz V'Shalom, Jerusalem, 1984. Essays from rabbis of various backgrounds on Jewish teachings related to peace and non-violence.

LERNER, MICHAEL. *Jewish Renewal: A Path to Healing and Transformation.* G. P. Putnam's Sons, New York: 1994. A rethinking of Judaism by a Jewish Renewal leader with the aim of building spiritually rich Jewish lives and a more just society.

──────. *Embracing Israel/Palestine: A Strategy to Heal and Transform the Middle East.* Tikkun Books, San Francisco, 2012. Excellent summary of the issues and possible peace settlement. Especially valuable are the 25 challenging questions and answers from both side's perspectives.

LEVINE, AARON. *Free Enterprise and Jewish Law: Aspects of Jewish Business Ethics.* Ktav, New York, 1980. A comprehensive analysis of Jewish teachings on business-related issues.

POLNER, MURRAY, AND STEFAN MERKEN, EDITORS. *Peace, Justice and Jews: Reclaiming Our Tradition.* Bunim & Bannigan, New York, 2007. A gathering of voices demonstrating the remarkable depth of thinking and commitment by Jews seeking justice and peace.

ROSE, AUBREY (EDITOR). *Judaism and Ecology.* Cassell, New York/ London, 1992. Collection of very readable essays on environmental issues, from Jewish perspectives.

SACKS, RABBI LORD JONATHAN. *The Dignity of Difference: How To Avoid the Clash of Civilizations.* Continuum, London/New York, 2003. "...a plea — the most forceful I could make —for tolerance in an age of extremism."

SCHWARTZ, RICHARD H. *Judaism and Vegetarianism.* Lantern, New York, 2001. Argues that Jewish mandates to show compassion to animals, preserve health, help feed the hungry, preserve the earth, conserve resources, and pursue peace point to vegetarianism (and even more so veganism) as the ideal diet.

————. *Judaism and Global Survival.* Lantern, New York, 2002. Jewish teachings on involvement and protest, justice, the environment, energy, climate change, peace, population, and vegetarianism.

SEARS, DAVID. *Compassion for Humanity in the Jewish Tradition.* Jason Aronson, Northvale, New Jersey, 1998. Statements from classical Jewish sources on universal issues.

————. *The Vision of Eden: Animal Welfare and Vegetarianism in Jewish Law and Mysticism.* Create Space Independent Publishing Platform; 2nd edition, 2014). An almost encyclopedic treatment of vegetarianism and all aspects of Jewish teachings on the proper treatment of animals.

SEIDENBERG, DAVID. *Kabbalah and Ecology: God's Image in the More-Than-Human World.* Cambridge University Press, New York City and Cambridge, UK, 2015. A groundbreaking book that challenges our anthropocentric reading of the Torah, showing that a radically different orientation to the more-than-human world of Nature is not only possible, but that such an orientation also leads to a more accurate interpretation of scripture, rabbinic texts, Maimonides, and Kabbalah.

SHATZ, H., CHAIM I. WAXMAN, AND NATHAN J. DIAMENT (EDITORS). *Tikkun Olam: Social Responsibility in Jewish Thought and Law.* Jason Aronson, Northvale, New Jersey, 1997. Wide variety of essays by leading Jewish thinkers on the Jewish mandate to heal and repair the world.

SLIFKIN, NATAN. *Man and Beast: Our Relationship with Animals in Jewish Law and Thought.* Yashar Books, 2006. Israel's "zoo rabbi" examines many animal issues from an Orthodox halachic perspective. Not a vegetarian book, but nevertheless an excellent resource with well-reasoned arguments and materials.

STRASSFELD, SHARON AND MICHAEL. *The Third Jewish Catalog — Creating Community.* Jewish Publication Society, Philadelphia, 1980. Contains sections on social justice, ecology, and compassion for animals.

TAL ALON. *Pollution in a Promised Land: An Environmental History of Israel.* University of California Press, Berkeley, California, 2002. Very comprehensive analysis of environmental developments in Israel by the country's outstanding environmentalist.

TAMARI, MEIR. *With All Your Possessions: Jewish Ethics and Economic Life.* Jason Aronson, Northvale, New Jersey, 1998. Torah teachings on a range of economic issues.

VORSPAN, ALBERT AND DAVID SAPERSTEIN. *Jewish Dimensions of Social Justice: Tough Moral Choices of Our Time.* Union of American Hebrew Congregations Press, New York, 1998. Reform Jewish perspectives on social justice, environmental, peace, civil liberties, and other issues.

WASKOW, ARTHUR I. *Godwrestling — Round 2: Ancient Wisdom, Future Paths.* Jewish Lights, Woodstock, Vermont, 1996. Excellent application of Jewish tradition to "wrestle" with current problems such as injustice and violence.

WASKOW, ARTHUR I. (ed.). *Torah of the Earth: Exploring 4,000 Years of Ecology in Jewish Thought.* Jewish Lights, Woodstock, Vermont, 2000 (two volumes). Wide variety of essays on various environmental issues.

YANKLOWITZ, SHMULY. *The Soul of Jewish Social Justice.* Urim Publications, 2014. The book explores how spirituality, ritual, narratives, holidays, and tradition can enhance one's commitment to creating a more just society. Readers will discover how the Jewish social justice ethos can help address issues of education reform, ethical consumption, the future of Israel, immigration, prison reform, violence, and business ethics.

————. *Bringing Heaven Down to Earth: Jewish Ethics for an Evolving and Complex World.* Indie Publishing, April, 2014.Jerusalem. Has thoughtful essays on many topics, from Jewish theology to interfaith relations, labor fairness and prescription drugs, to illegal immigration and women's rights.

GENERAL BOOKS ON GLOBAL SURVIVAL ISSUES

BINGHAM, THE REV. CANON SALLY G., *Love God, Heal Earth: 21 Leading Religious Voices Speak Out on Our Sacred Duty to Protect the Environment*. Saint Lynn's Press, Pittsburgh, Pennsylvania, 2009.

BROWER, MICHAEL AND LEON, WARREN (EDS.). *The Consumers' Guide to Effective Environmental Choices: Practical Advice From the Union of Concerned Scientists*. Three Rivers Press, New York, 1999. Discusses the contributions of various human activities to environmental threats. (The worst are driving cars and eating meat).

BROWN, LESTER R. *Plan B 4.0: Mobilizing to Save Civilization*. W.W. Norton and Company, New York/London, 2009. Excellent analysis of climate change and other threats to humanity and a comprehensive, well reasoned plan to avoid a global catastrophe.

CAMPBELL, T. COLIN WITH THOMAS M. CAMPBELL II. *The China Study: The Most Comprehensive Health Study Ever Conducted and the Startling Implications for Diet, Weight Loss and Long-term Health*. Benbella Books, Dallas, Texas, 2004. Excellent discussion of the ramifications of what the NY Times called "the grand prix of epidemiology" and the factors that prevent shifts to healthier diets.

FOER, JONATHAN SAFRAN. *Eating Animals*. Little, Brown and Company: Back Bay Books, New York/Boston/London, 2009. Very readable account of Foer's journey to vegetarianism, with many thoughtful arguments.

FRENCH, HILARY. *Vanishing Borders: Protecting the Planet in the Age of Globalization*. W.W. Norton, New York/London, 2000. How to respond to societal problems caused by globalization.

GORE, ALBERT. *An Inconvenient Truth: The Planetary Emergence of Global Warming and What We Can Do About It*. Rodale Press, Emmaus, Pennsylvania, 2006. The book version of the Academy Award-winning documentary, with valuable pictures, charts, and discussions.

HOGGAN, JAMES. *Climate Cover-Up: the Crusade to Deny Global Warming*. Greystone Books, Vancouver/Toronto/ Berkeley: 2009. Prepare to get very angry while reading of the major steps some corporations are taking to mislead the public about climate change to maintain their huge profits.

LAPPE, FRANCES MOORE. *Diet For a Small Planet*. Ballantine, New York, 1991. Twentieth Anniversary Edition. Shows the tremendous wastefulness and inefficiency of animal-based agriculture.

LAPPE, FRANCES MOORE, ET AL. *World Hunger: Twelve Myths.* Grove Press, New York, 1998. Dispels myths like 'overpopulation is the main cause of hunger' that make it difficult to find solutions.

LEQUIRE, STAN L. (editor). *The Best Preaching On Earth: Sermons on Caring for Creation.* Judson Press, Valley Forge, Pennsylvania, 1996. Eloquent Christian sermons on environmental issues. Many arguments based on Jewish scriptures.

PATTERSON, CHARLES. *Eternal Treblinka: Our Treatment of Animals and the Holocaust.* Lantern Books, New York, 2002. Explores how the Holocaust was rooted in the 20th-century automation of slaughterhouses, and how treating people "like animals" leads to dehumanization, desensitization to suffering, and genocide.

REGENSTEIN, LEWIS. *Replenish the Earth: The Teachings of the World's Religions on Protecting Animals and the Environment.* Crossroads, New York, 1991. A comprehensive discussion on the teachings of the Bible and the world's religions on protecting and preserving animals and the natural environment.

RIFKIN, JEREMY. *Beyond Beef: The Rise and Fall of the Cattle Culture.* Dutton, New York, 1992. Powerful analysis of the many negative effects related to the raising of cattle and the consumption of beef.

ROBBINS, JOHN. *The Food Revolution: How your Diet can Help save Your Life and the World.* Conari Press, Berkeley, California, 2001. Documents health, animal rights, and ecological reasons for not eating flesh, eggs, and dairy.

TUTTLE, WILL. *The World Peace Diet: Eating for Spiritual Health and Social Harmony.* Lantern Books, New York, 2005. Very comprehensive, eloquent analysis of the many reasons for vegetarianism and of the cultural factors that support the widespread eating of animal products.

WORLDWATCH INSTITUTE. *State of the World 2015: Governing for Sustainability.* W. W. Norton, New York/ London, 2015. Highlights obstacles and opportunities, a clear eyed but optimistic assessment of society's efforts to obtain a sustainable environm4nt.

————. *Vital Signs 2015: The Trends That Are Shaping Our Future.* Worldwatch Institute, Washington, D.C., 2015. Valuable analyses and instructive graphs and charts that provide insight into the issues that will affect the world's future.

What People Are Saying about
Who Stole My Religion?

The many endorsements below are included to show that it is not just the author, but also many other people – of various perspectives – who think their religion has been "stolen," but who still believe that religious values have relevance to current issues. It is our hope that the voices of the people who submitted the statements below, as well as many more voices, will be raised to help revitalize Judaism and other religions and to apply religious values effectively in response to the many threats to humanity today.

"For many years now, Richard Schwartz has been a clear, unwavering voice for a more compassionate, more humane and holier Judaism. *Who Stole My Religion?* offers Jews and non-Jews alike a critique of many of the unhappy trends in the Jewish world today and an authentic and inspirational view of what traditional Judaism is and should be."
> – PROFESSOR ALON TAL, BEN GURION UNIVERSITY OF THE NEGEV,
> CHAIRMAN OF "THE GREEN MOVEMENT" (ISRAEL'S GREEN PARTY),
> AND AUTHOR OF POLLUTION IN THE PROMISED LAND AND MANY
> OTHER BOOKS AND ARTICLES ON ENVIRONMENTAL ISSUES IN ISRAEL.

"This is an inspirational and prophetic book that explores the deep issues that are facing us today, not only for the purpose of healing the ecological world, but more importantly saving the soul of Judaism. The essential question Richard Schwartz, a modern Orthodox Jew, is asking is: 'Why has my Orthodox Jewish community moved away from following the deep God-centered and, consequently, moral and ethical way of life in which humanistic ideals and actions are essential out-flowing of a God-centered way of life?'"
> – RABBI GABRIEL COUSENS, MD, MD(H), DD,

DIRECTOR OF THE TREE OF CENTER AND FOUNDATION, AUTHOR OF TORAH AS A GUIDE TO ENLIGHTENMENT, SPIRITUAL NUTRITION, CONSCIOUS EATING, AND CREATING PEACE BY BEING PEACE.

"No one has been more creative, committed, and consistent than Richard Schwartz in arguing for a Judaism that can address in all its depth the world crisis that all humanity and all the life-forms of our planet face today."
— RABBI ARTHUR WASKOW, DIRECTOR OF THE SHALOM CENTER,
AUTHOR OF DOWN-TO-EARTH JUDAISM, SEASONS OF OUR JOY,
AND MANY OTHER WORKS ON JEWISH THOUGHT AND ACTION.

"The challenging title of this welcome new book by Prof. Richard Schwartz, one of the most insightful commentators on Jewish scriptural interpretation, says a great deal about his struggle to reclaim Judaism in the 21st century from those who would narrow its scope to ethnocentrism and self-interest. Schwartz is a major protagonist in the battle to present the humanitarian insights and universal truths that have been part of the Jewish tradition, from its earliest holy texts to the present day."
— RABBI GERALD SEROTTA, FOUNDER, RABBIS FOR HUMAN RIGHTS
IN NORTH AMERICA,
AND EXECUTIVE DIRECTOR OF CLERGY BEYOND BORDERS

"I commend Dr. Schwartz for his courage and integrity in reminding the Jewish community of its historic mission to serve as a light unto the nations. While it is always safer to tell people what they want to hear, I am thrilled that at least one person has the guts to challenge our people to live up to the highest ideals of the prophets by acting as responsible stewards of our planet, fighting to protect those who need our help, and practicing kindness to animals. His book *Who Stole My Religion?* will serve as a lightning rod to stimulate critically needed discussion about what it means to be Jewish and how we can live an ethically Jewish life."
— RABBI BARRY SILVER, RABBI OF CONGREGATION L'DOR
VA-DOR IN LAKE WORTH, FLORIDA, FORMER FLORIDA STATE
REPRESENTATIVE, AND FOUNDER AND CO-CHAIRMAN OF THE PALM
BEACH COUNTY ENVIRONMENTAL COALITION.

"Once again Richard Schwartz has produced a thought provoking book. *Who Stole My Religion?* will be a very positive addition to our libraries. His writing is powerful and thought provoking. As always, Richard is not afraid to challenge us."

– RABBI MICHAEL M. COHEN, DIRECTOR OF DEVELOPMENT AT THE
FRIENDS OF THE ARAVA INSTITUTE FOR ENVIRONMENTAL STUDIES

"As a Jewish animal rights activist, I have always considered Richard Schwartz to be a mentor and someone I admire tremendously. His book only corroborates that opinion as it passionately and persuasively goes beyond even the most important 21st-century concerns into the heart of Judaism itself. Every Jew – and non-Jew who is concerned with the future of our planet – should read *Who Stole My Religion?*"

– PAULINE DUBKIN YEARWOOD,
MANAGING EDITOR AT CHICAGO JEWISH NEWS

"In this time of ubiquitous polarization and demonization of 'the other,' *Who Stole My Religion?* makes a cogent, compelling call for Jews to turn from unquestioning acceptance of particular cultural and political positions back to core religious values of wisdom, compassion, and self-examination. No nation or religion is automatically good; frequent comparison of values with behaviors is a huge part of what makes good people, good nations, and good religions. Professor Schwartz weaves a readable and interesting tapestry of current and historical facts, scriptural citations, study findings, authoritative quotes and heartfelt common sense, all in the cause of finding the best course for Jews, for peace, and for the world. Highly recommended."

– KARIMA VARGAS BUSHNELL, CO-AUTHOR OF CULTURAL
DETECTIVE ISLAM (TM) AND TEACHER OF INTERCULTURAL
COMMUNICATION AT METROPOLITAN STATE UNIVERSITY

"Tekiah! The venerable Richard Schwartz once again sounds a shofar blast of warning to wake up the Jewish community and the world. As unabated greed and climate change threaten life and religion as we know them, Schwartz urges actions rooted in the very heart of Judaism. We all would be wise to heed the call."

– DAVID KRANTZ, PRESIDENT AND CHAIRPERSON AT AYTZIM: ECOLOGICAL JUDAISM

"There are woefully few examples in history of lone individuals who bravely rose up to identify the underlying causes of problems that have plagued nations, societies, and indeed, the world at large. All too often those voices were rapidly silenced, either through political subjugation, ignorance, or indifference. Fortunately, despite overwhelming odds, there are those who have made a profound difference to the reigning status quo. Richard Schwartz is one such man. His new book identifies much of what we as Jews have failed to recognize as our planet heads inexorably towards an ecological meltdown. Politically, ethically, morally, economically, and scientifically, we are guilty of wearing blinkers when we look around and perceive what is happening to our world, especially in the face of global warming and also in our inability to obtain a just and peaceful settlement to the Israeli-Palestinian conflict.

Soundly basing his views on the profound teachings of the Torah and the inherent wisdom and compassion of our ancient faith, he provides an alarming analysis of how we are failing not only ourselves but also our duty to be a 'light unto the nations.' This book should be essential reading for everyone. I applaud Richard as a maverick and as a tzaddik, a truly righteous man in every sense of the word. He is one of the few individuals who gives me a sense that there is still hope if we act now to reverse the trends that are pushing us towards disaster."

– LIONEL FRIEDBERG, EMMY AWARD-WINNING PRODUCER, DIRECTOR, WRITER, AND DOCUMENTARIAN, AND PRODUCER OF *A SACRED DUTY: APPLYING JEWISH VALUES TO HELP HEAL THE WORLD.*

"If you think Judaism consists of occasional visits to a synagogue or Temple where congregants perform rituals and recite prayers without feeling and attend mainly to socialize, then this book is a must read. Schwartz reminds us that the very essence of Judaism is to struggle to find what is right and to have the courage to do right, including speaking out against evil. Worship accompanied by indifference to evil, the prophets said, is an abomination to God. Schwartz fulfills the best of Judaism by urging us to cry out against immorality, injustice, deceit, cruelty, and violence toward all living beings, rather than condone it with our silence. For in condoning empty rituals and standing silent in the face of immoral deeds, we make a mockery of Judaism itself."

— NINA NATELSON, DIRECTOR OF CONCERN FOR HELPING ANIMALS IN ISRAEL (CHAI).

"Provocative! Magisterial! Titanic! Richard Schwartz is the most knowledgeable person alive on the teachings of Judaism on protecting animals and nature. His writings are brilliant, and his books are always valuable and worth reading and discussing. I say this as a conservative, even a right-winger, who strongly disagrees with Richard's devotion to liberal tenets. But when he discusses the fate of our planet and the many environmental issues that threaten human civilization, and the responsibility of Jews to take action, there is no one better."

— LEWIS REGENSTEIN, 40 YEAR VETERAN OF THE ANIMAL PROTECTION MOVEMENT AND AUTHOR OF REPLENISH THE EARTH: THE TEACHINGS OF THE WORLD'S RELIGIONS ON PROTECTING ANIMALS AND NATURE.

"Richard Schwartz has been a consistent, clear, compassionate voice for the planet. This book once again illustrates his wisdom, insight and willingness to speak up. If the Jewish community takes this book to heart and makes the necessary changes, the world can follow. We can co-create a world that respects all life."

— RAE SIKORA, CO-FOUNDER PLANT PEACE DAILY; INSTITUTE FOR HUMANE EDUCATION, AND VEGFUND.

About the Author and Contributors

Richard H. Schwartz, PhD, is the author of Judaism and Vegetarianism, Judaism and Global Survival, and Mathematics and Global Survival. He also has over 200 articles and 25 podcasts online at JewishVeg. com/schwartz. He is president emeritus of Jewish Veg – formerly known as Jewish Vegetarians of North America (JVNA) – president of the Society of Ethical and Religious Vegetarians (SERV), a patron of the International Jewish Vegetarian Society, and a member of the Board of the Farm Animal Rights Movement (FARM). He is associate producer of the 2007 documentary *A Sacred Duty: Applying Jewish Values to Help Heal the World*. In 1987 he was selected as Jewish Vegetarian of the Year by JVNA, and in 2005 he was inaugurated into the North American Vegetarian Society's Hall of Fame. He is a professor emeritus of mathematics at the College of Staten Island, has been married since 1960, and has 3 children and 10 grandchildren.

Rabbi Yonassan Gershom is a freelance writer and author of *49 Gates of Light, Beyond the Ashes, From Ashes to Healing, Jewish Tales of Reincarnation, Eight Candles of Consciousness, Jewish Themes in Star Trek*, and *Kapporos Then and Now*, as well as many feature articles. He was born in Berkeley, California, grew up in the Philadelphia area, and graduated from Minnesota State University at Mankato in 1975. He received his ordination from Rabbi Zalman Schachter-Shalomi, the B'nai Or Rebbe, in 1986; later became a Breslov Hasid; and currently teaches as a Maggid (storyteller-preacher) through his writings. He lives on a 15-acre hobby farm in northern Minnesota with his wife Caryl, three dogs, two geese, 13 cats, a flock of chickens and guineafowl, and a bunch of wildlife. His blog "Notes from a Jewish Thoreau" explores connections between traditional Judaism, animals, ecology, and his personal nature observations.

Rabbi Dr. Shmuly Yanklowitz studied at the University of Texas as an undergraduate, at Harvard University for a Master's Degree in Leadership and Psychology, at Yeshiva University for a second Master's Degree in Jewish Philosophy, and at Columbia University for his Doctorate in Moral Development and Epistemology. He has taught as an instructor of moral philosophy at Barnard College and at the University of California, Los Angeles School of Law. Shmuly was ordained as a Rabbi by Yeshivat Chovevei Torah as a Wexner Graduate Fellow. Rav Shmuly has served as a congregational rabbi and as a campus Senior Jewish Educator and Hillel Director of Jewish Life.

As a global social justice activist and educator, Shmuly has volunteered, taught, and staffed missions in five continents and over 15 countries, including Israel, Ghana, India, France, Thailand, El Salvador, Britain, Senegal, Germany, Switzerland, Ukraine, Argentina, South Africa, and Haiti. Shmuly serves at the World Economic Forum in Geneva and Davos, Switzerland as the rabbinic representative, a facilitator, and motivational speaker. Rav Shmuly is the Founder and President of Uri L'Tzedek, the Founder and CEO of The Shamayim V'Aretz Institute, and is the author of eight books.

In 2012 and 2013 Newsweek rated Rav Shmuly one of the top 50 rabbis in America. Shmuly, his wife Shoshana, daughter Amiella, and son Lev live in Scottsdale, Arizona.